Foreign Exchange

Studies in Missionaries and Christianity in China

General Editor: Kathleen L. Lodwick,
Pennsylvania State University/Lehigh Valley, Pennsylvania

Publishing interdisciplinary, innovative scholarship, this series extends our understanding of the Christian missionary movement in China from the time of the Jesuits in the Ming dynasty to the Protestants in the nineteenth and early twentieth centuries and explores its impact on both the Chinese people and on the countries that sent missionaries to China.

Other Titles in this Series

Jessie G. Lutz, ed., *Pioneer Chinese Christian Women: Gender, Christianity, and Social Mobility*

Kathleen L. Lodwick, *The Widow's Quest: The Byers Extraterritorial Case in Hainan, China, 1924–1925*

M. Cristina Zaccarini, *The Sino-American Friendship as Tradition and Challenge: Dr. Ailie Gale in China, 1908–1950*

Jun Xing, *Baptized in the Fire of Revolution: The American Social Gospel and the YMCA in China, 1919–1937*

Foreign Exchange

Counterculture behind the Walls of St. Hilda's School for Girls, 1929–1937

Judith Liu

With appendixes
by Donald P. Kelly

Lehigh
University
Press

Bethlehem: Lehigh University Press

Published by Lehigh University Press
Co-published with The Rowman & Littlefield Publishing Group, Inc.
4501 Forbes Boulevard, Suite 200, Lanham, Maryland 20706
www.rlpgbooks.com

Estover Road, Plymouth PL6 7PY, United Kingdom

British Library Cataloguing in Publication Information Available

Library of Congress Cataloging-in-Publication Data
Liu, Judith, 1950–
Foreign exchange : counterculture behind the walls of St. Hilda's School for Girls, 1929–1937 / Judith Liu ; with appendixes by Donald P. Kelly.
p. cm.
Includes bibliographical references and index.
ISBN 978-1-61146-004-9 (cloth : alk. paper) — ISBN 978-1-61146-005-6 (ebook)
1. St. Hilda's School for Girls (Wuhan Shi, China)—History. 2. Schools, American—China—Wuhan Shi—History—20th century. 3. Wakeman, Dorothea Kingsley. 4. Yeh, Yuanshuang. I. Title.
LG53.W84L58 2011
373.51′212—dc22

2010019757

♾™The paper used in this publication meets the minimum requirements of American National Standard for Information Sciences—Permanence of Paper for Printed Library Materials, ANSI/NISO Z39.48-1992.

Printed in the United States of America

To Donald Phillip Kelly
for his love and encouragement

Trade with the gifts God has given you.
Lend your minds to holy learning that
you may escape the fretting moth of
littleness of mind that would wear out your souls.

Grace your wills to action that they may
not be the spoils of weak desires.
Train your hearts and lips to song which
gives courage to the soul.

Being buffeted by trials, learn to laugh.
Being reproved, give thanks.
Having failed, determine to succeed.

—Homily of St. Hilda, Abbess of Whitby, 657–680 A.D.
Namesake of St. Hilda's School for Girls

Contents

List of Illustrations

Maps

Acknowledgments

I WAS RAISED ON STORIES THAT MY MOTHER GATHERED THROUGHOUT HER life. Instead of fairy tales, my mother mesmerized me with tales of her childhood, her school days, my father's family, as well as her courtship and marriage to my father. I never tired of them, and they were particularly powerful when I was growing up in tenement housing in Brooklyn and then in a predominantly Italian-Catholic and eastern European Jewish neighborhood in the Bronx. We were the only Chinese, non-Jewish, non-Italian, non-Catholic entities, and in the struggle to "belong," the thought of coming from a prominent, wealthy Chinese background fueled my imagination.

As the first branch of either side of the family to emigrate to America, there were no "blood relatives" here in the states. Our "family" was socially constructed. Beginning in 1956, once a month, a group of "Aunties," "Uncles," and their families would rotate hosting mah-jongg fests that would begin with fabulous home-cooked meals, endless cups of tea, Chinese pastries, sumptuous snacks, interjected amid the constant sound of shuffling mah-jongg tiles. These "Aunties" were a group of Chinese women who attended St. Hilda's School for Girls.

After graduating from college in 1972, I traveled to Taiwan where I met "blood" relatives—my mother's younger sister's children, and my mother's first cousin / "sister," Yuanlu. Also living in Taipei were a number of other St. Hilda's "Aunties" who related information about other fellow class/schoolmates living in the People's Republic of China. In 1982, after years of seeking information about her best friend, Cai Sumei, my mother learned from St. Hilda's connections that she was the deputy minister of light industry and was living in Beijing. Once contact was reestablished, my mother and I lived with her in Beijing, and this trip served as the basis for my dissertation. For eight months we lived and traveled throughout China. Wherever we went, we met with St. Hilda's graduates, and when we traveled to Wuhan, we spent days at the school. I began gathering the stories of St. Hilda's graduates at that time. Additional China trips in 1990 and 2009 completed the research on the school.

While writing may be a singularly solitary act, the finished product is anything but, and I have been helped by so many people. Many thanks go to the numerous graduates of St. Hilda's who have enriched my life with their stories. During my research trips to the People's Republic of China in 1982 and 1990, many of these "Aunties" extended their hospitality to allow me to live with them, and one, Liu Defu, became my godmother.

Thanks are due to the San Diego Writing Women, a group of dynamic women who have sustained me during the writing of the manuscript; Beth Bliss, Oberlin College; Martha Smalley, Yale Divinity School Library; Karma Lekshe Tsomo, University of San Diego; Michelle Liu, University of Washington; Richard Madsen, University of California, San Diego; Daniel Bays, Calvin College; Heidi A. Ross, University of Indiana, Bloomington; Duncan McCosker, University of San Diego, who masterfully reproduced the photographs; members of the Yale-Edinburgh Missions Listserve; Linda A. M. Perry, University of San Diego; Eleanor Wheeler, whose aunt was Hazel Gosline, and who provided me with photographs, letters, and correspondence from Hazel; Margaret Bowlus Stehle, for genealogical information about the Wakeman family; and the anonymous reviewer for Lehigh University Press. My special thanks to Kathleen Lodwick, University of Pennsylvania, a world-class scholar and friend, who has always encouraged and supported my research. I am grateful to my friends Lora and Pat Connolly, Elena Rodriguez, Ann Andrews, and Peter Fajkowski.

Funding for this research has come from the Henry Luce Foundation Incorporated, History of Christianity in China Project. Its weeklong 1989 seminar on Christianity in China was the impetus to seriously pursue this line of research by connecting me to a rich network of China scholars. I am also grateful for funding received from the University of San Diego that permitted me to travel to China and to conduct archival research.

The Archives of the Episcopal Church located in Austin, Texas, was "home away" from home for four major visits to use the enormous "China Mission Records—Record Group 64" (RG 64). My research began in 1985 with physically hand copying letters from the collection to the technological wizardry of a flash drive to store megabytes of information. I wish to thank the archivists and the entire staff for their invaluable contributions to this book.

Special thanks are due to my first cousins, Yuan Bao Jie, Yuan Bao Ying and her husband, Ting Yong Ch'ing, Yuan Bao Ping and his wife, Ren Mei Ling, who in June 2009 provided a magical three-week Yeh family reunion in Tianjin and Beijing featuring eating, laughing, and finishing touches to the manuscript. As their youngest cousin with the "accent of unknown origins"—an American accent with a mixture of Hubei and Henan overtones, they provided invaluable pinyin spelling corrections. We spent hours eating, laughing, and correcting the pinyin throughout the manuscript because my spelling was based upon my mother's Hubei accent, and "not proper

Mandarin" that resulted in an incorrect romanization of our grandfather's name!

When Dorothea died in 2001, her daughter, Catherine Howe Collato, and her son, Mark Howe, honored me beyond measure by giving me her four volumes of China letters that serve as the basis for much of this book. Their generosity has continued since that time by providing me with friendship as well as with family photographs, additional letters, personal effects, and other stories about their mother.

This book, however, would not have been completed without my husband, Donald Phillip Kelly, who has done yeoman service in getting this book published. As a scholar in his own right, he has written the appendixes and created the maps and genealogy charts, as well as meticulously read and edited the manuscript to the point that he truly knows more about St. Hilda's than he ever wanted. For his unwavering faith in me, his years of sacrifice while I traveled abroad and to the archives, and his care to detail in completing this manuscript, I am eternally grateful and lovingly dedicate this book to him.

Introduction

East and West

Protection for her daughters was utmost on Dexing's mind.[1] St. Hilda's School for Girls could provide that, but the school was temporarily closed, and Dexing wanted her daughters near. The primary school associated with St. Hilda's was St. Lois's, and even better, it was located near the mansion in Hankou. St. Lois's would have to do.

Shaded by three enormous parasols each borne by a male servant, the entourage entered the St. Lois's compound. Aided by a woman servant, Dexing carefully walked in her six-inch bound feet clad in embroidered slippers that matched her outfit. Accentuating her porcelain complexion, her lilac-colored silk tunic flowed over her black, midcalf silk skirt. Her hair was combed into a tight bun that sat at the base of her neck. Completing the outfit was a matching set of jade earrings and bracelet. All eyes, however, were drawn to the two young girls, on that hot, early October day in 1927.

Glittering in a golden glow, one was dressed in a bright yellow silk, floor-length traditional gown (qipao) with an enormous red and white bird elaborately embroidered on the front. Her long, jet-black hair cascaded down her back in one long queue wrapped in yellow silk cords that matched her gown. Her dainty feet were clad in handmade silk slippers which, when the feet were placed together, formed a dragon with luminescent pearl eyes. Her creamy-white skin was framed by a pair of ruby teardrop earrings dangling in each lobe, and on her finger, she wore an imported cameo ring. The other was wearing a light blue silk qipao elegantly embroidered with pink and white flowers. She, too, was clad in silk dragon slippers; her ears were adorned with blue sapphire earrings. Her hair was pleated and wrapped in matching blue silk cords. Like Chinese royalty, Yeh Yuanshuang, and her younger sister, Yeh Yuanquan, stepped into another world.

In the compound, young girls wearing short-sleeved, crisp white cotton shirts over mid-calf black cotton skirts, white stockings, and functional cloth shoes caught sight of them walking down the central path. As the entourage made their way to the principal's office, schoolgirls flocked around them forming a procession of white and black trailing the gold and blue figures. Whispering, giggling, and nudging one another, the girls called to others, "Come, come! Come see the qianjin xiaojie [thousand pieces of gold maiden]! Qianjin xiaojie at our school!" By the time the two precious maidens reached the building that housed the principal's office, a throng of girls surrounded them. Girls of the New China had just come face-to-face with remnants of the Qing dynasty.[2]

As the two women started their three-day journey from Beiping to Wuhan in March 1934, their excitement was palpable. Dorothea Kingsley Wakeman and her traveling companion, Mamie Lou Roots, were headed to Hankou—one for the first time; the other to rejoin her family for the pending birth of her first child.

At twenty-six years of age, Dorothea was a slender five-feet, eight-inches tall woman who towered over the average train passenger. She was striking in her newly tailored navy blue outfit that complemented her creamy skin tone and shiny, rich, wavy, mahogany-colored hair fashionably cut and styled in preparation for the journey south. Carrying recently purchased baskets, Dorothea and Mamie Lou began their rail journey. Recounting her trip in a letter to her parents, Dorothea wrote:

> We each had brot a lunch basket. Mine is a beautiful affair of tightly woven wicker and only cost 30 cents Mex. which is about 10 cents your money. We also each had a thermos of cold water. Then the boy brot us as much boiling water all day long as we wanted. (My thermos is a beauty, Chinese made and only cost $1.50 Mex. and is quart size.) Our meals were delicious. We made hot boulion with cubes and hot water. We heated delicious baked beans over a sterno stove for our meals. We ate tomato soup, thick and undiluted right out of the can, (I don't mean we ate right out of the can), with sardines and bread and butter. We had canned pineapple and tangerines, dried figs from San Francisco, dates, lots of hard boiled eggs and more bread and butter, hot postum with canned milk and sugar, marmalade and more bread and butter. It probably sounds most unhealthy put in this way, but each meal was very well balanced, perfectly delicious, and packs of fun. It wasn't the least bit messy because we just had a tin plate and spoon and knife apiece and a little kettle for heating over the sterno fire. When finished, we quickly washed the dishes in the little kettle of hot water and thru the dish water out the window. Every thing seemed so immaculately clean this trip too. The bath room was always scrubbed up and freshly supplied with boiling hot water. And I didn't hear any one spitting.[3]

As the train traversed the enormous landscape of China, Dorothea and Mamie Lou watched the landscape transform from the more barren and colder North to the more lush and hotter South. The train seemed to fly on its rails until seasonal rains forced the train to inch its way into Hankou.

During the next two and a half hours, Dorothea and Mamie Lou peppered the conductor with questions, "Are we there yet? What time will we arrive? How much longer is it to the station?" They asked so many times that the conductor, in exasperation, resorted to responding in French, "Not yet, but soon," in the hopes of ending their incessant inquiries.

Peering through the rain-drenched windows, Dorothea could see row after row of shiny gasoline tankers and their accompanying tin buildings emblazoned with Texaco, Union Oil Company, Sunoco Products, and Asiatic Petroleum Limited. For a brief moment she was magically transported back to her home in San Gabriel, California, but the huge Chinese billboards glistening in the foreground soon brought her back to China.

After a seemingly interminable wait, Dorothea and Mamie Lou stepped off the train in a driving rainstorm to be greeted by her friend, Mary Richards, the Episcopal bishop of Hankou's secretary; Hazel Gosline, a teacher from St. Hilda's; and two servants from the school. Scrambling into a taxi that wove its way to the bishop's house, hardy welcomes and a warming tea were extended to the group. Despite entreaties to spend the night, Dorothea could not wait any longer to reach her desired destination of St. Hilda's where she was to serve as an English teacher. That journey required a trip across the Yangzi River. Clambering back into a taxi, she and Hazel were transported to the wharf—the "Bund"—raced down the steps, and boarded a small wooden launch that was willing to brave the rough forty-five-minute trip across the river to Wuchang.

Aboard the launch that lunged up and down with the choppy waves, Dorothea embarked on what was to be the first of numerous trips across the river. Along the way, Hazel highlighted the Hankou sights: the Customs House with its large clock face; the "Surprise House," so named because strategically placed windows and a door gave the illusion of two eyes and a widened mouth; and foreign gunboats docked for the evening bobbing along the wharf. As they crossed the river, boats, launches, and other small crafts darted back and forth on the turbulent waters, but Dorothea's thoughts were on her new home.

In Wuchang, rickshaw drivers clad in brown fiber shawls to shed the rain, short trousers, and bare feet vied furiously for their fares. Hazel bargained for two, and the drivers trotted briskly down the slippery, narrow, winding streets, carrying their passengers to the outer gate of Wuchang Sheng Xilida Nu Xuexiao—St. Hilda's School for Girls in Wuchang. As they approached, the drivers shouted to the gatekeeper announcing the arrival of guests. Clutching two lighted sticks in his hand, the gatekeeper greeted the two women and excitedly explained to them as they entered through the gate and inner archway that the ritual welcoming of Miss Wakeman would need to be delayed. The girls were in chapel, and the usual welcome of firecrackers—the signal of their arrival—would disrupt the evening prayers. Rather than disturb Evensong, Dorothea and Hazel made a hasty retreat into the Ladies House, disposed of their things, and shook off the rain before madly dashing out to the front gate to make a second, formal entrance.

Carrying a long firecracker-festooned stick, the gatekeeper deftly scurried down the pathway with the exploding torch that sizzled, flared, and popped loudly in a blaze of light and sound. The girls streamed out of the chapel and stood shyly looking at the new American teacher standing in the driving rain. Sounds of a soft, melodic song of welcome filled the air. East and West were meeting on the chapel steps.[4]

This book is the story of two women and their experiences at an American Episcopalian missionary school—St. Hilda's School for Girls—during the period 1929–37.[5] One was a student; the other was a short-term teacher. St. Hilda's was located in Wuchang in the metropolitan area known as Wuhan (composed of the three cities of Wuchang, Hankou, and Hanyang), Hubei Province.[6] Their stories are being told because of my relationship with the two: Yeh Yuanshuang is my mother and Dorothea Wakeman Howe was my friend.

The choice of these years is significant in a number of ways. First, it is the time that Yuanshuang and Dorothea were at the school: my mother from 1929 to 1935, and Dorothea from 1934 to 1937. Second, the girls at St. Hilda's represent a unique cohort because they are within the first generation of Chinese to reach maturity after the founding of the Republic in 1912. They attended school during a time when few Chinese (much less women) received an education, and they attended school during what could be considered the halcyon days of Chiang Kai-shek's Nationalist rule—the years between the Northern Expedition (1926–28) and the War of Resistance Against the Japanese (1937–45). Third, the lives of Yeh Yuanshuang and Dorothea Kingsley Wakeman were inextricably influenced by their experiences at St. Hilda's. Each came from one world and entered into another when they stepped through the school gates. While their time there overlapped for a brief period, they did not meet with one another again until years later in 1997 in yet another world—San Diego, California. Each traveled a path to St. Hilda's that would leave an indelible mark upon her life. That imprint goes beyond the formal education that one gave and the other received.

Founded in Wuchang in 1875, the school that would eventually become St. Hilda's School for Girls was intended to provide a strong, Christian education for its students. Its creation, as well as other mission schools, was made possible when China's defeat in the Opium Wars during the mid-nineteenth century resulted in treaty provisions that allowed foreign "concessions" in many cities in China. Hankou became the most important inland treaty port, and it became central China's base for the Episcopal

Church's mission efforts. But as with many foreign, Christian schools, St. Hilda's floundered in its early years. American and Chinese values often clashed, and mutual misunderstandings abounded because of language and cultural differences. The inability to communicate effectively with one another created misinterpretation of meanings and actions that only served to reinforce the differences between the two cultures. The school's survival was also threatened by a severe teacher shortage and began thriving only when teachers were recruited especially for St. Hilda's beginning in 1899.

With the recruitment of teachers, the curriculum went beyond teaching domestic skills and basic English reading and writing to include mathematics, Chinese history, and geography as well as religious studies. St. Hilda's formal curriculum was intended to produce Chinese Christian women who could serve as role models in their traditional gender capacities as daughters, wives, and mothers.

While these goals were the manifest ones, there were latent, unanticipated consequences from a St. Hilda's education. Daily student-teacher interactions created an environment that allowed for a foreign exchange which led to the creation of a new culture that subverted both American and Chinese gender constructs. The walls that surrounded the St. Hilda's compound not only served to protect the school from outside danger, but those walls also served to screen what went on in the school from outside scrutiny. Whether they were aware of it or not, St. Hilda's was a citadel where the teachers and students were cloistered, somewhat paradoxically, from the confines of extant gender expectations. Thus, the American teachers as well as the Chinese students were acculturated and socialized in ways that liberated them from their respective patriarchal situations.

For the American teachers, serving as missionaries in foreign assignments allowed many of them to remain single yet still be engaged in a professional career that would not be as socially stigmatizing as it would be if they remained in the United States. As teachers at St. Hilda's, not only were they educating a future generation of Chinese women, they also served as exemplary role models by their sheer presence. As single, independent women who served in important positions, they were a source of daily reminders of what women could do when given an education. In the case of Dorothea Kingsley Wakeman, her four-year mission liberated her in a way that permitted her increased control over her own life.

For the Chinese students, their educations provided them with the means to aspire to roles outside of the culturally restricted positions of daughters, wives, and mothers by giving them the intellectual tools that enabled them to desire being employed in the fields of education, social work, and medicine. Their involvement in school activities developed self-reliance, independence, and leadership skills. For Yeh Yuanshuang, attending St. Hilda's provided an education that socialized her to American values and customs so that when she arrived in the United States in 1948, she was able to adapt readily.

In essence, the walls of St. Hilda's concealed a space where new gender expectations could be nurtured, hidden away from the gaze of prying eyes. As such, the education received by the girls and modeled by their teachers at St. Hilda's went far beyond the formal curriculum. Examining St. Hilda's through the experiences of Yuanshuang and Dorothea has the potential of illuminating the liberating qualities of female education, the power of personal narrative as an ethnographic/historical research tool, and how the stories of these two women are embedded in the historical circumstances of their times.

Yuanshuang's and Dorothea's stories also reveal the impact of the modern world on their parents' generation. Myths abounded about both countries regarding the status of women. In the early twentieth century, China was regarded as a once great civilization that was collapsing under the weight of its own corruption and decay. Chinese women were portrayed as suffering under centuries-old traditions of foot binding, arranged marriages, and concubinage. The United States was emerging as a world power and was a place where personal liberties were considered bountiful. Women were afforded education and could, in theory, freely marry for "love." In the case of Yuanshuang and Dorothea, it was the influence of their parents that played a profound role in why they ultimately went to St. Hilda's. The end of dynastic rule and the creation of the Republic provided cracks in the traditional Chinese patriarchal wall that confined a woman's place in Chinese society. It was through these cracks that Yuanshuang's mother sought to push her daughters into the modern world. Profound changes were occurring in the United States as well. The forces of modernization completed the United States' change from a rural, agrarian to an urban, industrial society. This transformation also created cracks in the traditional American patriarchal wall, and with Dorothea coming of age during the Roaring Twenties, her father tried to shore up the wall against the rising tide of gender-redefining social change.

The chapters in the book tell the respective stories of Yeh Yuanshuang and Dorothea Kingsley Wakeman. The circumstances in China during the 1920s and in Yuanshuang's family that led her to St. Hilda's School for Girls are told in chapter 1. How events in both the United States and in Dorothea's family resulted in her going to China in 1933 are told in chapter 2. Chapter 3 is a history of St. Hilda's School for Girls. In chapter 4 and chapter 5, Yuanshuang's and Dorothea's experiences at St. Hilda's are described. An epilogue continues their stories beyond 1937. Appendixes provide a social and historical context of events in China and the United States that ultimately affected the lives of both women.

Foreign Exchange

Yeh Yuanshuang (right) and Yeh Yuanquan (left) 1920.

1
Yeh Yuanshuang

YUANSHUANG WAS BORN OCTOBER 3, 1913, IN HANYANG, HUBEI PROVINCE to the prestigious Yeh family. The family's fortune came from the centuries-old, nationally renowned Chinese pharmaceutical firm Yeh Kai Tai, located at the inland port of Hankou. This wealth enabled the Yeh clan to educate its males to successfully pass the governmental civil service examinations and become mandarins. The family's most prominent official was Yeh Mingchen, who was the principal Qing official in South China from 1848 to 1858. He was appointed the governor of Guangdong Province in1848 and was named viceroy of Liangguang in 1852, which made him, in essence, China's de facto foreign minister during this period.[1] Two images surround him: to the Chinese he has become the heroic resister to foreign imperialism; to the British he remains the recalcitrant official responsible for starting the Second Opium War. More significantly, this war affected Chinese history. The spark that ignited the Second Opium War was lit when Chinese soldiers boarded the British-registered, Chinese-owned vessel *Arrow* off Guangzhou (Canton) in 1856. The vessel was suspected of smuggling goods, and in the British view of the incident, the soldiers were "disrespectful" to a ship flying the British ensign. When Yeh Mingchen refused to issue a public apology to the British consul Harry Parks, the situation escalated. In that same year, the death of a British sailor in Guangdong incited British forces to burn a Chinese village and, in retaliation, British-owned properties were torched by the Chinese.[2] By 1857, British and French commissioners demanded negotiations, the opening of new treaty ports, and reparations. Yeh's refusal to accede to these demands led the British and the French to begin military operations, and, paradoxically, Yeh ordered the army not to engage the foreign expeditionary force until it was too late. Yeh Mingchen was captured in 1858 by the British, "belatedly removed from office for being 'stubborn and presumptuous' " by the Xianfeng emperor, and exiled to India where he died of starvation a year later.[3] In 1860, the Treaty of Tianjin was ratified which officially ended the Second Opium War. In essence, the treaty opened eleven more ports to the West, legalized the importation of opium into China, and showed the world how militarily weak the Qing army and how ineffective the Qing government had become.[4]

Originally merchants from the Lishui region near Nanjing, Jiangsu Province, the Yeh branch that was to become the Hanyang, Hubei Yehs traveled to Wuhan in 1631 during Ming Chongzhen emperor's reign.[5] The faltering Ming dynasty's "Mandate of Heaven" was being questioned by droughts, floods, and open rebellions, and Yeh Wenji, his father, and his younger brother set up a small pharmaceutical dispensary in a Hanyang temple.[6] In 1637, Yeh Wenji then expanded the dispensary into the Hankou medicinal establishment Yeh Kai Tai, which ultimately moved to Da Jia Street.[7] Through a series of strategic marriage arrangements with prominent local families during the ensuing centuries, the Yehs gradually developed roots in the city.[8] However, the Yehs always claimed Jiangsu as their place of origin and home district, not Hubei, which they considered to be too backward a province for such a grand family.

Born into the eleventh generation since the founding of Yeh Kai Tai and with the generational name of Yuan,[9] Yuanshuang was to be a part of a quartet of children who would embody the Chinese notion of perfection, Fù, Gui, Shuang, Quan, which roughly translates to having wealth and honor (Fù, Gui) and producing perfection (Shuang, Quan).[10] Although the fourth child born to her parents, only Yuanshuang's elder brother, Yuanfù, survived infancy; two sisters died before her birth.[11] It was the death of her one-year-old sister Yuangui that became a source of friction between Yuanshuang and her father, Yeh Rongzai. According to family legend, Yuangui was frightened by a chicken alighting on her crib and developed "Mad Chicken's Fever," and she died just days before Yuanshuang's birth. Believing that Yuanshuang's "dark" spirit was somehow responsible for the death of his beloved daughter, Rongzai's initial suspicions of Yuanshuang seemed to be borne out by ensuing events.

It was a practice among women in the wealthy families to bear children close together; consequently, wet nurses were employed. When a child was born, Yuanshuang's mother, Gao Dexing, would send out a citywide call for a wet nurse, and when suitable young women responded, Dexing would meticulously screen each and every one of them for any physical diseases or sores as well as for any moral imperfections. Once selected, the young woman was scrupulously scrubbed and bathed before nursing the child.

Finding a suitable wet nurse for Yuanshuang, however, transcended the usual ordeal because she suckled her wet nurses dry. In a seemingly endless procession of inspections, scrubbings, and departures coupled with a constantly crying infant, Dexing frantically went through no less than eighteen women before a young mother who had recently lost her own child was able to sate Yuanshuang. Still grieving from the death of his second daughter, Rongzai's first impression of the newborn Yuanshuang was that she was a child with a "thief's eyes" whose large, dark, bright eyes seemed to shine in the dark and a "lion's mouth" that suckled women dry and did nothing but roar for milk. Yuanshuang's willful, stubborn nature in later years would do nothing to dispel her father's initial beliefs. Two more children—a girl, Yuanquan (1914) and a boy, Yuanli (1917)—were born in the next four years.

As was the custom in wealthy families in dynastic China, four generations of Yeh families lived together in a single compound in Hankou behind Yeh Kai Tai. During the 1911 Revolution, however, some of the houses and much of Yeh Kai Tai burned to the ground, and the family was forced to split up while the compound was rebuilt. Yuanshuang's great-grandmother, her three sons and some of their families remained together in the Hankou compound.[12] This unsettling situation also led the youngest son, Yeh Fengchi, to split his household.[13] Remaining in Hankou with his mother, Fengchi sent his oldest and youngest sons, Rongzai and Fanzai, along with his concubine—Tai—to live in Hanyang. All told, seventeen people moved to Hanyang. While Fengchi held his eldest son, Rongzai, in high esteem, both Fanzai and Tai had fallen out of his favor and were now to become Rongzai's responsibility.

In 1916, Rongzai became a provincial senator, and because the provincial capital was Wuchang, his entire household moved from Hanyang. Rongzai's position was made possible in part because of his strategic marriage to one of Wuhan's prominent, wealthy families, the Gaos, the owners of one of Wuhan's largest textile enterprises. When Rongzai married Gao Dexing in 1907, both were sixteen years old. As his financial contribution to the groom's family, Dexing's father provided a dowry of two thousand ounces of silver. This silver enabled Fengchi to purchase a short-lived, but highly lucrative Qing dynasty position in Wuhan which made him in charge of collecting contract fees on grain, tea, lumber, and silk as well as for collecting fees from the government-supervised salt market. After 1912, Fengchi returned the dowry to the young couple which allowed them to purchase a substantial mansion compound within Wuchang's city walls in 1916. Renowned for its gardens, the residence was known locally as the Ying family's garden—Yingjia Huayuan, and it served the family's needs ideally.

Within the compound were numerous living quarters and an expansive garden with a large gazebo surrounded by sweeping fishponds. Huge mulberry bushes and peach and cherry trees adorned the space. This formal garden was used almost exclusively by Rongzai to entertain dignitaries and other important guests in his role as provincial senator. Not permitted to play in this garden, the children were confined to the smaller back garden that was filled with flowers and bushes, another small fishpond, and gazebo. During good weather, the children played card games or ball with the servants' children, and strung beads on wire which was bent into elaborate shapes. The girls embroidered in the large gazebo shaded by bamboo or cloth curtains. More shade was provided by arbors draped with grapevines, and during the hot, humid summers, large mosquito-netted tents were erected there as sleeping quarters.

When weather no longer permitted activities outdoors, the bitterly cold winter days were spent in the enclosed dining room where a large charcoal-burning, copper brazier glowed continuously. There the girls whiled away the hours engaged in perfecting domestic arts such as embroidery, sewing, cross-stitching, crocheting, and knitting that would prepare them for their future roles as wives and mothers. The younger boys made origami figures, practiced calligraphy, and played cards. All snacked continuously on endless varieties of seeds, preserved fruits, and other delicacies stored in large porcelain jars.

Everything from combing Yuanshuang's hair to bathing her feet was performed entirely by servants who catered to her every request. She never had to concern herself with fixing a bed, cleaning a room, or preparing a meal. Despite her appetite, Yuanshuang was a sickly child, and therefore, she was treasured and pampered by Dexing and the servants. Whims and desires were indulged, creating a flurry of activity by the servants who strived to satisfy her wishes. In contrast to the quiet lives of the family, the servants were constantly in motion keeping the household functioning.

Although they did not live in Hankou, Rongzai and Fanzai and their families would frequently visit the Yeh family compound for birthdays, the Lunar New Year, and other special occasions. Their father, Fengchi, owned several residences up and down the Yangzi River,[14] but he preferred to spend time in Shanghai where he kept two concubines and sired separate families with each of them. While born in Hubei, Fengchi went so far as to always hang a placard on his residence that read, "The house of the Nanjing Yehs."[15]

When in Shanghai, as Fengchi frequently was, the entire family (except for his discredited concubine, Tai, and later, Dexing) would sail there on the family's private boats. Such gatherings were occasions for lavish banquets featuring the finest ingredients from around the world. Among Fengchi's many business enterprises were an international bakery and several merchandise firms; consequently, his house was filled with row after row of glass containers filled with domestic and foreign-made biscuits, candy, dried fruit, and cookies free for the family's taking. Small bottles of imported liquors lined the walls. Not permitted to drink alcohol, the children would nonetheless sneak a bottle or two. Freshly baked goods were delivered daily, and as a child, Yuanshuang would gorge on these treats. "I had my first bottle of Hennessy cognac brandy as a child, and to this day, it is my favorite brand. Each day, fresh fruit along with freshly baked bread, pastries, cookies—every conceivable kind—were delivered to the house, and we could eat as much as we wanted. That is why my teeth were so bad at an early age."

In Shanghai, Fengchi indulged his children and grandchildren with American movies featuring Hollywood stars such as Douglas Fairbanks, Stan Laurel and Oliver Hardy, Charlie Chaplin, and Mary Pickford; these films fascinated Yuanshuang and provided her first exposure to Western life. Fearing illness or disease transmission, Fengchi would rent the entire theater for private, undisturbed viewings. The family would also go shopping in the best stores, eat in fancy restaurants, and attend Chinese operas.

Most of these activities did not exist in Wuhan. During family gatherings there, acting troupes were invited to perform operas in the family compound to indulge Fengchi's mother's passion. On other occasions, musicians, acrobats, or storytellers were retained to provide entertainment. Intricate meals, fruits, and delicacies abounded, and the compound was abuzz with activity.

However lively life could be at times, day-to-day experiences in Wuchang were not, despite the considerable comfort the children enjoyed. As a child born into a wealthy, privileged class, Yuanshuang's childhood chiefly consisted of confinement in the family compound supervised by private tutors and family servants but with little parental attention. Rongzai and Dexing were frequently absent for a number of reasons.

In addition to being a provincial senator, Rongzai was, for a time, a government treasury official who was responsible for minting copper coins and printing paper money. Despite those duties, he also had to tend to the family business. The Yehs owned a river transport business that included four ships—two wooden, two steel. As the nominal captain of the two steel ships that transported goods on the Yangzi River—mainly the renowned porcelain from Jingdezhen, a town south of Jiujiang, Jiangxi Province—he made frequent monthlong trips from Wuhan to Jiujiang (to lade the porcelain) to Shanghai (the entrepôt for the porcelain). On one of these trips shortly after the birth of Yuanli in 1917, Rongzai began frequenting a Shanghai opium den with his crew, and he quickly became an addict. He also secretly took a young girl, Yu Suzhen, who worked at the den as his concubine. Her existence and his addiction were kept from Dexing until her personal servant, who embroidered most of her finery, cautioned her to count her jewelry. Daring not to make an outright accusation, the servant wished to not only alert her mistress to the fact that pieces of jewelry were being taken by her husband, but to avoid accusations of thievery as well.

As the daughter of a prestigious Hankou family, Dexing possessed a substantial jewelry collection as part of her trousseau. A piece missing here and there would not draw any suspicion at first. When a set of her favorite jade bracelets disappeared, however, Dexing confronted Rongzai who confessed that he had taken them to give to his young "ward" whom he claimed to have "rescued" from the Shanghai opium den he frequented. Although Rongzai and Dexing once had a warm, loving relationship, the concubine and opium addiction made Dexing miserable. Rongzai spent more and more time in Shanghai, and when he was home, he spent hours in an opium stupor. When Yu attempted suicide in Shanghai where she was living in a rented house, Rongzai moved in with her and spent even less time in Wuchang. A year later, Dexing allowed Rongzai to return home with Yu whom she invited into the house, but this event forever changed the family's dynamics.

With her husband and concubine now living under the same roof, Dexing spent more and more time away from home. Tempted to become an opium addict herself, but concerned for her children's and the household's welfare (which also included several Gao family members), Dexing sought solace with monthlong visits with her maternal second sister-in-law rather than succumb to opium's seductive high. This woman raised Dexing after the death of her own mother when she was only three months old. Her "mother" counseled her, provided support, and gave Dexing the strength she needed to endure the tribulations of her married life.[16] During those extended quarterly visits, daily care of Dexing's own children was given primarily to Tai, servants, and tutors.

Dexing's absence from the house had consequences. Managing a family in the traditional Chinese manner is an important function for a wife who has children. Not only does the wife have responsibility for managing the entire household, she must also hire, train, and supervise the servants. As the one who pays their wages, the wife maintains control over them. Working with the servants, Dexing had to plan the day's meals, arrange for the procurement of household food and goods, and attend to the myriad details of daily life as well as keep a detailed accounting of expenses down to the last copper coin. With as many as thirty people in her household, including twelve servants (four females and eight males), Dexing had enormous responsibilities. Well aware of the position's significance, Dexing would on rare occasion cede her authority to Tai during those few times she and the children traveled to Hankou or Shanghai on family business. This authority was never ceded to Concubine Yu. Her arrival ended Dexing's ability to freely attend family functions and was the primary reason why Dexing rarely joined the family on their Shanghai excursions.

All too aware of her secondary status, Concubine Yu sought every possible means to conceive since bearing children—especially male children—was the sole means to elevate her position so that she could create a separate household, and therefore challenge Dexing's authority on overall household matters. Losing control of the head servants, who were essential for the smooth functioning of the household, would spell disaster for Dexing. Servants were the "arms, eyes, and ears" for their mistresses; they were privy to personal information about every household member. Little escaped their attention, and secrets were impossible to keep from them. In performing their duties, servants were permitted to leave the compound; hence, they also brought news of the outside world as well. Dexing guarded her position diligently and never relinquished her authority to Yu who chafed under the circumstances. When Dexing did leave for her extended natal visits, Yu made numerous attempts to foment discord among the servants to undermine Dexing. Warned of these attempts by trusted servants, when Dexing left it was Yuanshuang, as the older daughter, who was given principal responsibility for running the household.

Beginning at age seven, Yuanshuang not only made household decisions, but she also controlled the family finances during her mother's absence. As the designated "mistress" of the house, servants were expected to show her respect. At Yuanshuang's insistence, each morning servants would no longer need to prostrate themselves in front of her or Yuanquan; instead, they only needed to clasp their hands and thrice bow to them. Yuanshuang also began gambling with the servants during their off-hours. She paid when she lost but forgave their debts when she won. As a consequence, Yuanshuang was affectionately referred to as Guanyin—the Goddess of Mercy—for her generosity. Yuanquan, on the other hand, was derisively called Yeng-Wang-Yeh—the God of Punishment—for her constant tattling and for the fact that she was far more attuned to the social distance between herself and the servants than Yuanshuang was.

With the guidance of the family's majordomo, Chen Bingchen—a third, generation Yeh family head servant—Yuanshuang was able to run the household. Bingchen was the only male servant who was permitted to personally interact with the girls and to call them by their "little names"—Shuangshuang and Quan-quan. Because he was truly fond of them and respected Dexing, he ensured that Yuanshuang's and Yuanquan's wishes were obeyed and that proper protocols were kept. He insisted that all expenditures—including the gambling money—be diligently documented and skillfully interceded so that Concubine Yu did not overstep her place or undermine Dexing's authority during her absence. Thus in her mother's frequent absences, decisions about the household were determined by Yuanshuang.

> Each day, Bingchen sent the cook who would inquire about the meals. He could not come into our room but spoke through the maid. Only the maid could come in and talk to us. The maid would come in and say, "Xiao jie [little miss], tomorrow the vegetable money is due." I would give the money, and then I would order the next day's menu, what we wanted to eat. . . . The cook who was standing behind the screen would say, "Xiao jie, vegetables are so expensive and difficult to buy. Add a little more money. Add a little money." So, I would give a

few copper coins more. Then I would order what? I would order hot peppers with fish and chives and two other dishes. After wandering into the kitchen to see what the servants ate, I gained a love of anything made with hot peppers. The cook would say, "Okay." He was happy because I gave him more than what he needed for the three dishes. The servants all loved me because I was generous. They referred to me as the Goddess of Mercy because my mother would be upset about the household expenditures, and I would always defend them. I could be generous—afterall, it wasn't my money, now was it!

When my mother returned, I had to provide an accounting of the household expenses that Chen Bingchen helped me keep, and, ah, how that would trouble her so because I was not as conscientious as she, and I spent money so much more freely. Because I was learning to read, write, and do sums, she would ask me to help her with her accounts, but I had no patience for doing such things and would begrudgingly help. My mother would sigh and say, "Asking you to do such a little thing produces this response. Someday you will know just how difficult it is to run a household and how it feels to be regarded as a nuisance by your children."

As was the practice in wealthy families, private tutors were hired to teach the children, especially the males. Since tutors were provided with room and board, Rongzai decided that all of the children in his and Fanzai's households should be taught. Hence, beginning at age seven, Yuanshuang's formal education commenced. Until the age of ten, girls were permitted to have male teachers; after that age, only female teachers could be employed. From age seven through ten, they had a string of male tutors all of whom quit in rapid succession; the Yeh children were not model students. Their distaste for schooling was to play an important role in Yuanshuang's future. When she was seven, as a ruse to escape lessons, the children convinced their tutor to visit his friend who was the tutor to the children of Wuchang's warlord commander, Cai Hanqing.[17] When Rongzai was away on one of his numerous business trips and Dexing was visiting her family, the children cajoled their tutor into taking them on an excursion. Ordinarily, the young girls would not be permitted outside their gated compound; however, since the tutor was escorting them, Tai and Chen Bingchen relented.

Commander Cai lived in the "House on the Lake"—a fortress—in the center of "East" Lake, the largest lake within Wuchang's city walls.[18] Accessible only by boat, one was hired and rowed to the fortress where the Yeh children and their tutor were granted permission to land.

It was a summer day, I remember. Commander Cai and his wife—everybody—was in the garden eating watermelon when we arrived. Watermelon! Suddenly, the Commander saw so many children—his children and us. The Commander called out to his children, "Why aren't you studying?" And his children said, "Father, it is because our teacher said that we have guests. We are taking them to view the water lilies." Their island was surrounded by beautiful water lilies,

> and we were going to view them. The Commander asked his tutor, "Who are these children?" He said, "That's the family of Yeh Kai Tai." That was my family's store name; everybody knew it. "That's Yeh Kai Tai's family." When we dropped off his children, the Commander invited us to eat some watermelon, "Come, come, eat some watermelon." But we didn't go; we rushed home instead. The Commander invited us all back to the island, but we were afraid to go because my family did not know we were out.

Commander Cai must have been suitably impressed with the girls, because soon after that outing, Yuanshuang's uncle and younger paternal aunt approached the family on behalf of the Cai family requesting a marriage between his eldest son and one of Rongzai's daughters. Childless herself, the aunt not only pressed Dexing to permit her to serve as the marriage broker, but she also wanted to adopt Yuanshuang who bore a striking resemblance to her.[19] Initially, Dexing resisted both requests; however, when Rongzai's elder sister heard about Commander Cai's inquiry, she made a "counteroffer" and proposed a marriage between her second son and Yuanshuang. Dexing felt, not unjustly, that marriage between two first cousins was "inappropriate." Yuanshuang and Yuanquan were not in the best of health, and her own marriage was faltering, so Dexing wished to postpone engagements for her daughters as long as possible. Greater and greater pressures were brought to bear, and when the patriarch, Yeh Fengchi, pressed for a decision, Dexing had no recourse but to choose between the two options. Rather than have Yuanshuang marry within the family, Dexing chose the Cais' marriage proposal. It could be seen as a strategic move for the two families. The Cai family would gain even more respectability by marrying into a family whose wealth and fame predated their own, and the Yeh family businesses would now fall under the military protection of one of China's most powerful warlords—Wu Peifu—under whom Cai Hanqing served.

After a series of negotiations followed by consultations with a diviner to determine the suitability of the match and the most propitious date to seal the marriage contract, at eight years of age, Yuanshuang was engaged.

> My mother said to my younger Aunt, "Yuanshuang can be engaged but not adopted by you." Within six months—very fast—an engagement was announced, and I was forbidden to even say the surname of "Cai," much less say the words "engaged" or "marriage." It was considered improper and bad luck to speak of such matters. At dinner time, when I asked for vegetables, because it is the same word as the surname Cai, all the servants would giggle. My face would flush with embarrassment, but there was nothing I could do if I wanted to eat vegetables.

As part of the marriage pact, gifts were sent. "The house was filled with the aroma of 800 red date moon cakes. How I loved red dates, and they

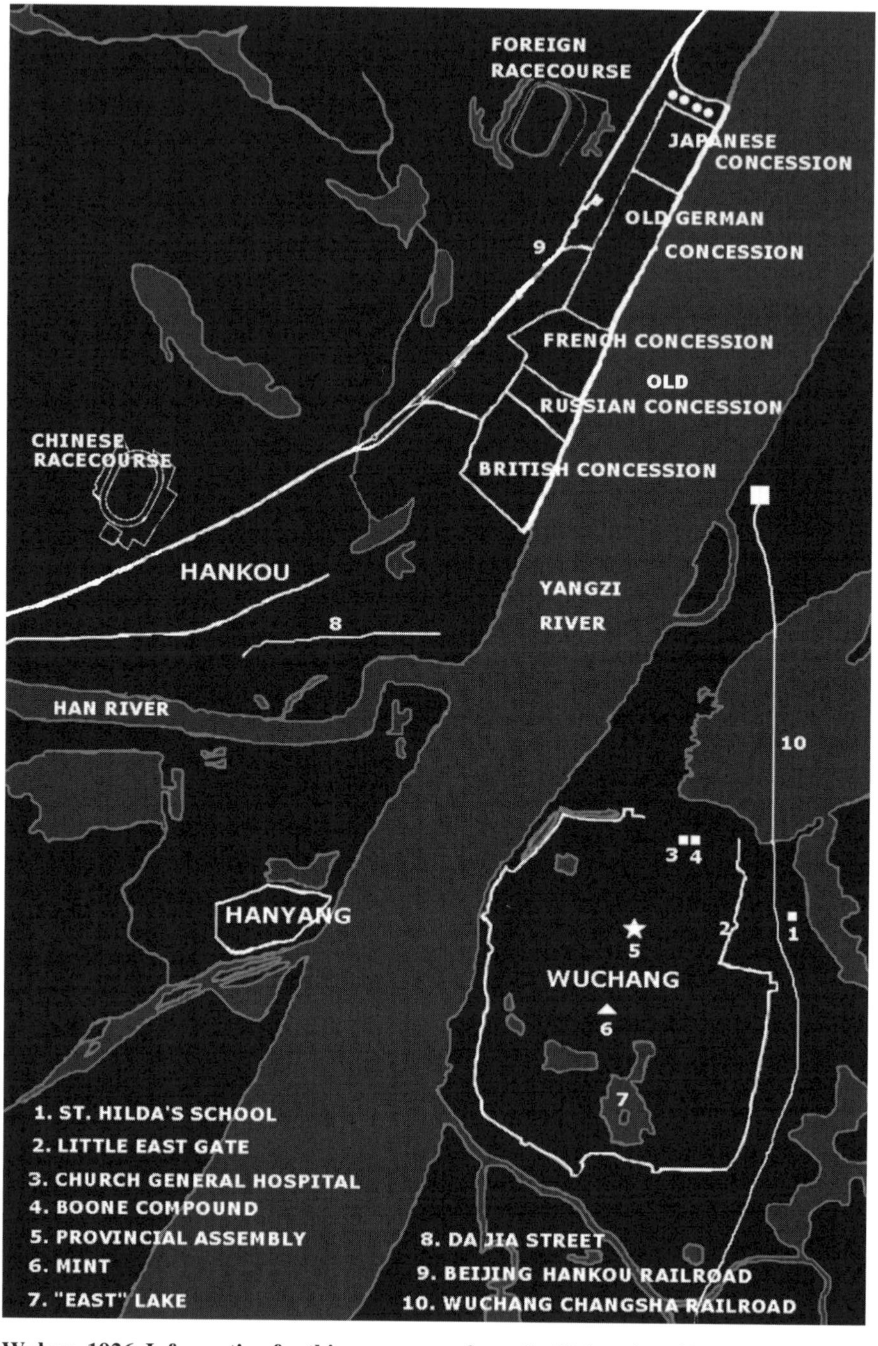

Wuhan, 1926. Information for this map comes from the University of Texas, Perry-Castañeda Library online maps: "Hankow with Hanyang and Wuchang 1915" (http://www.lib.utexas.edu/maps/historical/hankow_1915.jpg) and "Hankow 1945" (http://www.lib.utexas.edu/maps/ams/china_city_plans/txu-oclc-6566099.jpg). Additional information comes from Stephen R. MacKinnon, *Wuhan, 1938: War, Refugees, and the making of Modern China*, 7.

smelled so delicious. But I wasn't allowed to eat even one because they were part of the marriage negotiation, and I wanted to eat some. So, I told my sister, 'Steal some for me.' She brought back eight, and I ate every single one of them. I didn't care if it was bad luck to do so!" Along with bolts of silk, sets of earrings, rings, bracelets, and necklaces were sent.

> At that time, diamonds were very, very rare in China. I remember at that time, the diamond set looked like a Chinese flower and you could either wear it as a ring or as earrings. So my mother had to pierce my ears because those earrings were all for pierced ears. One set of diamonds; one set of jade; one set of rubies; one set of pearls; one set of sapphires. Whew, really beautiful things. From that time, I was only eight years old, and I started to really like jewelry!

A diamond and ruby watch and solid gold stocking garters inlaid with precious and semi-precious stones were part of the betrothal gifts as well.

Yuanshuang's education was frequently interrupted because she was a sickly child who suffered a serious case of measles which was succeeded by numerous bouts of contagious respiratory infections. In a desperate attempt to save her life, Dexing pledged Yuanshuang to a Buddhist nunnery where she had a lengthy stay during 1920 and 1921.[20] Not only would other family members be spared the risk of infection, but Dexing also believed that by sending Yuanshuang to the nunnery, she would be under the protection of the Buddha, share in the monastic life, and spend her days meditating. Reasoning that such a blessed environment would protect Yuanshuang from any harmful effects of previous lives, Dexing hoped that by accumulating merit and good karma, Yuanshuang would regain full health and vitality. While Yuanshuang was in the nunnery and when Dexing was visiting her family, Yuanquan was left to run the household. Following one of his river trips, Rongzai quizzed her about changes made in household customs, and Yuanquan is reported to have said (with her hands defiantly on her hips): "If you leave me in charge, then I get to make the rules." Such were the Yeh girls.

Being sequestered at the nunnery during her bouts of contagion and only returning home when healthy was also instrumental in preventing Yuanshuang from the ordeal of foot binding. Although formally banned with the founding of the Republic in 1912, the centuries-old practice of foot binding continued well into the twentieth century. Dexing's own experience with nearly losing her feet from an inadequate binding made her vehemently opposed to subjecting her daughters to the practice. So adamant was she that Dexing willingly risked Yeh family ire by breaking the tradition that held that only women with six-inch "lotus feet" could marry well. Yuanshuang's arranged betrothal in 1920 to Commander Cai's son dictated that foot binding commence. Sending Yuanshuang to the nunnery was Dexing's way of protecting her from the actual process. Dexing deflected attention by using elastic bandages that neither broke the bones nor inflicted the agonizing pain of the traditional foot binding technique. After spending most of her eighth year at the nunnery, Yuanshuang was formally released from her pledge; she returned home in good health. She was engaged, but her feet were unbound. Her formal education in the Chinese classics recommenced.

Yuanshuang disliked the discipline and effort required by formal schooling. Not permitted to administer corporal punishment to girls, the tutors had little recourse controlling Yuanshuang who was a willful and indolent child. A tutor's continued employment was dependent upon his teaching effectiveness not only for the boys (which was paramount), but for all of the children under his tutelage. Those who tried to deal with Yuanshuang often met with defeat and left the position out of frustration. The exit of one tutor was hastened by Yuanshuang. When he was especially brutal to her younger brother, Yuanshuang plotted to rid the household of him.

> We despised one particular tutor. If Yuanli made a mistake, he would hit him in the back of the head with a bamboo paddle—very hard. We could not say a word against the tutor, but I did not like what he did. Although tutors were permitted to strike students, except the girls, he was cruel.
>
> During one of my older brother's visits home from Shanghai, I told him about what the tutor was doing to our younger brother and solicited his help. Our tutor believed in ghosts, and I devised a way to get rid of him. My older brother's calligraphy was beautiful, and I had him write a statement on special worship paper in red ink, "Striking a student's head will result in a lifetime of headaches." We had one of the servant's sons climb a ladder and hang it high above a life-size painting of Kongfuzi [Confucius] in the study. He was frightened to do our bidding, but we made him swear an oath that he would not betray us. Each morning, before our lessons, we had to bow before Kongfuzi's image to honor him. That morning after the paper was posted, we went into the study. The worship paper was gone, but the tutor was very nervous and asked if we ever noticed anything when we paid our respects to Kongfuzi's portrait. I said, "Sometimes when I look at the portrait, Kongfuzi looks angry."
>
> We learned from the servant boy that earlier in the morning, the tutor had discovered the message and immediately began questioning the servants. The scholarly form and style of calligraphy was far beyond our abilities and certainly that of the servants—he knew that much. He never once suspected Yuanfù or the other adults. When the servants denied any knowledge of how that worship paper got to the top of portrait, the tutor became frightened. He thought it was a message from the heavens! He never hit Yuanli again, and he departed suddenly soon after that.

With each successive tutor, Yuanshuang would start anew with the first readers of Kongfuzi and Mengzi (Mencius) that she had already memorized, and this meant that she could expend minimal energy or effort with subsequent lessons.

Servants were responsible for awakening and dressing the children, but it was a task they soon dreaded when it came to Yuanshuang. Yuanshang was not one to enjoy her slumber disturbed, and each morning "Guanyin" was transformed into the "Empress Dowager" (who also appears to have shared a similar dislike for mornings). Cranky, ill-tempered, and unreasonable in the mornings, if Yuanshuang permitted herself to be roused, she would slump on her arms while the maid tried to braid her hair. Any tug of the comb was met with a snarl and a sharp rebuke. Most mornings, she would simply tell her maid to send a note to the tutor that read, "The Miss is ill."

> My maid would try to get me up, "Little miss, get up." "Get a slip saying that I'm sick." "No, yesterday you were sick," she would gently remind me. "Can't I be sick two days in a row? Can't I be sick tomorrow as well? Tomorrow I will be sick, too," I would snap. To save time, I even wrote a huge stack of excuse slips so that I could order my maid to pick one up from the stack. The maid could do nothing but deliver the note day-after-day.

These notes would prove to be her undoing with another tutor. Each year, Rongzai invited the teachers to the New Year's banquet where they provided a progress report. For Yuanshuang's evaluation, Rongzai was simply handed a thick stack of "The Miss is ill" excuses. Rongzai was furious since he was paying the tutor twenty taels of silver (approximately twenty-seven ounces) plus room and board a year for their education. Her punishment was to complete all of the missed assignments.

This anger turned to rage when on a subsequent visit home, Rongzai requested the written assignments for review. Reclining in his chair while smoking his opium pipe, he was puzzled by why parts of Yuanshuang's assignments appeared darker than others. Upon closer inspection, he noticed that the dates on each of the papers had been altered. He called Yuanshuang before him, demanding an explanation. When none was forthcoming, he used his walking stick to cane her backside. After several strokes, Yuanshuang's cousin, Yuanlu, pleaded with her uncle to cease because she said that she had suggested altering the dates of previous assignments. Not persuaded in the least, and even further annoyed that Yuanshuang was a bad influence on Yuanlu, Rongzai continued to beat his daughter. The beating was not only for Yuanshuang's current offense but also for complaints made against her by Concubine Yu. During the beating, Yuanshuang neither cried nor uttered a sound. Alarmed, Tai intervened on her behalf claiming that Yuanshuang's silence must be due to her having fainted from the pain; only then did the beating stop. "I never made a sound even though I could not sit down for a few days! From that time on, I really disliked my father and avoided him as much as possible," Yuanshuang remembers, "I also disliked studying even more!"

Yuanshuang's engagement further fueled tensions in the Yeh household. The excitement and flurry of activities surrounding Yuanshuang's betrothal only heightened Yu's lack of status and her resentment at how the children treated her. Although openly disrespecting an elder was impermissible, references to Yu were nonverbal. Behind her back, the children displayed their contempt by pointing their pinkies—a subtle way of alluding to the fact that she was a "little wife" (a concubine) and could never be the mistress of their house. Unable to discipline the children directly, Yu complained to their father who interceded on her behalf.

> She hated being reminded that she was just a concubine. Although we were supposed to refer to her as "Aunt Yu" or "Girl Yu," we ignored her. When we referred to her with one another, we made a face and just stuck out our pinkies. Her servant must have seen us and told her about what she saw. The concubine could never say anything to us, but she told my father instead about what we did. I was summoned and he warned me, "If you point that pinkie again, I am going to bend it backwards and break it right off!" I didn't say a word—I was fearful of my father—but even so, later when I was with Yuanquan, I just laughed; we didn't care. In fact, after he said that, we pointed both of our pinkies.

But a price was to be paid for such defiance. "My father always listened to his concubine; he didn't care about us. He spent all day with her smoking opium. If we ever did anything to offend her, she would tell my father who would then discipline us. We were scared to death of my father, but even that didn't stop us from pointing our pinkies when we were referring to her." Siding with the concubine against his children further strained ties between Rongzai and Dexing; Dexing now concentrated her energies on Yuanshuang.

Once Yuanshuang's engagement was official, fearing that the engagement jewelry might be taken by Rongzai for Yu as he had done before, Dexing entrusted the jewels to her father-in-law, Fengchi. "What a loss of face it would be if any of these items were missing when I got married; so, my mother gave them to my grandfather to store in his safe in his Hankou house." The jewelry was a means by which Dexing would counsel Yuanshuang.

> I really wanted that jewelry. Year-after-year, the Cai family would send more and more jewelry asking me to marry into the family sooner than age sixteen. Year-after-year my mother refused my pleas to accept it. "Don't look at that jewelry as all important; those are just for appearances. Look to the inside! If you have talent, you can earn anything you want. With talent and education, you can earn enough to buy your own jewelry, but you can't buy happiness. Happi-

ness is the most important thing! I don't want you to end up in the same situation as me—with no education and under the control of your husband's family."

Dexing's concerns were not unfounded. Through her own sophisticated information network of traveling vendors, servants, friends, and family, Dexing learned that Yuanshuang's fiancé, Cai Yinbao, was in poor health. Dexing knew all too well what the matriarch's responsibilities of managing a prominent family lineage entailed. With Rongzai's increasing health problems aggravated by his opium addiction, Dexing assumed more and more of the family's duties and obligations. As the eldest son in the first household, Yinbao would eventually assume the patriarch function for his portion of the clan upon the death of his father—a position that carried great demands. In traditional Chinese familial structures, typically, the eldest son of the eldest son (and not his brothers) became the patriarch upon the death of the father. (The Yeh family did not actually follow this classic example, however.)

In the case of the ninth generation of the Yeh family, it was Yeh Fengchi, the youngest of the three brothers and his second brother (Yeh Mengji) who were involved with Yeh Kai Tai. Their eldest brother, Yeh Zhongxing, who traditionally would have had the responsibility, did little for the business except to profit from its success. As an addict, he spent most of time with his concubine in an opiate-induced stupor. During the 1911 Revolution, much of Hankou was burned to the ground. Yeh Kai Tai also suffered much damage, but the main warehouse was miraculously spared which only added to its mystical stature and reinforced a local legend about Yeh Kai Tai. During one nineteenth-century fire that destroyed thousands of structures surrounding Yeh Kai Tai, "Some observers reported seeing several 'firebirds' fly up out of the inferno's center and hover protectively over the [Yeh Kai Tai] store, whose proprietor had a reputation for ministering to sick and injured animals. Not surprisingly, the Yeh family's medical reputation and their store's business immediately soared."[21]

Yeh Fengchi rebuilt Yeh Kai Tai utilizing money from his other businesses as well as from his endorsement from Sun Yat-sen to whom he provided considerable financial assistance during the waning years of the Qing dynasty, possibly with the money he received from his position as a Qing official! With Sun's endorsement, Fengchi became a Guomindang advisor. Fengchi assumed financial management of the business while his older brother, Mengji, served as the pharmacist because of his considerable botanical knowledge. All three brothers, however, had joint ownership and shared in its profits, but Fengchi and his eldest son, Rongzai, actually managed the numerous Yeh businesses, until opium addiction took its toll on Rongzai's abilities.

As a consequence, the responsibilities for managing a large family also fell upon Dexing who assumed the matriarch position with its tremendous obligations.[22] Well aware of the burdens accompanying the position, Dexing warned Yuanshuang of her future responsibilities, "If your husband is unhealthy and cannot work, he will always be dependent upon his family. Even though he is the eldest son, if he is unable to work, then the family will have less regard for you. And he comes from such a large family! Eventually, you will be the matriarch and will be obligated to serve your in-laws. Ten years from now, who knows how many in-laws you will have and how many you will have to serve!" Once Yuanshuang's engagement was officially announced, in addition to her formal education in the Chinese classics, her training to be a dutiful official's wife began in earnest as well. Dexing lovingly but persistently urged Yuanshuang to learn propriety.

> First, learn to control your temper. Second, improve your character. You must learn to be sweet and to try and get along with everybody. Now, with your foul temper, you can't get along with anyone. If you don't learn to control your temper, later on you will kill yourself because you can never escape the situation or you will have to hold everything inside of yourself. You will either die or go mad. I don't want either of those fates for you.

Tai was also crucial to her training. Both Tai and Fengchi's wife were originally from Beijing. When Fengchi's wife died, he returned to Beijing and brought back Tai, a woman of Manchu background. Most likely a courtesan as was his first wife, little was known about Tai, including her actual name. Both women's family histories were shrouded in secrecy—no natal family was ever mentioned, and both were literate and well-versed in Chinese history. According to stories told to Yuanshuang:

> My [paternal] grandma was from Beijing. In China during that time, there were several kinds of prostitutes. The first kind was called Qing guanren; they were girls of poor families. They learned to sing, play musical instruments, dance, and write poetry—similar to Japanese geishas. At that time, there were so many famous artists or poets such as Li Po and Du Fu; these men would go to this type of prostitute house. They didn't go to the prostitute houses for the common people; they would only go to this type of high-class house of prostitution. My grandmother was that type of girl. She was a virgin when my grandfather bought her. My grandmother was very young when she was bought; very young. That is why my grandpa loved her so much. No one ever told me exactly where she came from, but my grandfather brought her back with him from Beijing when he was an official. My grandfather was a governor, and when he was in Beijing, my grandfather saw this girl, married her, and brought her home. So nobody knew much about my grandmother, not even my father. But no one dared mention her background because my grandpa was the head of the family. She died very young. She died when she was only twenty-six years old. She had three boys and two girls. The younger girl was the aunt who was my matchmaker. When my aunt was only three days old, my grandmother died. When she died,

my grandfather went back to Beijing and brought back another woman. But my grandpa never married again; just had concubines. He said, "No one can ever take her place."

My grandfather had a portrait of her as a young woman hanging in the front room. Her hair was combed into two small buns on the sides of her head, each covered with a pearl-covered mesh—that was the fashion of the day for young women. Even after she died, he never removed that portrait. She was beautiful. My grandfather went back to Beijing, and the woman he brought back to care for his young children, my step-grandma, was Manchu. She wasn't pretty, but she was tall, lean, had a very nice figure; she had a face full of freckles that she carefully concealed with powder. She was also well educated; she could read; she could write; she also wrote poetry. But she never showed-off too much because she was afraid that people would say she was a prostitute because only those type of women had such abilities in the Qing Dynasty. She was referred to as taitai [lady]; I called her "Tai." She raised my father, his brothers and sisters, but she never had children of her own.

Tai came to live with the Rongzai's family when she was discarded by Fengchi. After the death of his beloved first wife, Fengchi took other concubines but did not bring them into the household as he had done with Tai. But in 1911, he decided to bring yet another concubine into the house. As is the custom, the concubine is introduced and in an act of deference, bows to the wife. Because Tai was herself a concubine but treated as a secondary wife, the new concubine bowed to her. Rather than accept the new concubine and welcome her into the household, Tai stormed out of the room in the presence of everyone. Such behavior caused Fengchi to lose face, and from that moment on, he banished Tai from his sight. He never saw her again and forbade any further mention of her existence.

Tai's training, however, was invaluable for preparing Yuanshuang for her future role as wife and matriarch. Each morning, Tai would sit Yuanshuang in her lap and read the Chinese newspaper and teach her Chinese characters. Breaking Yuanshuang of her tendency to be lazy and to avoid any schooling, Tai would reward Yuanshuang if she read the characters correctly and would punish her when she did not.

I was only nine years old when Tai began training me, but I was very lazy, you know. I was not a diligent student with the tutors, but I was with Tai, my step-grandmother. While pointing to the individual characters, Tai would read, *"Hankou Xiangwen Bao"* [*Hankou Daily*]. Then she would ask me to find characters on the page, "Which is *Han?* Which is *kou?*" If I missed too many characters, she would make me stand on the chair until I learned. My grandmother was really good. That is why I know who were such men as Zhang Zuolin, Wu Peifu, Feng Yuxiang, Liu Zhenhua—all well-known warlords during my youth. They were all in the newspaper. Because I read every single day, I knew these men's names. She taught me a great deal. She also counseled me to "Remem-

> ber to control your temper; become educated. In case your marriage fails, you can do anything independently." That is why I was so independent; my step-grandmother and my mother taught me that.

Once engaged, the intensity of Yuanshuang's training increased as well. She learned how to eat, to sit, to use her hands, and even to sleep.

> Tai taught me how to sleep; not to sleep with your arms and legs spread out. She would check me at night, and if I was sleeping in an incorrect position, she would gently rap me—pong, pong, pong—to awaken me and to show me the correct way to sleep. Once a month I had to sleep with her. Oh, how I hated that. If I thrashed about at night or slept in the wrong position, she would awaken me. I had to continue sleeping in the same bed until I slept through the entire night in the proper way. So, I was trained. Now, I have gone back to my bad ways (laughs), but then, I was trained.
>
> I was also taught to be still, not to move too much. I was taught to use slow, graceful motions—nothing rushed. No laughing out loud, but instead, to drop and tilt my head and raise my hand to cover my mouth. And how to eat—to take small mouthfuls, to close my mouth while chewing; how to use my hands—to keep my fingers held in the lotus position gracefully in my lap. Tai taught me more than my own mother because my mother was frequently gone. My mother was also not literate, and she did not know all of these manners but Tai did because she had been a courtesan.

Yuanshuang's life was changing, and the world in which she was living was about to change as well.

Wuhan had always been at the forefront of nationalistic movements in central China. After all, the Revolution of 1911 that led to the overthrow of the Qing dynasty began in Hankou, and with the Northern Expedition, Wuhan would again become the locus of social change in China. In the summer of 1926, rumors of a military action forming in the south began filtering north and as the days progressed, the rumors turned into reality. The newspapers carried stories about a young military figure—Chiang Kai-shek—a protégé of Sun Yat-sen, who had marshaled together troops in a bold plan to continue Sun's vision of a "reunited" China by wresting political control from the northern warlords. In 1917, Sun led a successful military expedition to defeat the Guangxi warlords, but his second expedition to Hunan and Jiangxi failed. After Sun's death in March 1925, Chiang proposed another military action to unify China. This resulted in the so-called "United Front" between the Nationalists (Guomindang) and the Communists (Chinese Communist Party) who joined together to eradicate warlord control, and the Northern Expedition began in July.

As news of their impending arrival reached Wuhan, Commander Cai warned Rongzai that Wuchang's city gates would soon be barricaded to

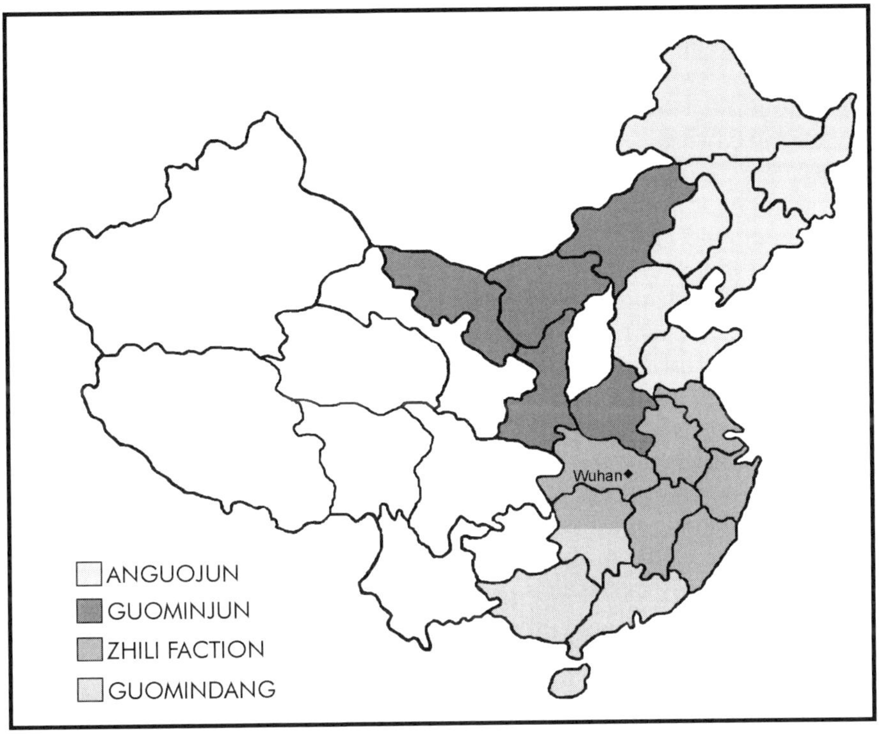

Warlord China, 1926.

thwart the imminent arrival of the Expedition's forces. No longer living in the Yingjia Huayuan residence but in a rented mansion in anticipation of moving into Yeh Fengchi's recently completed, new family compound in the Hankou's French concession, Rongzai had to leave immediately or risk being barricaded within Wuchang's city walls.[23] Servants, Tai, and Yu were left behind in Wuchang to protect property that could not be moved.

By August the Northern Expedition's army was nearing Hubei, and soon the battle for Wuhan would begin. While Hanyang and Hankou were liberated from warlord control quickly, Wuchang resisted behind its great city walls. In a vain attempt to dissuade any Nationalist support, Commander Cai's soldiers executed suspected sympathizers.

> Life was cheap those days, at least the life of any thought to be in league with the South [Guomindang], and many was the student given short shrift, if we are to believe a quarter of what was said. Heads of such victims were suspended from the telegraph poles etc at the site where the two main streets of the city cross, as a warning to others, The sight was indeed gruesome. I had often heard of this custom in China but had never before seen with my own eyes.[24]

Wuchang's massive gates were barred, and when the Expedition's troops arrived at Wuhan in late August of 1926, the fierce battle of September and October was about to begin.

The fighting was bitter, and American eyewitnesses seeking refuge at the Episcopal Church General Hospital within Wuchang's city walls documented the siege. Despite the American flag and large Red Cross painted on the building, stray shots were fired into the compound, airplanes dropped leaflets demanding the surrender of the warlord's troops, and bombs exploded perilously close to the hospital because "Wu Pei Fu's Commanding General, of Wuchang [viz., Cai Hanqing] taking advantage of this probability, tried to shelter himself by moving next door to [the hospital] and making the compound across the alley at the rear of the hospital his ammunition dump."[25] Cannons shelled the city walls daily. Doctors worked through the night operating and caring for the wounded at the hospital. As the assault wore on, fresh food and water ran out.[26] After a fierce forty-day siege, Wu Peifu's troops finally capitulated on October 10, 1926.

While Wuchang was under siege, another drama was occurring in the Cai family. With his military position becoming untenable, Commander Cai and his family fled the city in large river boats that his family owned. The plan was to reach Shanghai and transfer to a seafaring ship bound for the relative safety of Tianjin. En route to Tianjin, Yuanshuang's fiancé, Yinbao, fell ill. The family desperately tried to reach a hospital first in Dalian and then in Tianjin, but despite their desperate efforts, Yinbao died in Tianjin from acute appendicitis.

The Cais sent a telegram to Yeh Fengchi who, in turn, summoned Rongzai and Dexing to inform them of the death. In the message, the Cais implored Fengchi to honor the marriage contract. In return for their consent to marry Yuanshuang to the Cai family, the Cais would actually pay a brideprice and double any agreed-upon amount.[27] A wedding ceremony would take place as usual but with a wooden effigy of Cai Yinbao in his stead. Yuanshuang would become a nun and spend the remainder of her life in a nunnery respected as a member of the Cai household. Yuanshuang would be provided with a "son" born to one of Yinbao's younger brothers. Yuanshuang's sacrifice would be immortalized on a large stele commemorating her virginal purity and virtuousness as well as the union of the two great families. Yeh Fengchi presented Rongzai and Dexing with the marriage contract jewelry that he held in custody. "My grandfather told them to bring me the jewels; all of it would belong to me, and if I accepted them, that would mean that I agreed to the marriage contract. But if I did not accept the terms, I would have to return the jewels except for one piece to serve as a remembrance. The piece, however, would have to be damaged signifying a broken contract."

Dexing did not utter a word until she saw Yuanshuang and presented her with the two options.

At that time, I was so bored living at home; so I thought, "What difference would it make if I lived here at home or with the Cai family?" I was willing to go, but my mother was insistent that I think it over carefully. "Don't marry under these circumstances. This is not something you can change your mind if you don't like it. This is for the rest of your life—forever. At home you are indulged; we try to please your every whim. With your temper and attitude you won't last very long in that situation because you will have the burden of pleasing someone else's every desire." My mother said: "The demands of marrying into a large family are hard enough without these conditions; this marriage would be equivalent to prison. The demands will break your spirit. If your spirit is broken, then you will die. If you want to live, you have to think of another way."

Because I loved my mother, I listened to her. I asked her: "What do you think I should do?" My mother said: "Send all of the jewelry back. Don't keep even a single piece. If you want jewelry then develop your skills, obtain an education, then you can have all the jewelry you may ever want. If you want to marry, we will arrange another marriage, but you can only be a 'secondary wife,' [concubine] because you are now considered to be bad luck. Improve yourself instead." She was always saying that to me, but I really wanted some of that jewelry and wanted to keep just one little piece but my mother insisted: "Not even one small piece. Send it all back." Because I loved my mother more than I loved the jewelry, we sent it all back.

Yeh Fengchi was none-too-pleased with the decision and was furious with Dexing for ruining what he thought would be a powerful alliance with one of the wealthiest families in Wuhan and for further straining relationships within the family. Even more radical was the fact that Dexing now encouraged Yuanshuang to "be independent and not marry" rather than to spend the rest of her life as a "concubine."

Once the left Guomindang and Communist forces gained control of Wuhan in October 1926,[28] they began propaganda campaigns and also began to dismantle Wuchang's city walls, making a "siege, like that of 1926 . . . practically an impossibility."[29] Declarations were posted throughout the city threatening imprisonment for any warlord sympathizers. When Cai Hanqing was declared a criminal for barricading the city gates and executing suspected Nationalist sympathizers, it was possible for those with any association with him to come under suspicion as well. Fearing reprisals, especially since a member of the family had been engaged to Cai Hanqing's eldest son, the Yeh family men decided to leave the city. Boarding one of their own ships, all the males over the age of fifteen fled to Shanghai which was under right Guomindang control. Only the women and young children remained in Fengchi's Hankou compound which became habitable just prior to the Northern Expedition.

For less than a year, the multistoried, Western-style housing within Hankou's French concession was filled with the various generations of Fengchi's extended family. The ground floors contained the accounting offices, guest bedrooms, and a huge ballroom. Rows and rows of glass shelves housing various kinds of crystal glassware lined the walls; several huge crystal chandeliers graced the ceilings. The second floor housed Fengchi; his second son, Yeh Zhizai; his wife and surviving children—Yuantong and Yuancui; Yuanshuang's older brother, Yuanfù (the future family patriarch); and the household teachers. This floor also contained many bedrooms, sitting rooms with patios, and studies. Rongzai's family lived in the front part of the third floor, and Fanzai, his wife, and two children—Yuanfú and Yuanlu—lived on the fourth floor along with the household servants. Guests stayed in the fifth floor bedrooms, and the storage rooms were located on the sixth floor. Thus, the sudden departure of the adult Yeh men left Dexing to tend to the compound and the remaining women, children, and servants as well as to undertake the task of trying to remove any incriminating artifacts in the house.

> In the ballroom there were eight enormous elaborately embroidered panoramic scenes of Cai Hanqing's house on the lake. They were embroidered in Hangzhou [Zhejiang Province] and they were beautiful. Each one was in a magnificent gold-gilded carved frame. These silk embroideries filled one entire wall of the ballroom. But because they contained the name of Cai Hanqing on each one of them, they had to be removed. The glass was broken, the frames dismantled and burned, and the silks embroideries cut apart into smaller scenes with all traces of Cai Hanqing's name removed. Such a pity. But we didn't dare keep them in our possession. Afterall, Cai Hanqing was now a criminal, and if the house was searched, it would be disastrous if the silk embroideries with his name on them were found.

Workers from Yeh Kai Tai were summoned to help the women manage the house and to give the impression that the compound was occupied to prevent looting. One hundred workers in two shifts of fifty came daily and brought word of events occurring throughout the city. Bands of uniformed civilian police roamed the streets; members of the left Guomindang/Communist alliance held rallies railing against the capitalists and warlord sympathizers.

At first, the women were terrified. But as the days turned into weeks, and weeks turned into months and no one came to the compound, the women began venturing out, but only by car. Yeh Fengchi owned two American cars—a Lincoln Continental and a Chevrolet—and they were used for excursions outside of the compound which included attending the horse races in the spring. The chauffeurs would drive the women and children to the races where they would dine and watch the races. Although Yuanshuang, Yuanquan, and Yuanli had attended the races with their grandfather in previous years, they never had the opportunity to join the winner's circle if one of their grandfather's horses won. That privilege was reserved exclusively for Fengchi's favorite relatives. "I always wanted to be in the winner's circle; have my picture taken; receive the flower wreath that they place around the horse's neck—be a part of that ceremony, but my second Uncle's [Zhizai] daughter [Yuancui] was my grandfather's favorite; only she had that privilege. We could only watch from the stands. And, oh, how I wanted to taste that thrill."

The quest for a thrill proved to be their undoing. One late spring day in 1927, out in the Chevrolet for a day at the races, the car was stopped by the civilian police, and the car was confiscated.

> "Get out of the car, get out!" they shouted. "There are people starving to death and you are going to the races! You are the reason why we need a revolution. You are capitalists and have enough. Get out of the car; we seize this car in the name of the government! You can walk home." Two brothers, the Ma brothers, were our chauffeurs—one drove and the other took care of the cars. We referred to them by their surname and number—number four Ma, our actual chauffeur, and number five Ma. They pleaded with the officers to allow them to take us home explaining that within the car were young girls who had never been in the streets before. We were so frightened, and that was the first time in my life that I was ever on the street before. By then, a crowd had gathered around us. We were standing in the street surrounded by people staring at us. It was so embarrassing and frightening. There we were standing with the officers shouting at us that we were capitalists and commanded us to walk home. Number four Ma pleaded and pleaded and finally convinced the officers to let them drive us home.

With officers riding on the running boards and an ever-growing crowd running alongside, the car slowly wove its way back to the compound. The car, along with chauffeur Ma, was confiscated but not before the police and the crowd looked around. For many of them, it was the first time they had ever seen the inside of a wealthy person's mansion much less one built in the Western style.

> Our chauffeur Ma—he was a wonderful man—warned us, "Today they are confiscating the car, but they will be back to confiscate the house next. If I can, I will come back to warn you if I hear anything." And then one night, he took a huge risk by coming over to tell us about what he had overheard. "Be careful. I have heard them talking; they held a meeting about your case. They intend to confiscate the house. Gather your valuables and send them to your relatives' homes as soon as possible."

Heeding his warning, Dexing assembled what jewelry and other goods she could manage to pack at that time and had servants quietly deliver them to her husband's cousin who also lived in the French concession for safekeeping. The very next morning, signs were posted everywhere.

> In the morning, we never would have believed it could have happened so quickly, but there it was just as chauffeur Ma told us the night before. We were still asleep and when we arose, there was a steady stream of people going around the house. Everywhere we looked, we saw wooden placards stating that this room was to be an office, that room was to be a meeting room, and so on. Not only did they post the signs, but they evicted us immediately as well when they found a scroll of calligraphy that Cai Hanqing had written while searching the house.[30] Even the Lincoln and the race horses were confiscated.

Dexing sent the children over to their other paternal aunt's house in another part of the French concession taking with them whatever personal goods the servants could carry. Guards surrounded the entire compound, and Dexing was forced to employ a system of bribes to allow her to remove larger items while the guards turned a blind eye. Enterprising guards began changing hourly, and the next round of bribes ensued. Fortunately, the large number of Yeh Kai Tai workers who came to the compound worked tirelessly to remove much of the furniture and personal items.

Evicted from their home, Dexing moved temporarily to a hotel that the civilian police surrounded to ensure that no one tried to smuggle anything in or out. With no servant having the abilities of the deceased Chen Bingchen, Dexing spent two desperate days seeking a large, affordable place to rent because she still had seventeen people under her charge. As the events at Fengchi's mansion showed, even the foreign concessions were not totally safe from the heightened nationalistic Zeitgeist in Wuhan,[31] but nonetheless, Dexing was able to rent suitable accommodations in the Japanese concession from a mochi shop owner who owned a four-story building. Dexing rented the upper three floors for the household and one-half of the ground floor for the few remaining servants and cooks.

Residing in the Japanese concession essentially freed the Yeh household from the surveillance of the left Guomindang, but living there was fraught with its own perils. Under the pretext of insuring that no Communists were infiltrating the quarter, all Chinese citizens passing through the concession were subject to search at anytime, and men were required to bow in respect to any Japanese who crossed their paths. Cars were permitted to pass without inspection, but passengers in rickshaws or on foot were subject to interrogation. Any slight—real or imagined—to any Japanese person resulted in swift retaliation. If any Chinese man failed to display sufficient deference, he could be thrown to the ground and have his face trod upon while being verbally ridiculed and mocked. Although women did not have to bow, they were subject to body searches at whim. Soldiers would purposely grope and fondle attractive young Chinese women during the inspection; any resistance or complaint would result in further abuse. Consequently, Yuanshuang and Yuanquan were forbidden to walk in the area unescorted, especially since across the alley from their apartment was a brothel. A steady stream of Japanese sailors and marines would wander in there at all times of the day and night.

> There was an alley directly next door where there were prostitutes. Many of the women were Koreans who were brought over from Korea to serve the Japanese soldiers—they were called "military women" or "comfort women." There were also Chinese women who were sold into prostitution as well. The lives of the prostitutes was harsh, but the lives of Korean prostitutes were especially terrible, terrible. They were kept naked at all times. They were kept naked so that they could not escape. If they wore clothes and managed to escape, they might be able to pretend they were Chinese or to be mistaken for a Chinese; but they were naked and could go nowhere. They were treated so badly, worse than animals. Our servants would talk with some of the Chinese prostitutes in the alley who told them about how they were all treated. On the other side of the alley was a Geisha house. These women were beautifully dressed and had elaborate hairstyles and make-up. They were reserved for the high-ranking Japanese officers.

Even avoiding public appearances as much as possible did not spare Dexing and the children from problems. While watering the plants lining the front window ledge, the overflow dripped upon pedestrians down below who made the accusation that someone above was urinating upon them. The authorities came to arrest the offender and thoroughly searched the premises. Their Japanese landlord interceded on their behalf.

Their landlord, whom Dexing called Dong Wu, owned the mochi shop on the first floor of the building. At first, Dexing was fearful of him as she was of all Japanese. "The first time I ever saw a tomato were ones that Dong Wu grew in his garden. My mother forbade us to eat them because she said they were poisoned. But we were all too curious. We blanched the tomatoes to remove their skins, and ate them coated in sugar anyway."

During the time that Dexing lived there, the fear and suspicion ceased and she befriended the Japanese landlord to whom Dexing gave homemade preserved meats, fish, and vegetables. In return, he would give them mochi and fresh vegetables grown in his garden. So, when the authorities came to arrest the person for urinating on the pedestrians, it was Dong Wu who intervened, personally reassuring the police that only women and a small boy lived in the upper apartments. An old family cook was the sole adult male associated with the Yehs, but he lived in the downstairs kitchen and never went beyond the ground floor. Only after the landlord argued that it would be physically impossible for the girls or the young boy to urinate from the window ledge and vouched to the authorities that the water was not intentionally poured upon the people walking below was the furor settled, and the authorities left. The potted plants, however, were henceforth banished from the ledge.

Chinese Provinces, 1926.

The second time Japanese authorities came was more disturbing. Buildings throughout the concession and especially those rented by Chinese were frequently searched and used during military maneuvers. Simulated attacks and escape tactics were often conducted by Japanese military personnel. Houses could be entered at will, and when a group of armed Japanese soldiers entered the floors rented by Dexing thrusting written orders she could not read, the whole family became frightened. Running to the windows, they called to Dong Wu who came up from his shop immediately. "Our landlord was a good man. He told the officers that he owned the building and that we rented the floors above his shop. He promised that if ever he saw a suspicious person enter the building, he would immediately notify the military police. He personally vouched to provide surveillance for the building since he was the landlord and his shop faced the street."

The third incident involving interaction with the Japanese was the proverbial straw that broke the camel's back. Bored with their confinement within the apartment, and freed from the normal restrictions that would have confined them to their family compound, Yuanshuang and Yuanquan pestered their mother to the point that she relented and allowed them and their cousins to venture out to the miniature golf course across the alley that was next door to the brothel. There they could play golf and enjoy ices in the shade of the covered pavilions. Slouched in a garden chair with her head tilted back while eating her ice, Yuanshuang looked up to see a drunken Japanese soldier staring in her face.

> I will never forget that time. I can close my eyes even now, and I can recall that day so vividly. There I was lounging in the chair eating my ice with my eyes closed when suddenly a Japanese soldier was in my face saying in fractured Chinese, "Pretty girl, pretty girl." He was drunk because I could smell the alcohol on his breath—that's how close he was! He didn't mean me any harm, but seeing his face looming above frightened me. I jumped up; the chair fell behind me, and I ran to the edge of the pavilion. We raced home immediately. My mother was horrified when we related the tale.

Shaken by these incidents, Dexing's resolve to find a safer place for the family was strengthened. She sent the girls immediately to live with her brother who resided in the ex-British concession while she searched for new housing in another quarter. Now that Chen Bingchen was dead, Dexing's continuing trials further convinced her of the importance of literacy. Her inability to read and write hampered her every move, and she was determined that her daughters would not suffer the same fate. No longer able to hire a private tutor because of the housing situation, Dexing enrolled the girls in a local public school for the fall term 1927. Dexing, the women, and Yuanli continued to live in the Japanese quarter, and Dexing visited her daughters whenever possible until she, too, was able to find suitable housing in the ex-British concession where the family continued to live throughout the War of Resistance with the Japanese.

Almost immediately, Dexing was dissatisfied with the public schooling arrangement. Now forced to regularly leave the newly rented mansion to tend to family matters, she witnessed an increasing change in attitudes and behaviors during her excursions. Schoolgirls had their hair bobbed instead of braided in long queues. The left Guomindang encouraged social and political reforms. Young female students freely traveled in public, wore new fashions, and had boyfriends—behaviors that Dexing regarded as inappropriate for young ladies. Fearful that her daughters would be seduced by the "wild" environment, Dexing explored other alternatives.

Dexing's grandnieces were attending an American Episcopalian missionary school in Wuchang—St. Hilda's School for Girls—and upon questioning them about their school, she learned much about the missionary school experience. The girls wore uniforms, were not allowed to wear make-up, were not permitted to have boyfriends visit or even correspond with them, and, most importantly, they lived in a compound situated in a remote agricultural section in Wuchang away from the dangers of the Japanese and left Guomindang's influences. Even so, during the unsettled times of the "revolution," Dexing did not want her daughters to be separated from her especially since the men were still in Shanghai. Moreover, St. Hilda's was to become a solely junior/senior high school in 1928, and it really did not matter because the school was temporarily closed because of the current political situation.

St. Lois's, an elementary school in Hankou's ex-British concession where the elementary students for St. Hilda's were transferred in 1928, would have to do. Located in the same compound as St. Phoebe's Training School for Deaconesses and St. Lois's School for Primary Teachers,[32] it was the only school in Hankou to provide a complete upper and lower primary education. Although founded as a day school, during the period following the Northern Expedition, St. Lois's became a boarding school and an expensive one at that. Supported by Americans, the school was largely operated by the Chinese except for the key administrators who were Americans, but they had little interaction with the students.[33] When Rongzai finally returned from Shanghai in late 1927, Dexing approached him for the tuition, but he refused given Yuanshuang's past performance with private tutors. Money was now tight since Rongzai was neither a senator nor the treasurer and Yeh Kai Tai's business was being adversely affected by the political turmoil. As such, it would be public school or nothing at all. If Dexing wanted to spend her own money that would be fine, but he certainly would not throw good money after bad for the "little miss" who was always "ill."

Undeterred, Dexing took five thousand ounces of her own silver and invested it in Yeh Kai Tai which helped it survive the tumultuous time, and she would be able to use her monthly interest payments to pay for the tuition. Dexing had two elaborate traditional silk qipaos—one in bright yellow for Yuanshuang, one in light blue for Yuanquan—made by her seamstress. Using the requisite shoe-making skills that women of the upper class used to prove their "worthiness" by making shoes for their future mother-in-laws, Dexing now made elaborate dragon shoes for her daughters. She was ready to present them outfitted in the grandest of dynastic fashion for their audience with the principal of St. Lois's.

Entrance into missionary schools was not automatic: an examination was required of all students, and only those with sufficient scores were normally accepted. Funding was a chronic problem for missionary schools; intermittent suspension of school terms from 1926 to 1929 placed even greater financial burden on their fiscal budgets which were already pared to a minimum. Consequently, when Dexing brought her two qianjin xiaojie to see the principal of St. Lois's, he was most understanding. Being a Christian minister and a father himself, he understood Dexing's plight and her desire for Yuanshuang's and Yuanquan's safety. Since the fall term was well under way, the girls would not be admitted; however, the principal agreed to admit them for the next term without the usual requirements, but he suggested some modifications in dress and hairstyle.

> There the two of us sat—my sister and I—dressed like two actresses in our silk qipaos. The principal said, "We will admit them on a trial basis. They will have to wear uniforms; they certainly won't be able to dress like that. And their hair must be cut." My mother refused, but the principal urged her to give us a more modern haircut. "At least trim their hair to shoulder length; their hairdos are from dynastic times," he implored my mother who, after much convincing, finally agreed to trim—not cut—our hair and only to the middle of our backs.

A list of the required goods was given to them, and Dexing purchased what they would need.

> My sister and I went to special stores that sold the required goods that students needed for school. The list was quite long, several pages in length—we had to provide all of our own personal things. We were fitted for uniforms that had to be hand tailored, even they had to be made of a certain type of cotton cloth—no fancy embroidered silk gowns there. My mother proceeded to purchase everything new—new combs, new underwear, new stockings, new shoes—everything was brand new. From the top of our heads to the soles of our feet, we had everything new, new, new. New wash cloths, new towels, new sheets, new wash basins, new blankets—everything we needed for school was brand new. Anything she could think of, she purchased. "This is your dowry," my mother said, "you are marrying your future. You don't have to rely on anyone, and you don't have to marry if you are able to take care of yourselves. Remember that. Be diligent and study hard."

To ease their adjustment into a foreign-run private school, the girls were placed together in the fifth grade which was lower than their ages would warrant and despite the fact that Yuanshuang was a year older than her sister. Since their school, St. Hilda's, was temporarily closed, Bao Xunfang and Bao Xunyi (Dexing's grandnieces) were frequently invited to the Yeh household to prepare Yuanshuang and Yuanquan for their impending status as students in the New China. Since they already attended a foreign-run school, they were available to provide some additional tutoring. The idea was to coach Yuanshuang and Yuanquan in subjects that they had never encountered, such as English grammar and conversation and geography, as well as to further socialize them to foreign customs and habits. Although Yuanshuang and Yuanquan's grandfather had frequent interactions and business partnerships with foreigners, built a foreign home, and used foreign products, the girls had never interacted with Westerners let alone Americans before. Their exposure was confined to seeing American movies and seeing "white foreigners" in the streets once they moved to the ex-British concession. But these encounters were sporadic and they did not involve any personal interaction.

Following the 1928 Lunar New Year, the two sisters moved into the dormitories at St. Lois's. Because St. Lois's was near their rented mansion, every Saturday, Dexing would visit and bring washbasin-sized bowls that were filled to the brim with seasonal fresh fruits. Other times she would bring or send steamers filled with dainty meat and vegetable dumplings, steamed bread, and other snacks so that Yuanshuang and Yuanquan could share them with their classmates. To help them acquire grade competency, two St. Lois's teachers were hired as tutors. Dexing sent the house matrons and the teachers/tutors gifts so that they would not mistreat her daughters. Dexing's hope was that by providing so much food and so many gifts, her daughters would become popular and this would help them adjust to an environment far different from their previous existence.

And different that environment was. Never exposed to physical education nor Western music, they found those subjects to be bizarre. "All that jumping around with your arms going up and down, the first time I saw that, I thought, 'They have lost their minds!' And singing out loud. I was familiar with Chinese opera, but this was entirely different—standing and singing together was too much. I refused to participate. When my report card had two big fat zeros in those two categories, my mother was concerned and went to speak to the principal. Eventually, we got used to singing, but I still refused to participate in physical exercises, and my grades in that subject continued to suffer."

By the end of the 1928 school year, Yuanshuang wanted to attend the sixth grade. Embarrassed by the fact that she was at least four years older than the others in the fifth grade, Yuanshuang pushed to take the examination for the sixth grade. Although not quite prepared, Yuanshuang was nevertheless placed in the sixth grade when the new school term began in fall 1928. Yuanquan was also placed in the same class so that the girls could remain together. Every evening and on Saturdays, they continued their remedial work in an effort to reach their grade level. At first, she was diligent, but as time went on, Yuanshuang fell back into her old habits.

> Two women teachers from St. Lois's were hired by my mother to tutor us every evening after classes. Shi Meiling tutored us in English, history, and geography, and Qiang Peifen was especially talented in mathematics. Every night we went for tutoring. We spent more time together on Saturdays preparing for the following week's courses and homework.
>
> Qiang Peifen was an excellent teacher—strict but patient in how she taught mathematics. She was a quiet woman who encouraged us whenever we were at a loss. Shi Meiling was a more lively, attractive young woman, and although she was hired to teach us English during the summer as well, she spent most of the time playing mah-jongg with my mother, Tai, and Concubine Yu. Meanwhile, in the other room, we would practice our English loud enough so that our

teacher and, especially my mother would hear us. "Is this a book?" "Yes, this is a book." "Is this is a pen?" "Yes, this is a pen." It sounded so convincing, that everyone was impressed remarking, "Oh, their English is improving" when in reality, we merely repeated the simplest English phrases over and over again.

By the summer of 1929, Yuanshuang and Yuanquan wanted to attend junior high school despite the fact that their sixth grade competency skills were below par. Requirements for entrance into St. Hilda's were more rigorous and no leniency would be given. That summer, Xunfang and Xunyi coached Yuanshuang and Yuanquan warning them that St. Hilda's entrance examination was difficult. Undaunted, the two took the examination.

Unbeknownst to Yuanshuang, fortuitous happenstance occurred in her favor. Once control of China was wrested away from the warlords and unified under the Nationalists, the status of all foreign schools changed. No longer would there be separate and unequal school systems. Foreign schools either had to register with the government or cease operation altogether, and foreign schools would now be subject to government regulations. Included in those regulations were specifications that all classes other than English had to be taught in Chinese by Chinese teachers. Thus, the entrance examinations prior to that time were in English. In order to comply with this regulation and to enable St. Hilda's to reopen its doors in time for the fall term, the teachers hastily constructed an entrance examination. Instead of the previous lengthy essay-type examination designed by the chair of the English Department of Central China University,[34] the test was multiple choice or short questions written in Chinese. In the case of Yuanshuang, it was more multiple guess than multiple choice.

I heard so many stories about the entrance examination that I was dreading it. My English was still inadequate. All I really knew was "Is this a pencil?" "Yes, it is a pencil," but not much more. Oh, how I regretted not studying English more diligently at that moment. But when the examination was passed out, it was nothing like what [Xunfang and Xunyi] had described. It was just little squares that you filled in, and it was entirely in Chinese! I did not need to know one bit of English. No grammar, no conversation, no reading comprehension, no spelling. Even so, I did not know the answers to most of the questions. I just sat there randomly filling in the little squares. . . . No one was more surprised than I when the test results were returned, and I learned I had passed. I passed! To this day, I don't know how I passed, but I did.

Yuanquan was less adept at guessing and did not pass even though she was far more diligent and conscientious about her studies; she remained in the sixth grade at St. Lois's before retaking the entrance examination and moving onto St. Hilda's the following year. For Yuanshuang, a whole new world was about to open.

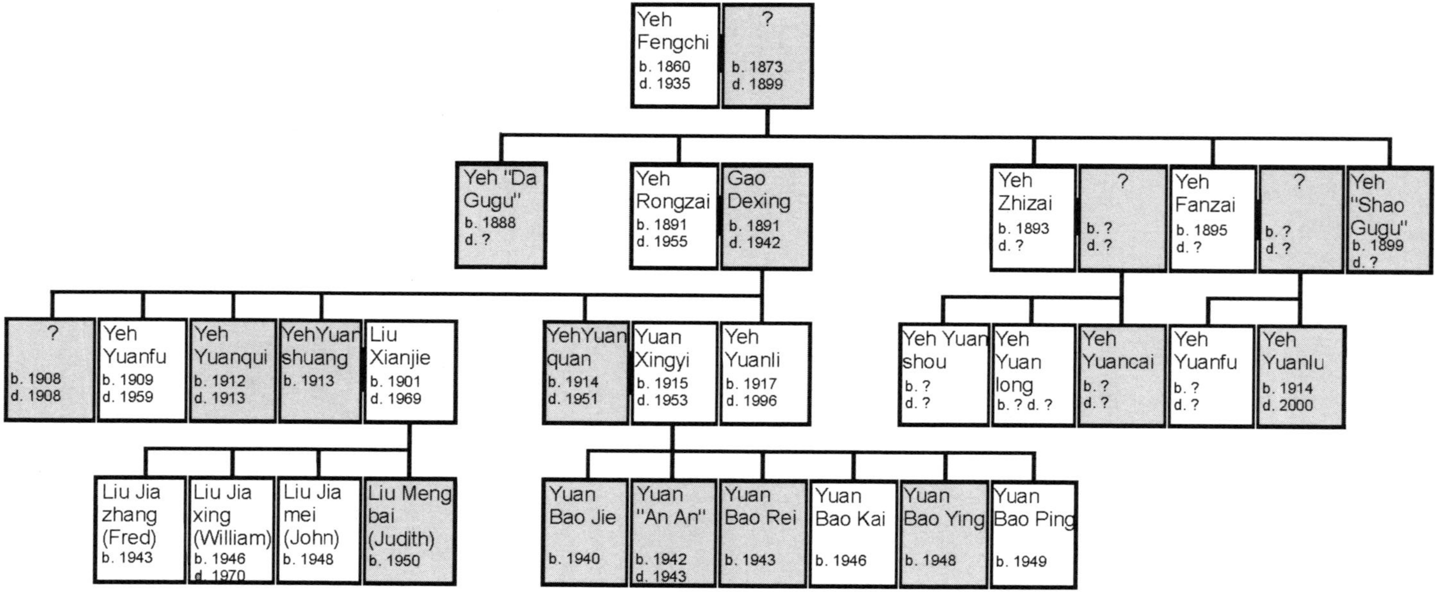

Descendants of Yeh Fengchi.

Gao Dexing and the Yeh Children, 1928. Left to right: Yuanfù, Yuanli, Yuanshuang, Gao Dexing, Yuanquan.

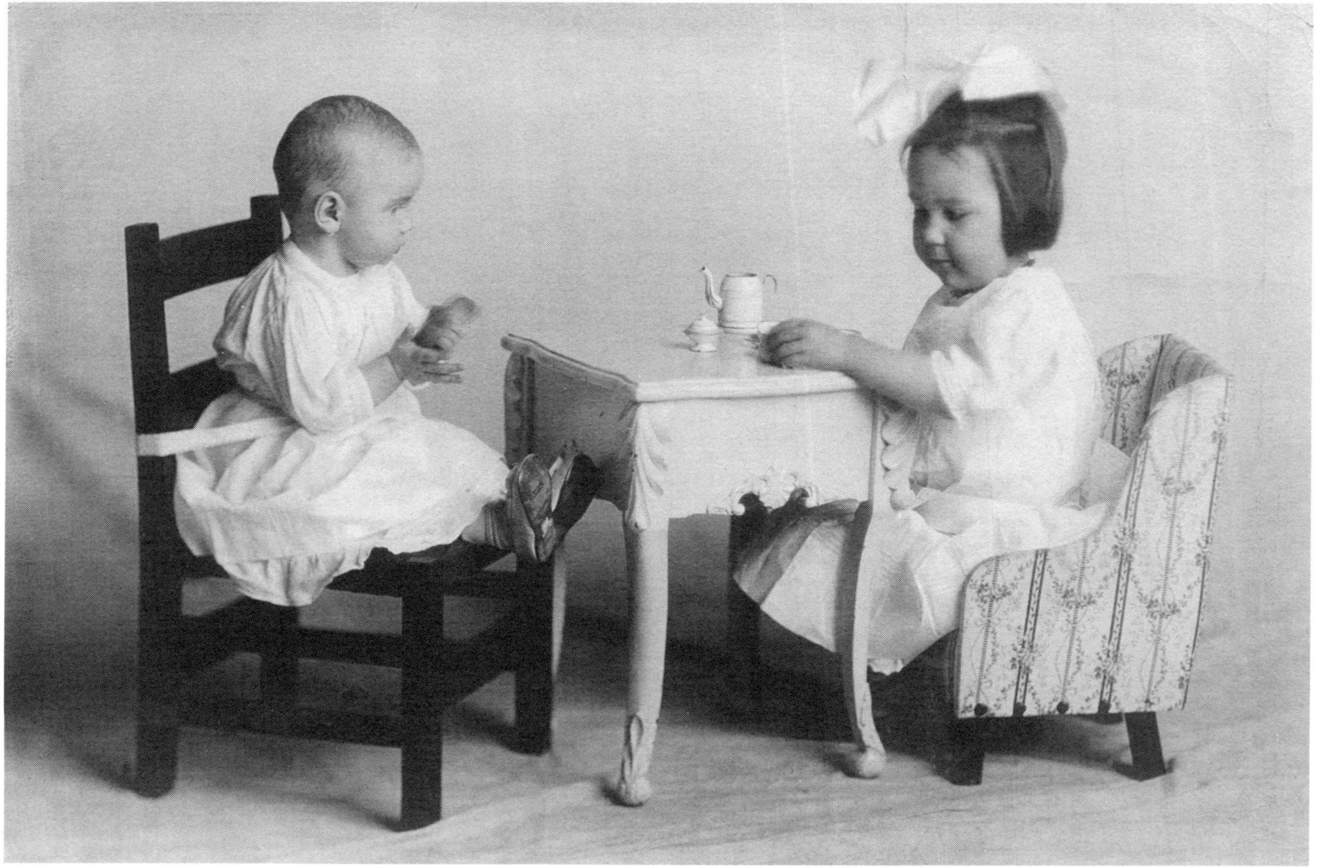

Dorothea and Norman, 1912. Courtesy Catherine Howe Collato, Private Collection of Dorothea Wakeman Howe.

2

Dorothea Kingsley Wakeman

DOROTHEA WAS BORN TO EARL SEELEY WAKEMAN AND HARRIETT ALICE Stillson Wakeman on July 3, 1907, in Oberlin, Ohio. As avid music lovers, Earl and Harriett met when both were members of Stanford University's campus choir. Although a nondenominational service was offered each Sunday, it was Episcopalian in essence. With each successive choir practice and service that Earl and Harriett attended as choir members, their interest grew not only in terms of the ceremony, but also in each other. During his courtship days in 1904, Earl would pick up Harriett who lived on Kingsley Street with her aunt who had come out from Nebraska "to provide a home" for her.[1] Within six months, they were engaged. Dorothea's middle name would forever commemorate those fond days of courtship. When they married in 1906, Earl, who was a Congregationalist, and Harriett, who was a Presbyterian, decided to wed in "the only place possible"—the Stanford Chapel that they had grown to love so much.[2]

Other mutual interests quickly bonded the couple together. Both shared a passion for learning and teaching. The two enjoyed reading literature, poetry, and the Bible which they would read aloud to one another. More importantly, Earl and Harriett shared a deep abiding belief in their respective faiths, a complementary concern for the current social conditions they witnessed not only in the United States but in the world as well, and a profound desire to remedy those social ills. That they would share such a similar worldview was not surprising since Earl and Harriett were born during the tumultuous end of the nineteenth century—Earl in Riceville, Iowa, on April 11, 1881; Harriett in Craig, Nebraska, on May 7, 1884. Earl and Harriett grew up during a time when Protestant movements directed specifically at youth were beginning to become more commonplace. Two were particularly important—the YM/WCAs and the Student Volunteer Movement for Foreign Missions (SVM). The YMCA founded a student department in 1877 to work with colleges and universities and the SVM was founded in 1888 to recruit volunteers who would pledge their lives to missionary service. Earl and Harriett were part of that large contingent of students who were inspired by the YM/WCAs and the SVM. Passions to become crusaders for Christ were fueled during large, revivalistic student conventions which both Earl and Harriett attended. As members of two denominations—Congregational and Presbyterian—where "the social gospel became especially conspicuous," the call for foreign service was a natural extension of their religious faith.[3] Travel to the far corners of the earth and the fervent desire to bring God's word were the impetus for so many college-aged students of the time to join and to answer the riveting call to social service through "evangelization of the world in this generation"—the battle cry of the SVM.[4] Using this catchphrase as the title of his book published in 1900, John R. Mott's work became the essential "must-read" book for the movement. In it, he challenged individual Christians to take personal responsibility to implement this worldwide goal.[5] And Earl and Harriett were two of many who not only read Mott's book but who answered the call to serve as missionaries—Earl wished to be a preacher; Harriett wished to be a teacher.

Earl's desire to become a preacher was also consistent with the Social Gospel movement in that the Social Gospel not only called for social action and social responsibility, it was also an evangelical movement promoted by charismatic speakers from the pulpit. Its leaders were "preachers, proclaimers, and educators" who "sought to change men's views and attitudes, to win them to a new religio-social faith. The movement was strong in the pulpit and on the platform, and in the seminaries."[6] As an excellent orator with a dynamic, powerful personality and commanding presence, Earl was a natural.

Coming-of-age during the heyday of the Social Gospel movement profoundly influenced the youth living through those times. Harriett, who was the more ardent of the two, was the first to submit her SVM application on June 4, 1904. In her application, she wrote that she "was lead to think of becoming a foreign missionary by two student volunteers [on] December 1, 1903," and by attending the "missionary convention at Oakland, California, December 4, [1903]," where she "felt that God told me to sign the [Volunteer Declaration] card" which she did on May 16, 1904.[7] Harriett's conviction was further cemented when "at the last Student Conference at Capitola, California," she heard "Mr. Hotchkiss from Africa. He was a wonderful power at the Convention. Those who had never thought of volunteering volunteered when they heard him."[8] In that same application, Harriett proposed a course of study to prepare her for such work. "My major course in college is German and my minor courses French and drawing. I intend to take up Spanish this fall. Languages & drawing I specialize in. After I graduate I intend to take two years in music. I also intend to form my course so that I have as much Bible Study as possible. I shall begin Vocal Interpretation before graduation and courses in English Composition."[9]

Reading about "those poor women in India—of their early marriages and widowhood . . . [and] how they die without knowing a single thing about

Jesus Christ" inspired Harriett to select India as a preferred mission field—if the Presbyterian Mission Board had a site in "Northern India"—to serve as a teacher. She also sought advice from the SVM for courses to take and for books to read that would strengthen her knowledge of mission studies. "Could you tell me what would be best for me to read for gaining more knowledge concerning India? Could you suggest any alterations in my course of study? I have several good books. 'The Evangelization of the World in This Generation'—Mott. Medical Missions, 'The Call, Qualifications & Preparation of Missionary Candidates,' 'The Volunteer Bared,' & 'Do Not Say.' "[10]

Although she had "done very little work in my Association at Stanford" in terms of training for missionary work, Harriett did "have a little Deputation work" with the intention of doing more "next summer." She planned to "teach a Mission Study Class" in the fall of 1904, and continue "private teaching of children" and studying music to prepare herself for a teaching position anywhere that there was "the greatest need in the whole missionary field."[11]

Earl's desire to be a missionary was first kindled by his early church experiences, and his later association with Harriett had a profound effect on not only his personal life but on his future plans as well. He joined the SVM on April 5, 1906, as a "result of an evening walk and talk about Christ with a Stanford man who opened his life to me and told me he wanted to believe in Christ the Son of God and in the forgiveness of sin, and could not." People who possessed such a spiritual lacuna were in need of help and guidance. His friendship with two friends who had "gone to Africa"—"Augustine James and Charley Duncan"—as well as his involvement with Harriett, were also instrumental in his decision to become a missionary, especially in Africa.[12]

> When a boy of twelve I joined the church & wished to become fitted for the ministry. When I was eighteen my aged pastor—Dr. William Windsor of Campbell, Cal, took me and my father aside after church one Sunday and told my father that he believed I should find my life work in the ministry. I did not however decide to take his advice. I first considered becoming a foreign missionary seriously when a year and a half ago, I came to know and love an earnest student volunteer of Stanford. We have been engaged a year. During that time we have prayed to know God's will, and I have become greatly interested in missions; Africa especially.[13]

Although he was majoring in English, Earl had "made a thorough study of South America from Pool's index, maps and books of missionary libraries . . . read 'Do Not Say,' 'World Evangelization in this Generation'. . . and all of 'Livingston in Africa' in various leaflets on missions."[14] To prepare for the ministry, Earl proposed further study in a "Theological Seminary, also what medicine I can get" as well as continuing to study and collect various "talks and readings" in his file case.[15]

Their ardent desire to become missionaries led Earl and Harriett to transfer to the great midwestern institution founded by abolitionists, Oberlin College, in 1906—Earl to attend the Theological Seminary, and Harriett to study at the music conservatory.[16] However, upon graduation from Oberlin, their first assignment was not to be their desired sites in Asia or Africa but to a home missionary station in North Dakota. Ironically, their applications to the SVM were rejected because they had "family." Realizing that Harriett's pregnancy and the subsequent birth of Dorothea in 1907 were contributing factors to their home missionary assignment did not decrease their disappointment at failing to receive a foreign mission assignment. Nevertheless, they accepted their home mission assignment and spent two years teaching English to immigrant miners before they decided upon another course of action. After some deliberation and a sense of purpose that extended beyond teaching English, the decision was made to decline renewal of the home mission assignment and instead, for Earl to pursue more education. Earl decided to become an attorney and applied to Stanford Law School, and upon his acceptance, the family moved back to Palo Alto.

Earl and Harriett's passion for their faith fostered in their youth and roused during their undergraduate days never cooled. Even while attending law school, Earl's desires to preach the gospel and to contribute to the community were evident. In between studying diligently, on evenings and weekends, he pursued evangelical work. Purchasing what was once a large chicken coop, Harriett and Earl completely remodeled it not only into a home but also into a school. Recalling that house, Dorothea recounted, "Chicken houses in those days, were quite unique. They were more substantial and not just the type of chicken coops that might come to mind when you first hear the word, 'chicken house.' But I had very ingenious parents, and nothing stopped them ever, any time. They remade that chicken house into a home, built a living room onto it, all kinds of things."[17] Not only did the house serve as their home, but during the day, the living room served as a makeshift elementary school where Harriett served as a teacher. In addition to the usual subjects such as reading, writing, and arithmetic, the school would provide a strong Christian-based education. Earl invited one of his sisters, Ruth, to stay with them and teach kindergarten. "And I used to go in [Aunt Ruth's] pony cart each day to go out to collect the [neighbor's] children for the kindergarten," Dorothea recalled.[18] As a consequence, Dorothea was homeschooled initially by her Aunt Ruth and mother in kindergarten and first grade; from second grade on, she attended the Washington School.[19] During this time, a son, Norman, was born in Palo Alto on December 20, 1910.

On weekends, riding their bicycles, Earl and Harriett made home visitations and preached in Woodside, a community in the hills above Stanford. Riding on a seat attached to the handlebars of her father's bicycle, Dorothea was included on these excursions. Not only did Earl evangelize, but he also helped establish several churches for those congregations that did not have their own church. He would provide pro bono legal work by negotiating for the purchase of land, examining contracts, or providing legal counsel. Upon completion of his doctorate in jurisprudence in 1912, he was awarded his degree by David Starr Jordan[20] during graduation. Earl passed the bar examination and was admitted to the California Bar Association in 1912. When he was offered a position with the Title Insurance and Trust Company in Los Angeles, the family moved first to a rental in Pasadena before purchasing a home at 600 Broadway, San Gabriel.[21]

While renting in Pasadena, the Wakemans searched the local community for a parish and began attending St. Mark's Episcopal Church. There they met Stephen and Grace Clark whose son, Stephen, was the rector in another parish. The Clarks were responsible for Earl and Harriett becoming Episcopalians. With their previous exposure to Episcopalian services, as well as being "sentimental about having met while singing in the choir at Stanford Chapel," Earl and Harriett "became Episcopalians."[22] Wishing to baptize both Dorothea and Norman but belonging to no congregation of their own, the Clarks sponsored not only Earl and Harriett but also the children as well. At Earl and Harriett's baptism, Mrs. Hall—the rector's wife—sponsored Dorothea's baptism as well. Both Mrs. Clark and Mrs. Hall took a particular interest in and befriended Harriett who was pregnant with her third child. When Gwendolyn was born in January 1913, both of them visited Harriett in the hospital, and Mr. and Mrs. Clark were named Gwen's godparents. Once settled in their San Gabriel home, the Wakemans found a parish of their own—All Saints Episcopal Church in Pasadena—and Gwen was baptized there. Although Earl ceased giving formal sermons, he "never lost his missionary zeal" and continued to be active as a Sunday school teacher, a church elder, and a pro bono church legal counsel whenever needed.[23]

Following Gwendolyn's birth, another sister, Geraldine, was born in August 1919. The Wakemans had a loving home where Earl referred to Harriett as "Etta," "Lovey," or "Yuzziz"—all terms of endearment. Harriett and Earl were referred to as "Mummy/Mommie/Momsie," "Daddy/Poppie/Poppy/Popsie," "oozuz," "precious," and "sweeties" by the children even as adults; Earl was also nicknamed "Growley," "Punkin/Pumpkin," and "Poor Fish." Earl was the patriarch who provided an undisputed overall plan of operation; Harriett remained at home with the children and had primary responsibility for realizing that plan. Earl was the unequivocal "breadwinner" and was a strict disciplinarian who ruled the family in an orderly, traditional, and dominant fashion; Harriett was efficient and organized in her domestic responsibilities as wife and mother. When there were only the two children, Dorothea and Norman spent alternate weekday evenings dining with their father who wished to "have peace and quiet during his dinner meals after a long day at the firm."[24] When the other two daughters were born, either Dorothea or Norman would alternate turns caring for their younger sisters until they were all old enough to dine together. Dorothea and Norman coveted the privilege of dining with their father, and on evenings when it was Norman's turn, Dorothea would often sing or tell stories aloud in the nursery. In an effort to quiet his sister, Norman would run back to the playroom and chasten his sister but, unable to pronounce her name, would say, "Shh, Dortow; no noise. Dortow, quiet!" The moniker stuck, and Dorothea would use it throughout her life.[25]

Earl and Harriett's love of music and insistence on a quality education for their children were apparent everywhere from the large record collection and musical instruments to their substantial library of books and periodicals. Harriett's musical talent, training, and teaching were put to use, and she taught each of the children to play the piano, and each had the ability to read music and sing. Evenings would be devoted to completing homework followed by music either on the phonograph, singing, or live performances by family members. They read the Bible, poetry, literature, and members of the family wrote "cantos" and performed plays they authored for family entertainment. The children were expected to be diligent in their assignments, especially since Dorothea and Norman were homeschooled in their early years. All of the children became voracious readers and never questioned that they would obtain college educations. Dancing, riding, tennis, and sailing lessons rounded out their education. As a lover of the sea, Earl was a member of the Balboa Yacht Club, and all of the children became accomplished sailors.

Upon completion of her elementary schooling, Dorothea attended Pasadena Polytechnic. Directly across the street from the California Institute of Technology—Cal Tech—the school was founded by one of its scientists to provide a high quality education for children of faculty and staff. The commute to the school involved quite a journey that necessitated several transfers, but Dorothea was encouraged by her mother who "was bound and determined" that she receive a first-rate education.[26] Dorothea graduated from the eighth grade and attended Alhambra High School where she graduated with honors in 1925.

Dorothea was accepted into the University of California, Los Angeles (UCLA), when the campus was still located in downtown Los Angeles. At the earliest opportunity, Dorothea rushed the Sigma Kappa Sorority where she soon assumed leadership roles and lived in the sorority house which, as sororities do, played host to numerous social functions. Dorothea was popular, well-liked, and dated often. During one of the numerous sorority social functions, Dorothea—who was pretty, animated, and active as well as being intelligent—was introduced to a young man with whom she quickly became enamored. Throughout much of her last two years, she spent as much time with Merrill Tucker, a young man who was attending California Polytechnic, Pomona, as she could, and they were engaged—much to Earl's consternation and disapproval—in her junior year. They shared a "common interest" in "literature, music," and could "still thrill to the same thread of thot, bit of poetry, strain of music, beautiful scene, feel of wind, rain, or snow on [their] faces."[27]

Majoring in English as her father before her, Dorothea graduated in the last UCLA class on the Vermont Avenue campus before the entire school moved to its Westwood location in 1929. Because UCLA did not have a graduate program in education at the time, Dorothea attended classes at the University of Southern California (USC) in order to continue her advanced work in English and education and to obtain her teaching credential. Not wishing to "miss out on the brand new campus" or "the fun of a new sorority house," Dorothea continued to live at UCLA and commuted to USC by bus until she purchased a car six months later.[28] Although Dorothea completed enough units for a master's degree in English, she did not complete her thesis. Obtaining a teaching credential was paramount, and in order to "save money," she had to forgo enrolling in a "thesis" course.[29]

Her last two years at UCLA were marred with disappointment and frustration. Earl did not approve of Dorothea's fiancé, Merrill, even though he was a scholarship student enrolled at Cal Poly; he was a scholar-athlete who "did well academically and also played on the football team," but "Daddy did not approve of him; he just didn't think he would ever amount to much because Merrill, who had a terrific personality, was always somewhat reserved around my father."[30] Equally strong willed and opinionated, "Growley" and Dorothea argued frequently about Dorothea's future and Merrill's ability to provide for them. The general convention that married women did not work would have made it difficult for Dorothea to continue employment even with her teaching credential. Dorothea believed "the more courtly rather than the hard working, penny-pinching student seemed a good choice to Daddy—like Wesley V. who was polished and charming."[31] And when Merrill fell a few units shy of graduating in 1929, the recriminations flew fast and furiously. "Daddy said, 'I told you so. I told you that he would never amount to anything. And he can't even graduate on time. How will he ever be able to support you if he hasn't even graduated! He just isn't a suitable choice.' And on, and on, and on."[32]

When the stock market crashed in October 1929, Dorothea's engagement was a further source of tension between the two. Although the plan was to marry after graduate school, Dorothea called off both the engagement and the relationship. Tired of the constant friction at home, Dorothea "just sort of gave up and fell out of love." Although Dorothea and Merrill continued their friendship and corresponded with each other, numerous attempts by Merrill to reconcile and numerous discussions between the two failed; Dorothea had her mind set and did not relent, "My father won; I just gave up. The constant tension, arguing, and the disapproving looks just got to me."[33]

Despite the stock market's collapse and the ensuing economic depression that befell the nation, Dorothea continued her graduate education from 1929 to 1933. As of 1928, Earl was a senior partner of his own firm, Wakeman, Rogers and Brown. Finances were tight, but suspending the children's education was totally out of the question for Earl.[34] As the eldest child, Dorothea was expected to "pull her own weight," and while working toward her teaching credential during 1931–32, she taught at a public school in La Puente. Unlike her undergraduate days, her graduate days were marred with unhappiness. Visits home inevitably ended up in tears because of the arguments or "any time when things got tense for that matter."[35] At the end of her first term at USC, Dorothea plunged herself into her studies by "getting out for the summers" and taking classes at the University of California, Berkeley. Aside from occasional dates with a young Berkeley man, Joseph Stanley, Dorothea "didn't have a chance or didn't make one to meet people" which made her "lonesome and . . . irritable," particularly to her father.[36] The sometimes heated, verbal clashes between the two were now reduced to long periods of silence and tears. As the period of estrangement continued into the summer of 1932, a crucial turning point in Dorothea's life occurred that involved her family's friends, the Clarks.

Stephen and Grace Clark's daughter, Julia, was a missionary in China. So moved by the stark realities of poverty and economic injustices not only in the United States but around the world, Julia attended deaconess school. These schools emerged in the decades around the start of the twentieth century as an alternative to theological schools and seminaries that did not accept women.[37] After attending the Los Angeles School for Deaconesses and the Philadelphia Deaconess School, she was "set apart" in 1913. Julia applied for a China field assignment and was sent to the Missionary District of Hankou that same year.[38] Reports of her experiences in China were often a topic of discussion at St. Mark's (where Julia's brother, Stephen, became the rector in 1927), All Saints, and in the Wakeman household because the family often socialized with the Clarks. As was customary for all foreign missionaries, after four years in the field, mission workers were given a six-month-long home furlough. During her 1932 furlough, Julia engaged in her usual round of lectures and fund-raising. Mission boards were perpetually seeking funds to support their workers around the world—

never more so than during the Great Depression era—and missionaries home on furlough were expected to assist in any means possible which meant that they were frequently on the lecture circuit. Thus, it was not unusual for Julia to lecture at local churches when she was home.

As part of the Young People's Fellowship audience at All Saints, Dorothea heard "spectacular" tales of "Chiang Kai-shek's troops coming from the South and marching through Wuhan" and the bombardment of Wuchang in September and October 1926. Pictures and details of the harrowing great 1931 flood and how Julia "roped tin bath tubs together to use as boats" and how she swam the waters to rescue school property were also presented.[39]

Dorothea was so entranced by the lecture that she sought out Julia after the presentation and queried, "Do you think there's any chance that they [St. Hilda's] would need another English teacher?" Now in possession of an English secondary credential that permitted her to teach senior high school "and anything all the way down" through the elementary level, Dorothea was "thrilled" when Julia enthusiastically responded that her credential was exactly what St. Hilda's needed because "the government would not allow any foreigner to teach anything in English except English" and there was a current shortage of teachers. Dorothea's query and excitement prompted Julia Clark to write the Department of Foreign Missions, Church Mission House at 281 Fourth Avenue, New York.[40]

Dorothea herself wrote for an application which she returned on January 13, 1933. The department responded that due to "very serious financial difficulties" resulting from the Depression, "we are unable to secure many new appointments to the overseas work. We are very anxious to be in a position to meet the calls from the foreign field as we are able, and shall be glad to assemble the necessary papers for you and see what may be done about securing an appointment if you will understand that we are not in a position just at present, to make any definite promises." Dorothea was requested to obtain a "routine medical examination" and was provided with several Los Angeles area physicians' names from whom she could obtain the necessary examination.[41] An aptitude test was required as well.

> Hundreds and hundreds of questions, and to this day, I remember a few. One of the questions was, would you, if you came to church, I don't know how it was worded exactly, but if you were late and the only seats available were down in the front row, would you hesitate to go down, take that seat. And I answered, "No." And the other one was, if you saw a woman slapping her baby or her child on the street, would you just walk on by or would you do anything to help the child? And I said, "I would help the child."[42]

The Depression curtailed the ability of mission boards to send new personnel into the field, but Dorothea received a letter from the Department of

Foreign Missions inviting her to accept a position in China. The letter from A. B. Parson dated June 20, 1933, read as follows:[43]

> My dear Miss Wakeman:—
>
> The Bishop of Hankow has cabled us asking for your appointment to teach at St. Hilda's School in Wuchang. Ordinarily this would be the final step in the process and we would make sailing arrangements for you.
>
> The present financial situation is so desperate, however, that we will be unable to promise you the appointment as yet. It may be that we will have to wait until about August 1st to give you final assurances. I am sorry, but do not see how we can do otherwise.
>
> Most of the foreign mission boards are not making any appointments at all, and we may have to follow the same policy and tell you that we cannot send you this year. Would you mind replying and letting me know what your plans would be if we have to disappoint you to this extent, and also advise us as to whether you can wait until August 1st, and then be ready to sail?
>
> We can do nothing at present but hope that the situation will not be too bad.
>
> Very sincerely yours,
> A.B. Parson.

Dorothea promptly responded that she was still very much interested. In August, the Department of Foreign Missions sent a telegram offering her a temporary one-year appointment, and because Dorothea was in Berkeley, Earl opened it. He then forwarded the telegram by regular mail, but not before writing in bold letters across the bottom, "Of course you won't go."[44]

It took several days for the letter to arrive in Berkeley, but when Dorothea opened the letter, read the telegram, and the statement written across the bottom, she "simply went down to the telegraph office" and wired her acceptance. Then, she called her parents that she was coming home to "pack up her things."[45]

In an ironic twist, her parents who were so desirous of becoming missionaries in their own youth were now so averse to their daughter going to China. Earl adamantly opposed her decision to take the tentative one-year position and "demanded" that she immediately rescind her acceptance.[46] He was convinced that Dorothea's decision was merely a rash, rebellious reaction predicated on their estrangement instigated by the broken engagement with Merrill. Going to China was tantamount to "throwing her life away" by hampering her prospects of finding a suitable spouse and a meaningful life.[47] Despite Dorothea's reassurances to the contrary, Earl refused to give his approval. In letter after letter, he successively insisted, entreated, argued, and then implored his willful daughter to reconsider. Dorothea wrote in response:

Oh Mummy & Poppie darling—it is so wonderful to be alive. My heart just sings and I can't sleep or eat hardly I'm so thrilled over China. It makes me feel terribly to think of grieving you—but honestly, some day you are going to be rightly glad. It is by taking big steps that we live. Not by taking little cautious society worn steps. You wait & see. And dear as Julia Clark is—you don't need to worry about my life being like hers. I hope I can gain some of her beauty of spirit from doing for others—but I would never be content to stay single as she has. You see Julia Clark as a girl of 25 had an entirely different back-ground & make-up from mine. China meant one thing to her & some thing else to me. It is a very sacred trust but I can be true to it without overlooking another just as sacred. Oh Mommy & Poppy! If you could only be as thrilled & happy as I am. . . . I don't worry ever about being not married because "all the boys" fall in love with me. I'll have a regular line-up when the boat stops at S.F. but there is no sense in getting married just to get married. I want a husband that I'm very much in love with & that like to travel & we'll explore every inch of this great wide world. Haven't you heard that a woman is in her prime from 25 to 35? Well that's me. Just begun. You can expect big things from me.[48]

Home during a weekend to pack, Earl and Harriett realized that Dorothea was singularly determined about going, and in the end, her will prevailed but not without a cost. Earl made it clear that he hoped she "would not stay over a year." Harriett told Dorothea she wanted her to "stay in China until you [are] married" and went on to say that "she never wanted to see [her] again until [she was] married."[49]

With Dorothea scheduled to sail on Friday, September 8, 1933, from San Francisco, it meant that she had a scant few weeks to purchase necessities, pack her belongings, and tend to other matters pertaining to her trip. Dorothea needed a passport and visas; she required specific inoculations (typhoid/paratyphoid and smallpox); the board recommended that she have her "teeth put into good condition shortly before leaving"; and she needed an eye examination and a spare pair of glasses fitted in the short time she had before sailing.[50] Aware that Dorothea "meant business," Earl finally relented and took control of the preparations.[51]

In printed instructions, "Business Arrangements in Connections with the China Mission," Dorothea became aware of what her missionary commitment would be if her temporary one-year assignment became a full-time appointment. She learned that as an unmarried woman, her "first term of service" would be four years, followed by a six-month furlough in the United States, with a salary of $900 a year for the first three years to be paid in the "Mexican (or silver) dollar." For "newly appointed missionaries," the Mission Board allocated $300 ($150 "usually paid in the United States and one-half after arrival in China") to purchase necessities, but she was requested "to save $75.00" to complete any other purchases in China. The brochure ended with a final paragraph that read, "The Department of Missions feels that in justice to the work, it must ask that young women agree in writing not to be married within a period of three years after arrival in the field."[52] To reiterate that clause, a letter from the board stated, in contractual terms that

> because a surprisingly large number of our appointees have been married soon after arriving in the field, the Department of Missions feels that in justice to the work, it must ask that in the future young women appointees shall agree if the case should arise, not to be married within a period of three years after arrival in the field. This may seem like anticipating a question that is, to say the least, not uppermost in your mind, but we would like to have your statement that in the event of appointment, you are willing to agree to this request.[53]

A suggested wardrobe and necessities list was sent to prospective women missionaries as well. Created by Deaconess Katharine E. Scott in 1922, a longtime China missionary and headmistress of St. Hilda's from 1913 to 1923, the list provided a detailed list of necessities.

> Outfit for Women Missionaries
> Going to China.
> I. Clothing: In addition to the ordinary supply of clothes which one would use during a year in the country it is well to provide as follows.
> 1. For hot weather (May 15 to Sept 15th)
> a) a plentiful supply of white wash dresses. These may easily be made by Chinese tailors after arrival, either from material purchased in this country, or from Chinese grass linen—(a grass linen dress costs from $5.00 to 7.00 Mexican)—
> b) white shoes and stockings. Canvass shoes can be made in China if you have a good model.
> 2. For cold weather (January and February probably December and Early March)
> Serge or other woollen dresses for every day wear (thin waists are out of the question)
> A velveteen or light cloth frock for evening wear.
> Remember that few houses are well heated, and churches and school rooms are not heated at all.
> Wool or silk and wool underwear.
> Woollen stockings.
> A furlined or very heavy wool coat for general wear.
> Warm gloves.
> At least one nice, fairly warm sweater for wear indoors.
> Outside the cities of Hankow or Shanghai, galoshes.
> Flannel night dresses (or material for the same)
> 3. The following articles while they may be bought in Shanghai and sometimes in Hankow, are rarely satisfactory and are usually disproportionately expensive. It pays to take a good supply—or to have replacements sent out.
> Shoes (other than canvas)

Corsets
Stockings
Handkerchiefs
Knit or woven underwear.
Overshoes (sometimes these cannot be got in Hankow at any price).
The following can not be got in Hankow—
Good bone hair pins or combs.
Fine needles or sewing cotton.
Good blotting paper.
II. Living conditions and expenses—

A single woman usually lives at first in one of the "Ladies Houses" that is with two or three other women workers who form a family, and share expenses. Or she may live with a married couple. Whether she pays board or shares household expenses, her actual living cost will be about 50.00 Mex. (Gold 25.00) in Hankow or higher in Shanghai.

It should be understood that while the mission provides houses or other living quarters it does not provide furnishings. The older "Ladies Houses" particularly those attached to institutions are now pretty well equipped at the personal expense of present and former residents and some only ask of newcomers a fixed money contribution towards replenishing the common stock for kitchen, dining room and living room. The newer houses may still be in need of equipment, in which all the residents should share. The new missionary should, if possible, ascertain in advance what is desired of her in this respect.

In any case she will have to furnish her own bedroom and probably also a study.

Bedding i.e., sheets, pillow cases, blankets, quilts, should be taken out. Also towels—price for table bed is cheaper in this country than in Shanghai but freight costs are heavy.

Furniture of all kinds can be made in either Shanghai or Hankow—or bought second hand—with the present high freight rates there is no advantage in sending out furniture except such articles already possessed as may be specially desirable. It is well to take ones books and pictures.

Miscellaneous.
Hot water bottles (metal) are almost a necessity and are cheaper in this country.
Toilet articles are obtainable in China but usually at an advance in price.
The same is true of retail drugs.
Hair nets are made in China.

Notes: Missionaries spending the first year in Language School will require their own bedding and towels but not furniture till the second year.

In any case the new missionary may be assured that the household to which she goes will expect to make her comfortable till she can collect her own things.[54]

Purchasing as many of the items as possible, Dorothea and her parents corresponded back and forth about how to get a steamer trunk to Berkeley —should Dorothea come down or should the trunk be shipped? In the end, Earl loaded the remaining items in the car and drove up north a mere five days before Dorothea was scheduled to sail. A second, used trunk, purchased from a Berkeley thrift shop, was packed "right there on the street with the people staring the entire time."[55]

To the very end, Earl tried to dissuade Dorothea, and she wrote a lengthy response to his entreaties.

> Daddy dear—please don't say "it seems terrible to have you going into all this." It doesn't make me feel as jubilant as mother's darling letter did yesterday because I never am completely happy when I think I'm worrying or grieving you. I remember once when I was going to a dance with M. and I remember I had left without telling Gerry or Mother or some one I was sorry for something I'd said & M. said driving right up to a pay phone "Well you're going to phone right now. I can see that or you'll be unhappy all evening." I had to know your happy. If you'll think hard you'd realize that if this were happening to someone else & I didn't have a chance of going that you'd wish I did. What earthly use is it to putter around doing common place drudgery things like every body else when you can get out into the whirl & do good to. I know there is lots to be done here but you sacrifice much more (if it comes down to that) by staying here and working. Sometimes you become obliviated. But out there you come in contact with just the most outstanding people—the courageous hearts. As for marriage you're running right into it in China. Everyone says that. They say every girl they ever knew who went over—was married as a direct result. I've heard of dozens. The first thing May Wood said was how she envied me because China is full of young Americans & Englishmen & no women out there at all. It is quite common for them to fall in love with Chinese girls because their own kind are so scarce. . . . But please don't take what I do so seriously. You can't worry forever about what I do. I wouldn't be doing it if it didn't make me happier than anything else. I'll never be lonesome. You ought to realize how quickly I Get acquainted. Then think of me in a place where they seek you out. Oh if you could just be as thrilled as I. I can always come home. I'm not going to be imprisoned in China. Oh I love it love it love it!![56]

On Friday, September 8, 1933, Dorothea set sail from San Francisco aboard one of the Dollar Steamship Lines's "newest, finest and largest electric liners ever built in America"—the SS *President Coolidge*—with a flurry of telegrams from well-wishers, boxes of candy, flowers, and accompanied by a full entourage of friends and family to see her off.[57] She would share "stateroom 142," "best in section— . . . near middle of ship—outside porthole,"[58] with Miss Broadbeck. Wearing a new fur coat purchased by her parents, with a note from Earl tucked within a pocket cautioning her to be careful about not losing such a valuable coat, and thirty dollars in cash, Dorothea left port. Because her parents could not attend the sailing, a small band of friends, her Aunt Grace, and her brother, Norman, who had the family's movie camera and recorded the event for them, saw her off.[59] Dorothea began a series of letters to her parents detailing her adventures aboard the liner as it crossed the Pacific Ocean with ports of call in Honolulu, Yokohama, and Kobe before reaching Shanghai.

Also aboard were twenty-seven other passengers headed for Shanghai most of whom were returning missionaries, and Dorothea was "treated as the baby" because she was "the only new missionary being sent out by any church."[60] The trip to China was filled with exciting conversations with missionaries returning to the "field" who warned her of the dangers of refusing "anything to the bandits. If they ask it—give it them, lest you lose a hand or an ear" and with "wild tales" about how she was "not to go up the Yangtze by boat . . . because it is too hot now to close the portholes & if you don't close them, the bullets shot by bandits at the passing boat will whizz in thro the port holes."[61] Dorothea met missionaries from the various denominations—Methodists, Baptists—and learned of the evacuations from the China inland missions during 1926 and 1928; she also observed how close-knit the Christian community was. Since much of the crew was Chinese, Dorothea had her first extended encounters with them.

En route there were "masquerade parties, fancy dress dinners, bathing beauty parades, deck sport tournaments, the well-known game of horse-racing, midnight sandwich parties, and dancing under the stars" as touted in the Dollar Steamship Lines's brochure along with deck sports, card tournaments, and tennis; Dorothea engaged in as many of these pleasures as possible with newfound friends such as Caroline Schulz, who was traveling to China to marry her fiancé, John S. "Jack" Service, and Helen Boyle, an Episcopalian missionary going to Japan.[62] At each port of call, church representatives met the missionary contingent where they were taken on grand sightseeing tours, and asked to take teas, have meals, and enjoy visits with the local Bishops during their brief layovers.

Upon the ship's arrival in Shanghai on Friday, September 29, Mr. Walker, the Episcopal treasurer in China, met Dorothea with the announcement that instead of going to Wuchang immediately, she was to be "sent to Peiping on the midnite train to Language School," and that evening, she boarded the "Tientsin—Pukow Railroad" for the train ride to Beiping.[63] The young woman who Dorothea was to replace had a miraculous recovery from her illness and was back teaching; consequently, Dorothea was now headed for six months of language training—the normal procedure for all missionaries entering the field for the first time. Accompanying her was Mary Richards, a young woman who was also obtaining intensive language training before assuming her position as Bishop Logan H. Roots's secretary in Hankou, and together, they whiled away the hours becoming acquainted with one another.

The College of Chinese Studies was the premier language school in China designed as an intensive, immersion-style language program. The student body at the language school was composed of students from all walks of life who came predominantly from Western countries, principally Americans, English, Irish, and Scots. The Department of Foreign Missions paid the $70 semester room rate and the $150 tuition; Dorothea was expected to pay her own board bill which was approximately $75 Mexican per month.[64] Although the program was rigorous and the daily schedule demanding, Dorothea had a wonderful time.

> Our day consists in arising at 7:15 and eating breakfast any time between 7:30 and 8:30. At 8:45 we must be in class. It is very strenuous at present. The Chinese language is a terrific one I can assure. Not a word of English is spoken in the language classes. We listen to one Chinese scholar for the first 45 minutes. . . . He introduces the new words. Then another Chinese comes in and repeats the new words. Then words steadily for 30 mins. in one sentence after another till your head is swimming. You can't imagine the concentration it requires. Then we have a 15 min. recess, which is well needed. We all play volley ball together and have lots of fun. Back to class at 10:15 for another half hour of listening to those Chinese words from another man. He, being well tired out, retires for his cup of tea at 10:45 and still another Chinese comes in to go thro the whole rigamarole again. Well from 11:15 until 12:00 we rest by listen[ing] to a lecture on Chinese History. You can't imagine what a relief it is. . . . [W]e go back to classes at 2:00 and stay in the same seat until 4:00. We have half hour periods of listening to different Chinese reiterate "This is a book, Whose book is it? Here are three pieces of money. This also is a piece of money. Give me three pencils. Is this yours? Not it is not yours." All in Chinese of course but terrible to get. We don't say one word. Just listen. Next week we are supposed to try to pronounce and go on to individual teachers. Then in the third week, we begin to learn to write the characters of the words that we have learned. . . . Sometimes we have four of those classes in the afternoon but the monotony is broken usually by a lecture on Chinese Geography from 3–4:00.[65]

Students were assigned an individual teacher whose responsibility was to increase their Chinese verbal abilities. Sessions began with the class meeting as a whole "first thing in the morning and first thing in the afternoon. That lasts half an hour each. The other half hour periods are spent alternately first with the individual teacher and then in groups of six students to a teacher."[66]

Despite long classes and the necessity for studying and practicing, Dorothea attended parties, went dancing, saw movies, visited the local sights, and went shopping with her new-found friends: Mary Richards, Dorothea's traveling companion to Beiping; John De Francis—"Yale graduate" out in China to "do business"; John Beck—"for missionary field near Wuchang"; Herbert Ruse—"an Englishman who has come out as a missionary"; and Norman Hanwell—graduate of UCLA, "also out for business."[67] Not only was Dorothea learning the language and creating networks, but her confidence was increasing to such a degree that she was determined to remain in China.

> I got scared over the Board's hiring me for one year only tho I don't suppose it would ever be limited to that actually. But I've decided that if they can't keep me out here, I'll get myself a job in China. They are really very easy to find if you're once out here. Kay Wilbur . . . has a perfectly marvelous job at $3.00 an hour for doing absolutely nothing but talk to two very wealthy Chinese girls giving them practice in English conversation and taking them with her to places like the University Club.[68]

After months of studying and surviving Beiping's cold winter, Dorothea received word that she was needed at St. Hilda's and headed south in mid-March. Accompanying her on the trip was Mamie Lou Roots, the daughter-in-law of Bishop Logan Roots. During the three-day journey, their excitement grew with each mile they drew closer to their destination. A new life was about to begin for both of them.

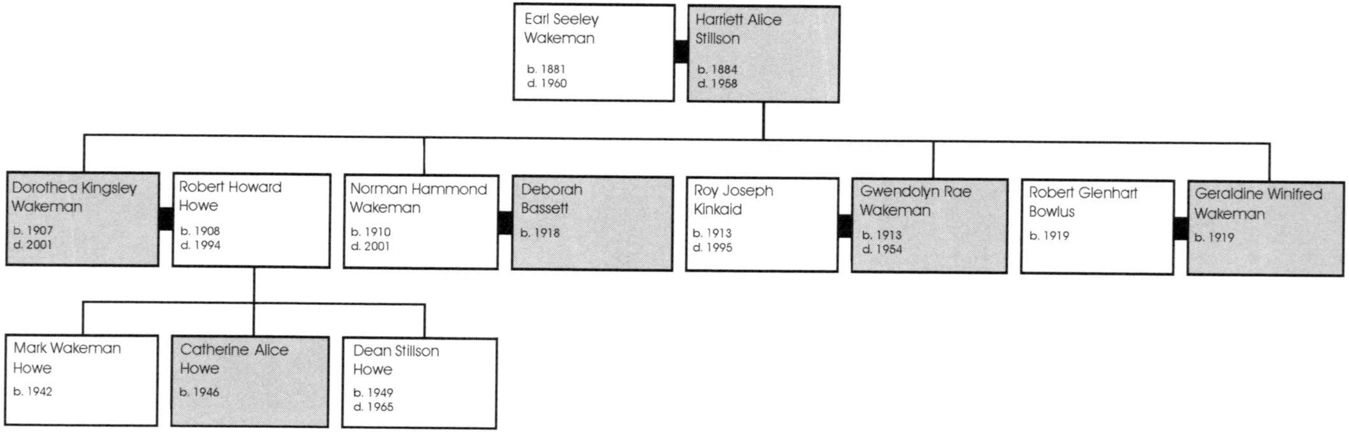

Descendants of Earl Seeley Wakeman.

Wakeman Family, 1931. Left to right: Geraldine, Dorothea, Gwendolyn, Harriett, Norman, Earl. Courtesy Catherine Howe Collato, Private Collection of Dorothea Wakeman Howe.

St. Hilda's School for Girls, 1934.

3

St. Hilda's School for Girls

THE TREATY OF NANJING IN 1842 ENDED THE FIRST OF THE SO-CALLED Opium Wars, and China was officially opened to the West by "agreeing" to the establishment of five treaty ports along the coast from Guangzhou to Shanghai. As a consequence, an American Episcopalian mission was established in Shanghai in 1845.[1] The Second Opium War (1856–60) ended with the ratification of the Treaty of Tianjin in 1860 which legalized the importation of opium into China and opened eleven more treaty ports including Hankou. Located about five hundred miles west of Shanghai on the Yangzi River, Hankou was China's most important inland treaty port, and hence the most likely place to establish a central China mission base. Episcopal missions were established in Hankou and Wuchang on June 22, 1868.[2]

Founded by Bishop Channing Moore Williams, a boys' boarding school, the Bishop Boone Memorial School, was established in Wuchang in 1871. It was named after the first bishop of the American Church in China, William J. Boone.[3] Although a school for girls was also envisioned, it was not until 1875 when the Jane Bohlen Memorial School for Girls at Wuchang was founded after members of the missionary community succeeded in purchasing the lot directly next to the Boone School.[4] The school was made possible by a bequest of $4,513.28 to the American Episcopal Missionary Board by the son and daughter of Jane Bohlen of Philadelphia.[5] The plan included building a structure at a cost of 2,500 to 3,000 taels[6] that could accommodate forty girls as well as a separate room for a foreign woman teacher.[7] Although the school was originally intended to open in 1874, a series of problems beset the project: the original contractor drowned, and the advance payment for the lumber was lost which delayed the completion of the school until 1875.[8]

The initial impetus for the school was to educate girls and to produce a Chinese women's Christian vanguard that would help, in the religiously militaristic language of the day, "conquer" China for Christ. But because women could not be ordained into the ministry, they would be ancillary to their minister-fathers and then, their minister-husbands. Hence, these educated women would represent the idealized vision of the good Christian daughter, wife, mother, and helper. In this way, it was believed that they would represent an alternative, positive role model for Chinese women.

That was the dream; however, the reality was quite different. By May 1875, Rev. William J. Boone[9] was concerned that as of that date, "no girl [had] entered, though 4 or 5 have signified a desire to come" because "no one likes to be first & then this is the 1st girls school up here."[10] Unlike the "Romanists" who were accepting "foundlings & infants," Rev. Boone wished to have "a school & not an asylum" and "to have a full school & do good to the women of the future in one time."[11] Convincing the locals, however, was not easy, as foreigners were accused of "kidnapping little children to take out their eyes for the gloss for foreign photographs"[12] and wanting young girls for illicit purposes. In a candid report to the home mission board, Rev. Boone noted:

> Remember first that many foreigners openly keep concubines. Still more somewhat secretly and hence Eurasian children abound at all the ports great & small. This leads the Chinese generally to believe that we [Westerners] have no morals. Sundry popular books also proclaim this and charge the Roman Catholic priest with indiscriminate intercourse and few [Chinese] distinguish Protestants or would believe us to be better. . . . When Mrs. Boone & Mrs. [Yung Kiung] Yen in 1874–5 tried to get girls for Bohlen Hall it was openly said to them that we only wanted the girls to train for foreigner's use and that by people right around us.[13]

Nevertheless, the school which had a capacity of forty girls, opened with one girl with a few others entering over time.

Almost immediately, pleas for scholarships and more funding began. Of greater concern, however, was finding a suitable woman teacher, and one was finally transferred from Shanghai in February 1877.[14] Henrietta Boone, William's wife, also actively involved herself in teaching sewing to the girls, and by the end of 1877, the school had thirteen girls.[15] Miss Henrietta Harris and Mrs. Boone, along with their uneducated Chinese helpers, taught the girls rudimentary educational skills and gave them the "requisite" girl's knowledge in cooking, cleaning, and sewing. In 1879, once funds were raised, Miss Josephine Roberts arrived to serve as a teacher at the Jane Bohlen School.[16]

A scandal embroiled the school in 1880 when the oldest girl in the school was discovered to be seven months pregnant. Although the child's father was the Chinese cook's son, the news of the girl's pregnancy rocked the mission and local community. Rev. William Boone's letter to the mission board detailed his concern because:

> By Chinese law the parents can kill the girl, hence the importance of Mr. [Yung Kiung] Yen's help to arrange matters as justly and yet as mercifully as possible.

> The great trouble is the Chinese said in advance that we Christians get up Girl Schools as a nursery for our lustful supply. So many foreigners live with Chinese that we cannot wonder at the suspicion. Hence we must protect this girl, and be able to do all that is possible that the living child may prove to all our Christians and to candid heathen that it is plainly of wholly native parentage.[17]

Rev. William Boone immediately requested another women teacher of at least "35 years, of churchly training, [and] ready to work" to assist the current teacher and matron, Josephine Roberts, who was regarded as "too young in **Chinese eyes**" and in his eyes for the position.[18] In the interim, a missionary's wife was sent from Shanghai to assist.

Just when it appeared that the school had weathered the worst of the storm generated by the scandal, yet another one arose in 1881. One of the missionaries was accused of fathering a child, and the girl and her Chinese fiancé's father spent several months in Shanghai with Rev. Boone before returning home to Wuchang.[19]

Other tragedies ensued. A new teacher who arrived at the school in October 1881 became ill six months later.[20] In a private correspondence to the secretary of the Foreign Committee, Rev. Boone provided the details of the incident. The missionary doctor who was summoned to examine the woman discovered she was in the final stages of labor. Pregnant before she arrived in China, she gave birth to a full-term baby boy who died that evening. Peritonitis set in, and five days later, the young woman was dead as well. Under the circumstances, Rev. Boone took immediate action.[21]

In the same letter to the secretary of the Foreign Committee, Rev. William Boone outlined the problems that plagued the school. Allegations against the missionary worker involving a number of Chinese girls proved to be true. A second case involving a young Chinese male student from the Boone School, who sexually assaulted a number of the girls, was equally verified. The death of the teacher and the negative publicity surrounding it both in the mission and local communities served as the impetus to first temporarily transfer the Jane Bohlen School to Hankou in early 1881, and then to shut it down on June 1, 1881.[22]

Moving the school to Hankou proved to be untenable, and the Jane Bohlen School was reopened in Wuchang after, yet another, brief hiatus, but it continued to struggle. Its viability was questioned when the school's third American-born teacher in eight years married and resigned in 1883, and no replacement could be found until 1894. As a consequence, home economics was the only education the girls received during this eleven-year period.[23] Bishop William Boone entreated the mission board to send only qualified, mature women, preferably married, to the field; however, Miss Lily Ward arrived at the school in 1894.[24] When she died in 1897 after three years of service, the continuation of the Jane Bohlen School was, again, in serious doubt.[25]

After further pleas from Bishop Boone, the American Episcopal Missionary Board finally decided to act. Following Bishop Boone's recommendations, the board would henceforth recruit teachers specifically for the school. Still recovering from the scandals, efforts to move the school away from the Boone campus to avoid comingling of the sexes, something that Bishop Boone was adamant about—"I do not believe any mission in China has single ladies in the same compound with single men"—began in earnest.[26] His admonishment for the separation was becoming a necessity; the school for boys was growing at such a rate, it was now encroaching upon the Bohlen School.

Bishop Boone also envisioned an expansion of the Bohlen school as well. Land was purchased outside of Wuchang's Little East Gate, about a mile from the Boone site, but while funds were sought for the completion of the new campus, the school remained on the Boone campus housed in a newly constructed brick building.[27] In 1899, after a two-year hiatus, the Jane Bohlen Memorial School became the Jane Bohlen building of the newly christened St. Hilda's School for Girls in Wuchang—Wuchang Sheng Xilida Nu Xuexiao—with Miss Pauline Osgood in charge.[28] That first year, eighteen students were enrolled—eight day students and ten boarding students—with most of the boarding students supported through a variety of scholarships.[29] "Why might not ten individuals, or ten Sunday-schools, or ten Junior Auxiliaries undertake to give $50 a year for the privilege of rescuing a Chinese girl from the degradation which awaits her as an uneducated woman!" read the call to action in an article in the *Spirit of Missions*.[30]

From its inception, St. Hilda's was anathema to prevailing Chinese culture. It existed to educate not only girls, but Christian girls. Furthermore, this education did not include the Confucian classics, the very basis of China's ethical system. Within the confines of traditional, dynastic China, St. Hilda's represented a foothold for disseminating Christian heterodoxy. Although the charge of advocating heterodox views could be leveled at all missionary schools, St. Hilda's could also be charged with cultural subversion. The perpetuation of traditional Chinese patriarchy depended upon the subservience of women, which, in turn, required that women remain ignorant. The very presence of St. Hilda's was a small crack in the wall of Chinese patriarchy. However, the girls who attended St. Hilda's during the dynastic period were the daughters of those who had already converted so the school had little impact in producing a large Christian vanguard, and therefore it and other Christian schools had limited success in promoting the religious doctrine of evangelism and its attendant goal of personal salvation.

In 1900, the Boxer Rebellion disrupted, yet again, the school's normal operations, and from September 1900 to March 1901, it was sealed shut, and the students scattered. Once reopened, St. Hilda's became a boarding school—the only one in Wuchang—enrolling eighteen girls largely sustained through scholarships provided by American donors.[31] By 1903, Miss Osgood was unbinding the feet of Christian girls in the school because "surely a Church school should not be the last to protest against such a cruel, and heathenish practice."[32] Consequently, in September 1903, "a rule requiring all Christian girls to unbind their feet, or pay heathen rates" was enacted. While such a ruling lost a few students, the end result was that there was a "noticeable" improvement in the girls' health because they could exercise more, and gymnastics along with "out-door sports" were added to the curriculum.[33]

Miss Osgood also instituted a "strict routine just as boarding schools" in America had. This routine would characterize the school in the years to follow:

> The girls rise at six, after they are dressed study until Church time, half-past seven. After Church comes breakfast, and then the dusting, and putting the rooms in order. Each girl takes care of her own bed, and it must be carefully made. . . .
>
> From nine to twelve are school hours. We are trying to introduce Western methods of education as much as possible that while it is a great value to train the memory, still to know the meaning of what they memorize, and to give it in their own words is important.
>
> After dinner they sew for a time. The girls have been taught to do various kinds of needle-work, and during the past year from orders taken have realized quite a little sum from our work. . . .
>
> The English classes are taught in the afternoon. At half past four comes the evening rice and the time is their own until half past six. Some wash their own clothes, others sit in groups to sew, and talk, and when the weather is fair the smaller girls go out in the yard, and have a good run, and play.
>
> Evening Prayer in the Church is half past six which we attend, after returning from this service the girls study until eight, this hour we meet in our Oratory, and have prayers, after which part of the girls retire, the others studying until nine.[34]

Enrollments continued to grow through the numerous scholarships provided for the girls; knitting and arithmetic were added for all students in 1904.[35] But by 1905, despite an enrollment of fifty-seven girls, the "largest number at the beginning of the term we have ever had," Miss Osgood was showing signs of strain. An outbreak of diphtheria that year resulted in the death of one student and the temporary closure of St. Hilda's to help prevent its spread.[36] When Miss Osgood returned to the United States for her regularly scheduled furlough in 1906 after seven years of dedicated service, she did not return. Deaconess Katherine Phelps assumed leadership of the school.

From 1906 to 1909, St. Hilda's continued to flourish to such an extent that a number of Wuchang Chinese officials approached the Episcopal bishop of Hankou, Logan H. Roots, requesting that he establish a school for their daughters.[37] Government schools for girls officially began in 1905. "At first the Mandarins' daughters had gone to one of these" but "the moral atmosphere" was regarded as "unwholesome"; consequently, "these officials desired to withdraw their daughters and entrust them to the Mission."[38] Because "St. Hilda's and its graduates were living witnesses to the quality of Mission work," another school, St. Margaret's, along with St. Hilda's School for Girls, began accepting the daughters of officials and wealthy families.[39]

In 1903, the former Bishop Boone High School (1890) became Boone College and in 1909, Boone College was incorporated as Boone University. A year later, Boone was expanding at such a rate that eligible male applicants outpaced the availability of space.[40] Also housed on its grounds were St. Hilda's School for Girls as well as the men's and women's hospitals. The decision was made to move both St. Hilda's and the hospitals to their own separate compounds; St. Hilda's would be moved to its new location on the previously purchased four acres outside Wuchang's Little East Gate.[41] A school building designed to accommodate three hundred girls was proposed—the largest school of its kind in the area, and in 1910, a ten thousand dollar gift from "the United Offering" given "as a memorial to the late beloved treasurer, George C. Thomas" permitted the construction of the school building.[42] The compound was situated in an ideal location. "On the east are hills and picturesque pagoda; on the south is a hillside covered with graves and crowned with a Taoist temple; on the west is the city wall and the Little East Gate; and on the north lotus ponds and gardens."[43]

The revolution that ultimately ended the Qing dynasty began in Wuchang on October 10, 1911. Before the Qing emperor, Puyi, abdicated on February 12, 1912, most of Hankou was burned to the ground as a result of the fighting between the Qing army and the revolutionaries, and it was this event that caused Yeh Fengchi to split up his family. Because of the instability, educational institutions ceased their normal functions, but schools and several church properties were converted into temporary medical facilities to accommodate the large numbers of wounded and ill within the Wuhan area.[44]

St. Hilda's reopened in 1912 with Deaconess Katharine E. Scott in charge, assisted by Deaconess Phelps. Enrollment for the fall was 168 students, and in the spring, 182.[45] During her tenure, St. Hilda's began to flourish. In 1916, the "Ladies House"—the residence for the foreign women teachers—was built.[46] After pleading with the mission board to allocate funds to build a chapel, Mr. John Bergamini, the mission architect, designed and supervised its construction beginning in February 1921.[47] With the building of the chapel, the compound contained "the school building itself which is well equipped, the residence for the foreign faculty, a small isolation hospital, a gymnasium, and the gate house where the Chinese men teachers live and where a small day-school is carried on for the benefit of the village children."[48] Women were recruited specifically for the purpose of teaching at the school.

While Deaconess Scott was on furlough, Miss E. Mildred Buchanan served as the principal and continued to do so even when Deaconess Scott returned to China in 1922. More improvements were made to St. Hilda's including partial electrification of the school in February 1923. Deaconess Scott's sudden death in August 1923 following surgery in Beijing was a severe blow to the school and to the Christian community, and Miss Buchanan was officially made the principal. Miss Buchanan entreated the mission board to send "two teachers . . . by September" 1924 to teach the 234 students subjects such as "History, Mathematics, and English."[49] During her tenure, the chapel's chancel furniture, pulpit, and choir screens were completed and installed, a new laundry built, the kitchen enlarged and screened, the old laundry in the school building converted into washrooms thereby allowing more dormitory space, the bedrooms on the third floor of the school building that housed the women servants were finished, and the construction of "two beautiful tennis courts" was completed.[50] By 1925, St. Hilda's had ten full-time Chinese teachers and seven foreign teachers on staff.[51] But St. Hilda's would not remain an oasis of tranquility for long.

Sun Yat-sen's death in March 1925 threw the country into turmoil, and after the May 25, 1925, Incident in Shanghai when Chinese police under British command fired upon Chinese students and workers during a demonstration, antiforeign and anti-Christian sentiments were such that the bishop was forced to shut down St. Hilda's before the June commencement. The families of students were notified and in "less than two days every girl had gone home properly escorted."[52] It was not the last time that political conditions would affect St. Hilda's.

Although a nominal cooperation among the Guomindang, the Chinese Communist Party, and their Soviet advisors was forged in 1924, factions abounded in this so-called "United Front." Military cliques formed and were at cross-purposes with political groups who divided into left- and right-wing factions; various warlords and warlord factions controlled the entire country. Slowly this situation began to change as the Guomindang sought to unify China. Beginning in its stronghold of Guangdong Province, the Guomindang and its allied armies began moving north.

By August 1926, news reports filtered up from the south about the coming Northern Expedition. Hubei's chief warlord, Wu Peifu, mustered troops to head off the southern advance. Hasty preparations were made in Wuhan in anticipation of the arrival of the southern troops. The foreign staff at St.

Hilda's—many of whom were at their mountain retreat in Guling, a place where foreigners spent their summers that was located in the mountains south of Jiujiang—rushed back to Wuchang. Miss Buchanan arrived at St. Hilda's on August 26 and for the next few days, rushed to pack important papers, money, and school and chapel valuables, as well as personal possessions. Miss Buchanan instructed the servants that "if the Southern soldiers came to be very polite to them and give them the gymnasium for sleeping quarters, and if the soldiers wanted to occupy our residence [i.e., the Ladies' House] to ask them please to stay downstairs."[53] She joined other members of the mission community, who had not fled downriver, at Church General Hospital near the Boone compound and encountered an ever-growing number of Chinese refugees confined within Wuchang's gated walls. Wuchang's main street had "its central telephone pole adorned by a dripping human head swarming with flies (one of the final efforts of the Northern Warlords here [principally Cai Hanqing] to intimidate those with Nationalist sympathies)" in an effort to dissuade any cooperation with the Southern troops.[54] The city gates were not only "barred, but reenforced with paving stones and sand bags," on September 2.[55] On the morning of September 3, heavy bombardment began outside one of Wuchang's main gates followed by ground fire throughout the next day. With casualties reported at one thousand, wounded men, women, children, and soldiers began pouring in Wuchang's Church General Hospital.[56] A telephone call to servants remaining at St. Hilda's on September 7 found them safe but that the school was "riddled with bullets."[57] Southern troops considered the campus as a potential headquarters and briefly occupied it, but when two of their men were killed, they decided not to remain. The door to the chapel's sacristy was blown in, "one shell . . . burst the attic of the Ladies' House," and Southern soldiers wanted to take the polished brass alms basins.[58] When the servants pleaded with them "not to take them as they were holy things," they were left untouched.[59] Being inside the city walls, the Boone compound was peppered with random rifle and machine gun fire, and bombs fell perilously close.

By October 11, the worst of the fighting was over, and Wuchang surrendered. Miss Buchanan returned to the St. Hilda's campus to find the entire servant staff safe. In her diary kept during the siege, she wrote, "Southern soldiers had occupied the Chapel, Gymnasium, Laundry and Verandahs of [the Ladies] house. School has one big hole on southeast corner and shell struck above Sacristy door breaking tiles and knocking bricks down into passage way."[60]

The cleanup of Wuchang began immediately. Once secured, martial law was in effect, and major renovations of Wuchang began. Many of Wuchang's city walls were dismantled to prevent any future possibility of barricading the city and were replaced with "broad cement sidewalks with proper curbstones, and up-to-date grating-covered drains" and paved "broad streets" able to accommodate motor vehicles were laid.[61] "A finely built macadamized road, fifty feet wide, well furnished with drains and bordered by sidewalks, now [ran] from the river to the Sz Men Ke'o [the fourth main city gate]."[62] The political climate appeared to be conducive to national unification under the Guomindang's banner, and the foreign concessions of Wuhan were temporarily occupied by left-Guomindang forces, and the British concession was seized.

While the Northern Expedition was a military success, it was a political disaster. The Guomindang was rife with political factions. The right Guomindang—primarily the military faction of the party—was commanded by Chiang Kai-shek, and this faction was seriously at odds with the left Guomindang, its Russian advisors, and its allies, the Chinese Communist Party—primarily the political faction of the party. This faction declared Hankou the new capital of China.[63] At this point the rift between the two factions was too great to span. Chiang, who declared Nanjing the new capital of China, appealed to Shanghai Chinese business leaders and to Western powers for support to strengthen his position, and they supported him. This strategy worked due to an innate fear of the left, particularly after the success of the Russian Revolution, and the left Guomindang began to lose support.[64]

While they were in power, the left Guomindang attempted to effect socialist doctrines. However, such actions provoked antiforeign incidents which brought foreign gunboats, including American ones, to the port at Hankou. Once again, nationalism was rampant throughout China, and strong antiforeign sentiments threatened Wuhan's foreign populations and other Yangzi valley cities; foreigners once again were ordered to evacuate to Shanghai and other coastal cities.

St. Hilda's, along with thirteen other foreign Christian schools, was closed for the turbulent fall of 1926, but Bishop Logan H. Roots considered reopening the school on St. Lois's campus in Hankou in 1927 and recalled Miss Buchanan back from Shanghai for that purpose "in spite of the protests of the naval and consular authorities in Shanghai."[65] Despite that turmoil, St. Hilda's managed to open briefly during spring term 1927 at Wuchang with 163 students, but was "given a vacation on March 25th" when the unrest continued, and "Miss Buchanan and the other St. Hilda's teachers went with the large party leaving Hankow on the 27th."[66] Again, Bishop Roots considered relocating St. Hilda's students to St. Lois's, but this suggestion was soon abandoned.[67]

At the end of the 1927 term, however, Miss Buchanan was so traumatized by the siege and continuous unrest in its aftermath that she took her home furlough and never returned to China. The school remained closed until September of 1928. Deaconess Julia A. Clark was recalled from her field work with Bible women at Yichang to serve as the acting principal for the 1928–29 school term and to deal with impending governmental changes directed at Christian schools.

While governmental regulation would cause consternation for the Christian community in China, St. Hilda's would finally have almost a decade of relative calm.[68] Once the Nationalists achieved nominal control over China, missionary schools became a target through mandated school registration. Registration meant the end of the two separate and distinct systems—the regular Chinese public schools and the foreign-supported missionary schools. With registration, missionary schools would become, in theory, secularized Chinese institutions, while maintaining their existence as private, but not foreign-run parochial, schools.

As early as December 1926, the Episcopal bishops of Hankou, Logan H. Roots and Alfred A. Gilman, suffragan, were both discussing the impact of registration and concluded that while procedures might change, the focus of Christian education would not; consequently, they did not oppose the possibility of registration.[69] In a lengthy report to the Department of Missions, Bishop Roots sent his justifications.

> I. The purpose of Christian schools. At the beginning of our meeting to consider the school situation in general and particularly the question of voluntary attendance at religious worship and instruction . . . the following four points are an approximate translation.
>
> (a) To make good citizens.
>
> (b) To develop a democratic spirit of co-operation.
>
> (c) To furnish vocational training "for life."
>
> (d) Especially by means of Christ's Spirit of brotherhood of service to build up high character of our students.
>
> 2. How to accomplish this purpose.
>
> (a) Teachers. The most important means to this end is that we should have for our schools Christian teachers believing in and moved by the Christian purpose of our schools as outlined above. If we have such teachers it will not make so much difference whether attendance at worship and religious instruction is voluntary or not and the Christian purpose of the school will probably be accomplished, whereas if our teachers are not really Christian teachers in that respect then the purpose of the school will probably not be accomplished even if attendance be forced at both worship and religious instruction.
>
> (b) Methods. Next in importance for the accomplishment of our purpose is improved methods in worship and in religious instruction. In both these points—that is in the teachers and in the improved methods—lies the real crux of the situation and I am afraid that we must admit that we have not solved these problems properly hitherto. Our religious education has been and is in many ways the weakest point in our schools whereas it should be the strongest.
>
> (c) Voluntary attendance. We agreed unanimously that attendance at worship and religious instruction at our schools should be voluntary on the part of the students. We reached this conclusion not because of demands made upon us. Our action was "self-initiated" and was based on the following grounds:

> (1) It is quite evident that whether the government be that of the North [northern warlord factions] or of the South [Guomindang factions] the official education enlists in the nation at large and in the various provinces are to require that any schools which they recognize shall grant entirely voluntary attendance at worship and religious instruction if either of these be allowed at all in our schools. This governmental action seems so certain that it is wise on this ground alone to give favorable consideration to the policy of voluntary attendance.
>
> (2) The attitude of students generally and our own students, either on their own or because of pressure from the outside, makes it quite evident that even where hitherto they have not felt the demands for voluntary attendance they are all deeply moved by the tide outside and are likely to feel it if their attendance at worship and religious instruction is not entirely voluntary. This is our second reason for giving voluntary attendance our considerate attention.
>
> (3) Our own convictions. We were unanimous that when required attendance is felt as compulsion, entire freedom with all its dangers is absolutely necessary if we want to achieve the purpose of our schools as Christian.[70]

Prior to 1929, St. Hilda's was a boarding school; this fact was a major attraction for wealthy, non-Christian families in the Wuhan region because traditionally in China, girls from wealthy families were sheltered from any contact with the world outside their family compounds. Ironically, it was only missionary boarding schools that were able to continue this practice of sequestering young, unmarried girls. The reputation of government schools being "mismanaged" with "many of the highly paid teachers in them" being "lazy and incompetent" and "the scholars . . . insubordinate" only strengthened the value of missionary boarding schools.[71] This cloistering was almost total: St. Hilda's permitted the girls to return home only for summer and Lunar New Year school breaks. The sense of separation from Chinese society was made even more complete since classes were taught in English and religious study was mandatory. Thus, the daughters of a select group of Wuhan's economic elite were being educated in an environment that was contrary to Chinese norms.

What further distinguished this Western-centered education at St. Hilda's were school regulations that forbade the girls from engaging in the political demonstrations that were prevalent in the public schools throughout the late 1910s and early 1920s. Confining the girls to the school's grounds effectively isolated them from the political realities of the times. This political isolation ended, however, after the Northern Expedition and following the requirement that all foreign schools must be registered with the government.

The basic regulations for registration were as follows:

> (1) The administration of the schools must be transferred to the Chinese. All Colleges must have Chinese presidents and all Middle Schools must have Chinese headmasters. All deans of departments must be Chinese.

(2) The control of the institutions must be in the hands of a Board of Trustees or directors, the majority of the members being Chinese.
(3) Religious worship and teaching must be put on a voluntary basis.
(4) The school or college must spread the doctrines of the nationalistic movement. Every Monday, the faculty and student body must attend a memorial service to Dr. Sun Yat Sen and listen to a lecture on his teaching.[72]

Given that the implementation of these regulations would completely challenge the independence of foreign-run schools, the issue of registration was widely debated throughout the missionary communities in China. Central to the discussions about the consequences of registration were its implications for Christian education in China. Opponents to registration argued against such an action "(a) because it is opposed to the principle of academic freedom and (b) because it makes the school a political agency."[73] Thus, a decision had to be made: "either to submit to the Government requirements or to cease to function."[74] Proponents of registration, such as Bishops Roots and Gilman, counterargued:

(a) The requirements may not prove to be so radical as they appear and in course of time they may be modified so as to allow greater freedom.
(b) The Christian Church in China would suffer a severe loss if deprived of its schools.
(c) The closing of the schools would appear to show lack of sympathy on the part of the Christian Church for the nationalistic movement.[75]

As the debate continued, the negative implications of registration were explored:

1. The school that registers ceases at once to be a private school and becomes a part of the government system; the control passes out of the hands of the mission.
2. The school must teach the party propaganda of the Nationalists as part of the curriculum.
3. The teaching of Christianity in the school is forbidden.
4. A teacher of the propaganda and another who is in charge of the discipline of the institution must be appointed by the government, but their salaries must be paid by the mission.[76]

The debate about the impact of Nationalist regulations prompted the creation, in 1928, of the Wuhan Christian Educational Association whose purpose was to "organize a Central Board for the Direction of the various schools for boys and girls."[77] It included all denominations, not just the Episcopal institutions. Incorporated in that plan was to make St. Hilda's a "senior middle school for girls."[78]

From the perspective of many missionaries, education was secondary to evangelism, and thus to accept registration would mean placing evangelism in a subordinate role; nonetheless, if the schools were to continue, then registration would have to be done. Regulations for private schools issued on August 29, 1929, by Dr. Chiang Monlin, minister of education for the national government, appeared to confirm their fears:

> Article 1: All schools founded by private individuals or incorporations are private schools, including those founded by foreign individuals or religious bodies.
> Article 2: Private schools may only be founded, reorganized or closed down with the approval of responsible educational authorities. For private universities, colleges and professional schools, the National Ministry of Education is the responsible authority for private middle and primary schools, the Provincial Educational Bureaux or Special City Government Educational Bureaux. Middle schools attached to private universities, colleges or professional schools, and primary schools attached to private schools of middle school or higher grade, are under the same responsible educational authorities as the ordinary private middle and primary schools.
> Article 3: Private schools must be registered with and placed under the supervision and direction of educational authorities. Their constitution, curriculums, etc, must comply with current educational promulgations.
> Article 4: Private schools, if founded by foreigners, must have Chinese as principals or deans.
> Article 5: Private schools, founded by religious bodies, must not count religious subjects as required subjects. They must not include religious propaganda in the curriculum. If they hold religious ceremonies they must not compel or persuade any students to take part. Religious ceremonies must be entirely excluded from primary schools.
> Article 6: When private schools are managed improperly or in contravention of promulgations, the responsible authorities may cancel their registration or stop their existence.
> Article 7: The names of private schools must show their nature and begin with the word, "Private."[79]

Outlined in the regulations were stipulations for private middle and primary schools that also required them to have a Chinese majority, board of directors, possess "definite property or capital yielding" that was sufficient to "pay the yearly current expenses," maintain "a competent teaching staff and more than three fourths of them whole-time teachers."[80] Many schools chose to close their doors rather than to register which was considered tantamount to capitulating to Nationalist secular propaganda, but St. Hilda's remained open and registered in 1929.

While church services, daily Morning Watch and nightly Evensong, and religious courses were no longer mandatary, life at St. Hilda's continued in its tradition of "whole-hearted, purposeful activity, proceeding in a social environment, an environment so fully social that it cannot be attained short of self-realization in terms of fellowship with God and man. To do this, we try to give the girls not only the necessary knowledge, but also to cultivate right attitudes and develop right skills, which involves every part of the school-life."[81]

This view of a Christian education's purpose can be seen in the teachers. The American women who taught at St. Hilda's were all college graduates, they were single, and they came to China imbued with the spirit to do good work. Because Episcopal women missionaries could not become ministers, they became educators. But these women were unlike many of their predecessors since most of them came specifically to be teachers who would teach the tenets of the Social Gospel.

A basic feature of the Social Gospel is the belief that social service is a legitimate expression of personal beliefs and that it could be an instrument for social change as well as a means to salvation. Unlike pure evangelism which focuses on personal salvation, the Social Gospel was focused on personal action for the transformation of this world. The Social Gospel was predicated on the belief that a fellowship can exist between God and humans and that this fellowship could be attained through the cultivation of correct attitudes and the development of the right skills.

The secular aspects of the Social Gospel legitimated the nascent nationalistic views held by the girls of St. Hilda's after 1927. No longer were they politically naive as they became aware of and, in some cases, participated in political demonstrations. Thus, from the period after 1929, political activities were frequent undertakings of the Student Self-Governance Association.

In compliance with government stipulations, once St. Hilda's registered and received final approval from the victorious, right Guomindang-dominated, Nanjing government in September 1929, the mandated changes had to be implemented. Prior to registration, classes were conducted solely in English; now they had to be taught in the Chinese national language (Putonghua) except for the classes on English conversation, composition, and grammar. The principal of the school could no longer be a foreigner, and the graduates would receive a Chinese diploma rather than receive ones issued through a foreign entity. Chapel attendance and religious instruction were no longer mandatory and any visible coercion placed upon students would be considered an infraction of the regulations. As an alternative to religious studies, a course in ethics had to be offered. Thus, beginning in fall 1928, Deaconess Clark began teaching a social ethics course that focused on

> studying existing social conditions and institutions and challenging all. And it is really most interesting to see how these same girls, who are deliberately avoiding a formal religious course, are constantly appealing to Christianity for

> their standards, and bewildered when I tell them they must try to find them otherwise. Of course, my whole joy is in their being constantly driven back to realize that they cannot keep on the same high level without what the Church has conserved for them and gives them.[82]

Christian students were still required to take religion classes in what was renamed "Religious Knowledge" courses.[83] Students were also now required to take government examinations for graduation, and the students in the 1931 graduating class were the first to take them.[84]

In addition to the above changes, the Three Principles of Sun Yat-sen were now part of the required curriculum, and they had to be taught by a Guomindang Party member. In May 1928, a Government Educators Conference was held in Nanjing to discuss and to determine how to integrate the Three Principles of Sun Yat-sen into the national curriculum. The Three Principles were discussed by a not-so-unbiased Western observer in his 1928 book in this manner:

> The central theme of the propaganda was without doubt the *Three Democratic Principles* (San Min Chu I), a book published by Dr. Sun Yat Sen which has rapidly become the text-book, or rather the Bible, of the Revolution. The book contains much irrelevant material, and gives evidence that the author was either himself warped in judgment by anti-foreign prejudice, or else deliberately wished to use it as a means of stimulating and consolidating the sense of Chinese nationalism. The Three Principles are, as stated by him, somewhat vague in their connotation; but may be briefly summarised as follows:
>
> (1) *The Principle of Nationality.*—The freedom and independence of China as a nation, and the equality of the various races comprised within the Republic.
>
> (2) *The Principle of Democracy.*—The people's right of suffrage, initiative, referendum and recall, and the rights of women.
>
> (3) *The Principle of Socialism, or the People's Livelihood.*—The equalization of land ownership by a heavy land tax, and the control of capitalism by nationalisation of the public utility services.[85]

A far more sympathetic English language newspaper's account of the conference listed the education goals through a fuller elaboration of the Three Principles for the New China as follows:

> 1. To develope the national spirit.
> 2. To elevate the morals of the people.
> 3. To give particular attention to the development of better health.
> 4. To develope the use of the scientific spirit and its practical applications.
> 5. To develope following educational efforts.
> 6. To see the girls have equal educational opportunities with boys.
> 7. To develope education among the Manchus, Mongols, Mahammedans Tibetans and Aboriginess.

> 8. To develope education among the Chinese abroad.
> 9. To make clear the limits of personal liberty and to develop the habit of obeying the law.
> 10. To increase the knowledge of governmental methods and train the people how to use powers.
> 11. To develope the power of organization in order that there may be created the spirit of co-operation.
> 12. To develope industrial education.
> 13. To develope the agricultural and silk raising education.
> 14. To develope the idea of co-operative production and co-operative consumption.
> 15. To work for every honest form of living in the way of public health, economy, order and asthetics.
>
> When we speak of the education according to the San Min Chu Ih [Sanmin Zhuyi] we do not mean putting a few words about the San Min Chu Ih into books or the use of the four characters in various educational notes but we mean the developing of the national spirit, raising the morality of the people and increasing the health of the people, with the liberty and equality of the people as an object and for this purpose we must develope a law-abiding spirit in the people, train them in co-operation and the use of governmental forms so that a modern government may be established. We must urge the use of scientific methods in labor operations to increase the production and use all forms of art in order to give the people a more abundant living so that what we call the peoples' livlihood may really appear.[86]

The socialist spirit of the Three Principles coincided with the Social Gospel beliefs held by the leadership in the Episcopal community in China; their concern was much more with the interpretation of these principles and the possible loss of autonomy in the governance of their educational institutions and less with teaching the principles themselves.

Deaconess Clark began tackling a number of issues facing St. Hilda's. One of the most difficult government regulations facing St. Hilda's was finding a Chinese principal. The Department of Missions itself was ambivalent at best about this regulation, and Dr. John W. Wood of the mission board expressed that sentiment when he wrote in 1929 in response to Deaconess Clark's request to find a suitable Chinese principal: "I do not know a Chinese woman qualified for the headship of St. Hilda's, and I see no sound and justified reason at the present time why the school should be turned over to a Chinese principal, even if one could be found. Some day, of course, I hope that will come about, but I hope it will come about in a period of good feeling and not in a period such as exists today."[87]

In order to reopen the school in 1928, Chen Jiang—a deaconess herself—was appointed to the position; however, she was not in residence and only occasionally visited the campus. On September 8, 1928, St. Hilda's reopened its doors with an enrollment of 155 girls—"instead of the usual

230"—supported by seventeen full- or part-time teachers.[88] In hopes of assuaging parental fears about the school and newly imposed governmental regulations, the suffragan bishop of Hankou, Alfred A. Gilman, and a teacher from Huazhong Daxue, Mr. John Coe, registered the students. On one of her rare visits to the school, the Chinese principal, Deaconess Chen Jiang, personally greeted the returning students and welcomed the new ones.[89]

The curriculum that year included psychology, sociology, literary criticism, history of the last hundred years in China, taught in Chinese, which "were going to be of great advantage to them [Senior Middle IIIs] on their entrance into college."[90] In addition to the aforementioned courses, Deaconess Clark noted that the "seniors are doing good work in their English Literature and study of English Styles. All the reading classes are taught by the American teachers."[91] English composition, mathematics, scripture, and music courses were offered as well.[92]

With the reopening of St. Hilda's in 1928, the chronic problem of insufficient foreign faculty was even more acute. Mr. John Coe, the Reverend Benjamin Yen (the chaplain), and "two Library Students [from Boone]" helped ease the shortages.[93] In spring, an additional five students joined the school pushing the enrollment to 160. Deaconess Clark made a strong plea to Bishop Gilman for help with teaching staff. Although the bishop "scoured the country" to find teachers, in the end, a graduate from Boone was hired "to carry the courses that must be carried in order to supply the work which the girls of the Higher Middle School must do."[94]

Additional accommodations to the current national regulations were needed as well. The newly created Wuhan Christian Educational Association designated St. Hilda's as the "center for the Senior Middle work" and as a consequence its primary school was moved to St. Lois's School for Girls in Hankou at the end of the school term. Chapel services were held only in the evening, and in place of the Morning Watch, a half hour of setting-up exercises conducted by the physical education teacher could be substituted in its stead.[95] In 1929, all chapel services and Bible classes were made voluntary. That year, enrollment was up to 181 students, and joining the student body at that time was Yeh Yuanshuang who transferred from St. Lois's.[96]

In 1930, with an enrollment of 200 students and "turning away girls every day, having already taken in our quota of two hundred,"[97] substantial improvements were made to the campus when a "light plant" was built that provided lights in all of the rooms, and the buildings on the main campus were finally screened thereby reducing the number of malaria cases. "This means that ever since, with light in the class-rooms and screens, we have evening study-hour in the individual classrooms, instead of all crowded up in the assembly-room, no proper desks, poor lights, and the air bad as well."[98] Funds for a music building were made possible by a generous donation by Miss Venetia Cox, the music teacher at St. Hilda's, and other sources that would cost about "$3000.00 Mexican silver" and construction of the five-room Cox Music Building with its additional two-room living suite was completed by June 1931.[99]

In 1930, Deaconess Clark had her hopes raised about leaving St. Hilda's because a suitable American replacement might be found. Miss Louise Boynton applied for a post in China but made it clear that her main interest was "in the administrative side of educational work and that [she] would not be willing to hold a teaching position for many years."[100] Responding to her application Bishop Roots replied:

> The place where we particularly wish to have your help at present is St. Hilda's School, although in our other schools somewhat lower in grade—that is to say kindergarten, primary and Junior Middle Schools as contrasted with the Senior Middle School work at St. Hilda's, we also need foreign teachers such as yourself. At St. Hilda's we have at present a nominal principal who is not resident at the school and who can do only a very small part of the work. The actual work of a principal is mainly done by Deaconess Clark who is the Assistant Principal. We have not yet found a Chinese principal although we have been trying to find one. We must find one if the school is to continue permanently and when we do such work as you prefer to do on the administrative side would be only part of the whole administrative task. It would be, I believe, an essential part of the task in that it would be the point wherein the school would be most directly related to the American Church through the American staff. Furthermore it would offer the advantage even in these difficult days of an opportunity for intimate co-operation with the Chinese principal. If you do not have a fairly strong appetite for such an adventurous undertaking, then I think you ought not to accept this position which we need to have filled at St. Hilda's. Deaconess Clark wishes to go back to the more directly evangelistic work as soon as practicable and would gladly and is in fact very eager to give place to some one else as soon as the right person can be found.[101]

Miss Boynton chose to accept the appointment and upon her arrival in August 1930, stopped in at St. Hilda's before heading to the College of Chinese Studies in Beiping for an intensive yearlong language training—now more necessary than ever since non-English classes had to be conducted entirely in Chinese. Deaconess Clark described Miss Boynton's visit in glowing terms: "It was like a fresh breeze in the midst of our August hot-spell, to have her appear and take over some fussy list that had to be made out, freeing me for conversations with the numerous parents, and many teachers, all of whom wanted something and wanted it at once!"[102] Without a Chinese principal in residence, "Miss Gwendolyn Seng," one of the Chinese teachers, would assume responsibilities when Deaconess Clark was occasionally unavailable.[103]

Deaconess Clark continued improvements to the school. A major need identified by Deaconess Clark and previous principals was the quality of the water. Water had to be hauled in to the campus. During the massive 1928 renovations following the siege of Wuchang, "Wesley School is filling our water-cart daily, instead of our having to find a new way to the distant river, with the main streets of Wuchang all torn up, and very good water it is. It makes us long for an artesian well of our own, so that we could always have good water and share with others, instead of having to seek ours outside, whenever a dry spell comes on."[104] Beginning in 1928, she implored the mission board to provide funds to dig a well on the campus because the poor quality of water was giving "sore mouths to some of the girls, and causes much talk among them," and when funds were finally appropriated, the well was dug in 1931 and "poured forth water at a depth of about ninety Chinese feet [sixty feet]."[105]

The completion of the well at St. Hilda's was perhaps an omen of things to come because in August 1931, a massive flood hit central China resulting in an estimated quarter of a million deaths with the most devastation occurring at the junction of the Yangzi and Han rivers where the three Wuhan cities are located. Heavy snowfall melting from the Tibetan plateau coupled with excessive rainfall in the Hubei area caused the river at Hankou to rise to "53.65 feet, two feet above the point recorded in 1860 which is the highest point found in modern records."[106] Returning from the Episcopal summer home in Guling, Deaconess Clark arrived in Hankou in August before the flooding reached its crest. Anticipating potential diseases in the flood's aftermath, she, as well as other members of the community, had typhoid and cholera inoculations.

At St. Hilda's, protective dikes were built around the school, and Deaconess Clark and a group of good Samaritans from Boone tried desperately to save as much as they could. Then

> five feet came in three-quarters of an hour, so that after saving records, office books, laboratory instruments, and putting books as high as we could, chapel things and all, I started back in over four feet of water, and the second rush caught the coolie and me half way over to the house, just near a convenient tree. The coolie could not swim, so we went up the tree, then I swam to the house, and Mr. Kemp and I towed a big book case over to the man in the tree.[107]
>
> Mr. Kemp made a great boat of three tubs lashed together with poles across the top and took me over to the school before he left with the cook. So I got all the rescued things sorted out and packed away upstairs, ready to open a temporary office there. Then went back on a raft made of several shutters, and helped at the house. We'd swim about and get a whole convoy of chairs, tables, stools, etc. started toward the stairway, then push them along, get ahead, and then haul them up, and at the top the amah was busy wiping them off.[108]

For over two months, the river level remained "at or above normal summer flood level," and "the action of the [Chinese] government in appointing and providing for the National Flood Relief Commission and in securing Sir John Hope Simpson as Director-General of the Commission is unprecedented in Chinese history and has been the chief factor in carrying out the major relief measures particularly the rebuilding of the main dykes."[109]

At St. Hilda's, Deaconess Clark sent notices for "an indefinite postponement of opening of school," and spent the next two months conducting relief work in Hankou.[110] When the school finally reopened on October 1, "it had to be upstairs [in the school building] only, so we borrowed the premises of the Christian Missionary Alliance in the city not far from Boone, and Miss Cox and Miss Gosline opened up there with some of the Chinese teachers and the seventy-nine children of the first two [junior] high-school grades."[111] In her letter to Dr. John W. Wood in New York, Deaconess Clark begged the Department of Foreign Missions to send out more teachers, particularly for the English classes because Miss Olive Tomlin was needed in Hankou at St. Lois's. Miss Margaret Spurr, a new teacher who joined the staff in September 1930, developed dysentery during the summer of 1931 and had to remain in Guling until the end of October recuperating, and her absence put a strain on the already over-taxed staff at St. Hilda's so that Deaconess Clark proposed:

> If we had someone at once, who could go into the second term of Language School when they give the beginning work again, or who would come out as Miss Spurr had just for English, and willing to get only such Chinese as can be picked up in an hour a day with a teacher, then I could leave the School next year with a freer mind. In the second case, it would do to have the worker come out in August to be here in Wuchang the first of September. I expect to leave in July [for furlough], and do hope to have the staff for the fall well arranged for before I leave.[112]

Deaconess Clark left on furlough in July 1932. It was a bittersweet leave because she learned in November that her father had died and that her mother was suffering from angina pectoris.[113] On a happy note, Deaconess Clark was finally able to leave her administrative position because a graduate of St. Hilda's and "first holder of the Katharine Scott Memorial Scholarship," "Dorothy Teh-tsen Tso," was appointed principal in 1932 and assumed the position in the fall with the assistance of Louise Boynton.[114] When she returned to China, Deaconess Clark would now be free to return to her evangelical work in Yichang—her first love.

While in the states, from August until December, Deaconess Clark "spent two and a half months speaking up and down the State of California," driving her deceased father's Ford, and "making an average of eight talks a week, the limit for one day being five," on "Mission Work in China. The greatest interest was evinced everywhere, though more asked what I thought of Mrs. Pearl Buck's books than of anything else."[115] Several of her talks were at her own parish as well as at All Saints in Pasadena, California.

At St. Hilda's, rebuilding after registration and the great flood of 1931 was crucial. This rebuilding was not only of the physical structures but of the curriculum as well. Self-sufficiency and independence would be further emphasized. In fulfillment of the action orientation of the Social Gospel, performing "good works" meant that the girls had to learn to be both self-sufficient and independent in a society where women were viewed as both dependent and subservient. Thus, instilling these values would be no easy matter, yet the mere presence of single, independent, self-sufficient women from America served as inspirations and as important role models for the girls. Creating a conducive educational environment as well as modeling the values that were being promoted were not courses in the formal curriculum but were, instead, part of the hidden curriculum and cultural fusion created at St. Hilda's. As such, the girls at St. Hilda's were being resocialized and reacculturated into a form of social organization that was neither entirely American nor entirely Chinese. Making the girls be independent was very Western, but the fact that this socialization process was occurring through foreign intercession made the girls feel proudly nationalistic at the same time. Interestingly, the culturally fused environment of St. Hilda's can be seen in the use of names. The girls were given English names for the benefit of their English-speaking, foreign teachers; while, the teachers were given Chinese names for the benefit of the students. This blending of East and West was a consistent feature of life at St. Hilda's following government-mandated registration.

Self-sufficiency and independence were fostered at St. Hilda's in a number of ways. Talents and abilities were quickly recognized and nurtured by the teachers who encouraged students to apply these strengths in the many student association positions or to act as dormitory and class leaders. Those with athletic abilities served not only on the teams but also were called upon to assist as the exercise leaders who conducted the voluntary daily calisthenics. Academically strong students became tutors and even served as teachers in the community. To provide teaching experience, a practice school was proposed by Bishop Gilman in 1933 by purchasing property adjacent to the school that "has on it a house which would be readily adapted for the Practice School. Miss Tso and Miss Cox agreed to write to you directly asking that you make a grant of $3000.00 to make this purchase and to put everything in order."[116]

When the practice school opened in 1935, the girls functioned as teachers and classroom aides. In the spirit of Christian service to others, a group of teachers and student volunteers regularly visited the homes of local families in a neighboring village near the school. They taught local residents

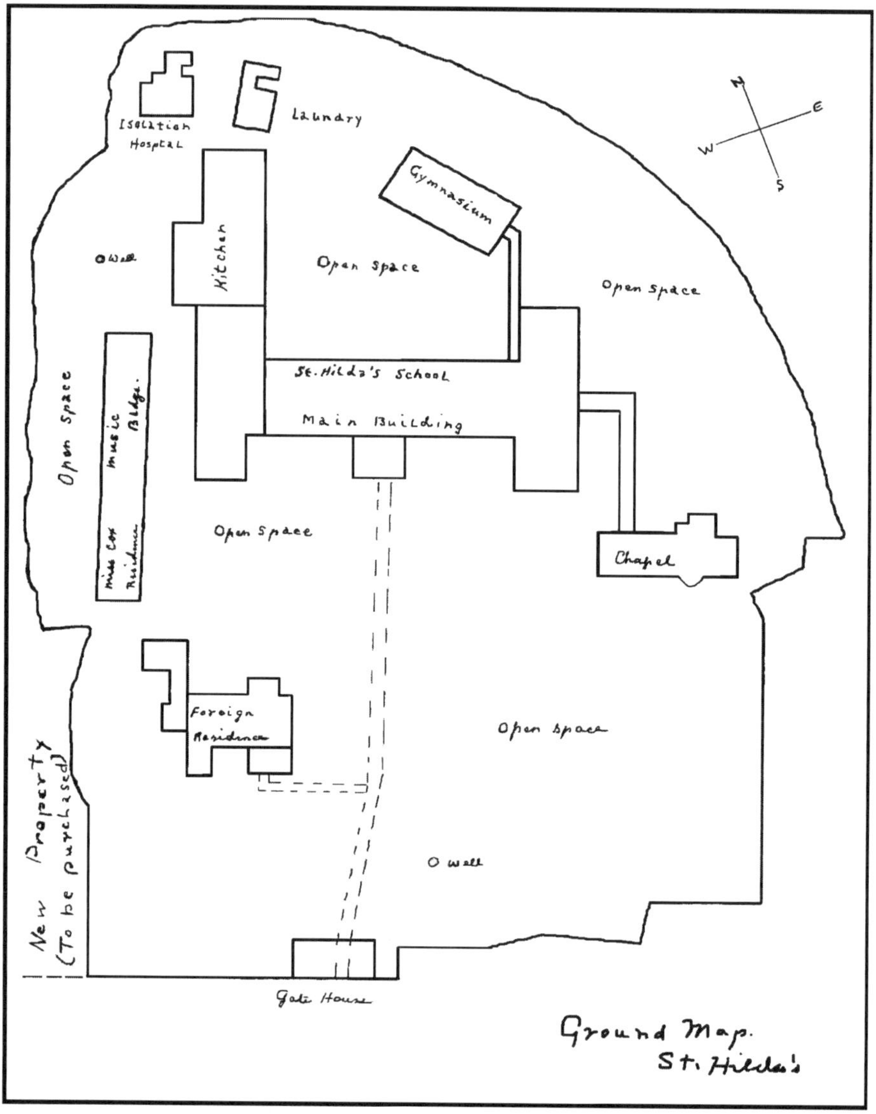

St. Hilda's School for Girls, Wuchang. Adapted from original drawing by Bishop Alfred A. Gilman, October 1931, Archives of the Episcopal Church, Austin, Texas.

about sanitation, nutrition, and hygiene; they tended to the ill and bathed the sick and elderly; they groomed young boys and girls; they administered minor medical attention under the supervision of a nurse from Church General Hospital; and on occasion, they cleaned the homes of local families.[117] In these ways, the values of self-sufficiency and independence were tempered by a moral code that stressed that the girls be conscientious and hard-working.[118] These service activities also made it possible for the girls to experience the only occupations that were available to educated Chinese women—teaching, social work, and medicine. It also showed the girls that these occupations could be beneficial to the whole of society; that is, the girls saw they could do well by doing good. As one of the graduates of the school stated: "Because of my work in St. Hilda's, the work I did with children" on Sunday afternoons, "I became interested in this work . . . and decided to do social work. When I entered [Ginling] college, I majored in Sociology."[119]

Activities within the school also nurtured these values. The Student Self-Governance Association sponsored a number of self-help organizations that provided many of the students the chance to earn some money. Rather than breeding resentment between the wealthier students and the poorer students, such organizations actually taught them to cooperate with one another.

Despite the fact that tuition-paying students were perceived as being favored by the school administration, the school actually sought to mitigate class differences. The inherent differences between the baptized Christian girls, who paid no tuition, and the non-Christian girls, who typically did, posed the greatest obstacle to creating an egalitarian atmosphere. Even though all the girls wore uniforms, they were far from equal in that the girls from wealthy families had nicer uniforms because their parents could afford to have them custom-tailored. Wealthier students could also afford to purchase leather shoes rather than make their own cloth ones.

Higher quality uniforms and shoes were the least of the differences. Most of the non-Christian girls came from wealthy families who wanted their daughters educated outside of the state schools, which they thought were Communist controlled; the Christian girls came from poorer rural areas where their parents were stationed as pastors or church workers.[120] The school instituted measures designed to create strong bonds between and among the girls. One way to create such a bond was to design a "sister class" system whereby an older class was responsible for a younger class. Thus, first-year senior middle girls (Senior I) were paired with first-year junior middle girls (Junior I); second-year senior middle girls (Senior II) were paired with second-year junior middle girls (Junior II); and seniors (Senior III) were teamed with third-year junior middle girls (Junior III). "Big sisters" were expected to help their "little sisters" adjust to the boarding school system and assist them in any way possible. Forging these strong bonds mitigated many of the inherent wealth disparities and created lasting friendships in their stead.

Improving the work of St. Hilda's required more teachers, and for the Department of Missions and the Hankou Episcopal Diocese, it meant American teachers. Each annual report placed a request for more American teachers, especially women teachers, "because they can live with the girls and enforce better discipline," but the plea became even more urgent once registration was mandated.[121] The lack of funds available to the Episcopal Church brought on by the Great Depression made funding American teachers that much harder. Thus, greater emphasis was placed upon the existing American staff to increase their Chinese language proficiency so that they could continue to teach their specialities in Chinese. An unanticipated consequence of registration was that there was now more interaction between the Chinese teachers and the American teachers.

This relationship was so much closer that by 1931, one of the American teachers wrote in her annual report, "There is much more of an effort to include the desires and ideas of the Chinese teachers [both men and women] in the plans for the school and they seem to appreciate and welcome it. This is especially shown in the monthly teachers' meetings where the teachers express themselves very freely."[122] In 1931–32, with an enrollment of 206, there were "twelve men teachers, half of them full-time and half part-time teachers, four living at the Gate House and four living in the city. We have nine Chinese women on the staff, six of whom are college graduates, three middle-school graduates, and all except one are St. Hilda's graduates. There were six foreigners: Miss Boynton, the treasurer; Miss Cox, the head of the Music department; Miss Spurr and Miss Tomlin, teachers of English."[123] Confidence in Dorothy Tso's leadership increased as well. In anticipation of Dr. John W. Wood's (who was initially opposed to having a Chinese principal) visit to the St. Hilda's campus in 1932, Olive Tomlin wrote: "And it will be a pleasure to show you our school under a Chinese principal. So far all goes well. We heartily approve of any changes Miss Tso has made. The students have responded remarkably well to the new regime (if such it could be called, for it is very much like former days) and Dorothy has shown tact in dealing with faculty and students, initiative, unexpected ability to assume responsibility, and a spirit of true Christian devotion"[124]

When Dorothea Kingsley Wakeman, a friend of Julia Clark and her family in Pasadena, applied to the mission board in January 1933, the wish for another teacher appeared to be granted, but the worldwide Depression made it difficult to send anyone new into the field. In 1933, Margaret Spurr suffered another bout of dysentery, and she was scheduled to return to Canada once she recovered sufficiently to travel. Her impending departure would leave yet another vacancy in the foreign staff at St. Hilda's, and an urgent plea for a replacement was sent to the mission board.

When Bishop Roots received a coded cable from Dr. Wood that read "Wakeman appointment opposed. Advise by telegram strongly your opinion emergency," a telegram was sent in response: "Wakeman essential survival of teacher training. Spurr, Jenner withdrawing next year."[125] In a follow-up letter, Bishop Roots explained in more detail what he meant.

> The first point is of course to state as strongly as I can the real emergency at St. Hilda's which in addition to the general need for the strengthening of the St. Hilda's staff is that Miss Wakeman is essential to the survival of the teacher training course at St. Hilda's since, as Gilman has already informed you, Miss Pritchard, who has hitherto helped us, has been withdrawn by the Wesleyans. If Miss Wakeman does not come we run the very great risk of having the Teacher Training Department at St. Hilda's condemned and closed by action of the Government authorities. I think we should welcome rather than reject this kind of strictness on the part of the Government and I hope we shall be able to meet successfully their requirements as the coming of Miss Wakeman will help us do.
>
> The point about Miss Spurr and Miss Jenner withdrawing next year I put in as indicating another element in the emergency. I trust that this will provide you with all that is necessary to enable you to show to the Department the necessity of appointing Miss Wakeman at once.[126]

In light of St. Hilda's urgent need, a letter offering Dorothea Wakeman some hope of a position was sent.[127] In mid-August, a formal appointment for a temporary, one-year position at St. Hilda's was made; Dorothea enthusiastically accepted the position and set sail for China on September 8, 1933.

St. Hilda's Chapel, Flood, 1931. Courtesy Eleanor Wheeler, Private Collection of Hazel F. Gosline.

St. Hilda's Chinese Women's Faculty and Staff, 1931. Top row, left to right: Zhou Yuying (Cultural Studies), Ying Ming (Mathematics), Li Dezhen (Philosophy), Shen Zuying (Class Advisor). Middle row, left to right: Dorothy Tso (Zuo Dezhen, Principal), Matron Nien, Nurse Li. Bottom Row, left to right: Science Teacher Tu, Yang Ailian (Gym), Yang Aimei (English).

Summer Break, Hankou, 1934. Top row, left to right: Yeh Yuanlu, Yeh Yuanquan, Yeh Yuanshuang. Bottom row, left to right: Gao Shenyu, Song Baozhen, Cai Sumei.

4

Yeh Yuanshuang at St. Hilda's School for Girls

ON SEPTEMBER 8, 1929, FORMAL NOTIFICATION OF ST. HILDA'S REGISTRATION with the Nationalist government in Nanjing was received. Acceptance by the Hubei Provincial Board would take an additional two months, and on November 9, approval was granted. With an enrollment of 181 students and "twenty-nine members of the teaching and executive staff," St. Hilda's reopened once again in September.[1] At age sixteen (seventeen in Chinese years), the year after she was to have been married, Yuanshuang was one of 94 girls in St. Hilda's junior middle school;[2] her sister, Yuanquan, and cousin, Yuanlu, were completing the sixth grade at St. Lois's before taking the entrance examination for St. Hilda's where they joined Yuanshuang in 1930.

Accompanied by her distant cousins, Bao Xunfang and Bao Xunyi, who were already students at St. Hilda's, Yuanshuang entered the outer wooden gate, passed through the inner wrought iron gate, and walked down the central path to St. Hilda's main school building. Dexing chose to remain at home because she felt it was inappropriate to accompany Yuanshuang to such a "fine school." Two servants dutifully carried the trunks filled with the required school supplies. No longer the "qianjin xiaojie," bedecked in a traditional qipao, Yuanshuang was dressed in the more contemporary look of the New China.

During the first week of classes, Miss Olive Tomlin, the teacher who taught junior middle English classes, gave her usual English comprehension assessment test. Devised by an English professor at Huazhong Daxue, John Coe, the assessment was used as a means of appraising grade-appropriate English comprehension. Xunfang and Xunyi warned Yuanshuang that she might not pass the test because Miss Tomlin "was a very strict teacher."

> I will always remember that test. We called Miss Tomlin the "cat" because she looked like a cat with her large eyes as well as being as sharp as a cat. My cousins had warned me, "Miss Tomlin is going to give you a competency test that you probably won't pass." First she showed us colored cards while saying the color, and asked us to write down what the colors were. And then, she named the days of the week, Monday to Sunday. And then she read the months of the

> year—January, February, all the way to December. I knew the months—the short ones such as May and June—but I didn't know how to spell all of them. And, sure, I could write "red," "white," and a few of the other colors. But she spoke so fast. We were supposed to put the words in the exact order she read them, but I just wrote down anything I knew. I got a big zero, a big fat zero on the test. I missed every single question because even though I had some of the words right, they were not in their correct order.
>
> After the examination, Miss Tomlin asked me to see her. She said: "Yuanshuang—at that time, I did not have an English name—Yuanshuang, how did you pass the entrance examination?" And I told her: "The same way I took your test; I just wrote whatever I could think of." Miss Tomlin laughed and said: "At that rate, you will never catch up with the class." She said: "I like you very much. You represent a classic young Chinese maiden from a traditional family that is so different from the others. I want to help you succeed." So she told me to come to the foreigner's house on weekdays at 4:00. Our classes finished at 3:30, and 4:00 was her tea-time. "Come during my tea-time in the afternoon, and I will help you with your English. But promise me one thing. You must practice." I asked her: "How should I practice?" And she told me: "Find two girls whose English is not very good, and you teach them what you have learned each day."

During that entire first year, Yuanshuang met with Miss Tomlin in the parlor of the Ladies Home. They would review the day's lessons and engage in general conversation. Miss Tomlin would have Yuanshuang read from magazines such as *Life* to help her with understanding English. The photographs in the magazine held Yuanshuang's interest, and she learned about American life from them. Following Miss Tomlin's advice and keeping the promise she made that first day, Yuanshuang did find two classmates whose English was weak and became their tutor/mentor.

Life at St. Hilda's was much more structured and regimented than at St. Lois's. Activities centered around the main building. The first floor contained the science laboratory, classrooms, and a large assembly room "used for a study hall."[3] While it was envisioned that three hundred people could be accommodated on the second floor of the building, it could only realistically house at most two hundred and fifty students; besides, enrollments were limited to about two hundred students during this period. Following a thorough physical examination by a doctor from the Church General Hospital when they first arrived, students who were diagnosed as being ill were assigned to the "fresh air porch"—a screened, airy room.[4] Using the seven characters of *jia, yi, bin, ding, wu, ji, gen*—similar to *A, B, C*, etc.—the others were assigned to rooms that were dormitory style, divided by age groups. The largest rooms—the first and seventh character rooms located in the two, large wings at the ends of the building—could house up to sixty junior middle students with the wealthier tuition-paying students living in the east-facing (*jia*) room and the students from poorer, non-tuition-paying families living in the west-facing (*gen*) room. The smaller, second through fifth rooms (*yi–ji*) that lined the long hallway tended to house the senior middle school students with each higher grade level housed in successively smaller rooms that could accommodate between ten and forty girls to provide increasing privacy. Once again, the better of these rooms tended to be assigned to the tuition-paying girls. Each year the rooms were reassigned by grade level; yet, the non-tuition-paying, senior middle school students tended to be assigned to the larger rooms, regardless of their grade level, which led to accusations by many of the students that the school administration "favored the wealthy, tuition-paying students."[5]

Each student was assigned a bed and a small locker in which personal items and clothing items were to be stored. Suitcases and trunks were stashed in a large storage room located on the third floor, and students were permitted access only during specified times; otherwise, the storage room was locked for safekeeping. Since the small lockers could not accommodate many items of clothing, the students were permitted more frequent visits to the storage room during the winter because their thick cotton uniforms nearly filled their lockers when stored at night. Students of means had specially made fur-lined winter uniforms in addition to their cotton ones, and they placed their little used, cotton-padded uniforms in between their mattress and bed frame during the winter because there was no room for them in their lockers. At the designated time, the school matron would sit at the bottom of the stairs and each student had to show her what was taken from her suitcases to help prevent thefts from occurring.

Elements of daily life were dictated by school regulations. Each student had to provide her own bed linens which consisted of two sets of white sheets, a white bedspread, and a cotton quilt that had to be purchased at special stores to insure uniformity among all of the students. In addition, two types of school uniforms with the school's name embroidered on the left side—white cotton, midcalf dresses for spring and summer; blue cotton padded midcalf dresses for late fall and winter—were required. Although wearing a uniform made with a certain type of cotton fabric was dictated, because these uniforms were custom-made by each girl's family, those students from wealthier families had uniforms that were better tailored. White cotton stockings were worn in the spring and summer; black wool stockings were worn in fall and winter. Girls from wealthier families had multiple pairs of each type of stocking while the other girls darned theirs when holes appeared. White canvas or leather shoes were to be worn in summer; black or brown canvas or leather shoes were to be worn in winter. Again, girls from wealthy families wore fine leather shoes; girls from poorer families wore cloth shoes. No jewelry or makeup was permitted. Hairstyles could not be elaborate—no fancy hairpins were permitted. Long hair, which could be no longer than the middle of the back, had to be braided or worn in a bun. Most of the girls chose to have their hair bobbed in the fashion that was made popular by college students during the May Fourth Movement—the literary and social movement that inspired a surge of nationalist sentiment in China following student demonstrations protesting the terms of the Paris Peace Conference that followed World War I.[6]

Not only were the students' appearances regulated, so were their daily routines. The day began with an orderly regimen. Awakened beginning at 6:00 a.m., the first shift of students would wash, brush their teeth, and comb their hair while the other girls engaged in "dusting and other domestic tasks."[7] Top sheets and blankets were pulled back to "air" them. Once a week, the students stripped the beds and the linens were washed at the school laundry. While the second group of girls groomed, the first shift made their beds and went downstairs for "setting-up exercises" conducted by the Miss Margaret Roberts (who taught the physical education classes) and designated student leaders at 6:30; the second shift began at 7:00. Although "many of the girls have not yet learned to enjoy exercise, and try to escape my watchful eye," Miss Roberts tried to make sure that all of the girls either did their morning calisthenics or attended the now-voluntary Morning Watch services.[8] Those students who chose to attend Morning Watch, which was held "between seven and seven-thirty each morning for private, or group, Bible-study," would go directly to the chapel.[9] Although registration prohibited mandatory religious instruction, Morning Watch was strongly encouraged, and pressure was placed upon students to attend. Between 7:00 and 8:25 a.m., the girls ate in the school dining room which was located on the first floor in the west wing directly below the *gen* sleeping quarters.

Once students departed the sleeping quarters in the morning, they were not permitted to return until they prepared for bed in the evening. Students who were ill had to report to the matron who then sent them to the school's infirmary where they spent the day.[10] Daily inspections were conducted by a designated "room leader" who reported to the house matron on a biweekly basis. Once a month, students were issued a "moral character (pinxing) grade. It was based on 100%. For sloppy beds, for instance, [students] were deducted two percent." Rooms were awarded gold or silver stars, and girls in rooms that were awarded "gold stars" for being particularly spotless and tidy were given high deportment grades on their report cards.

For all meals, eight students were assigned to a table. The Senior IIIs sat together at designated tables near the Chinese teachers at the front of the dining hall, and they were always the first students served. Seating at the other tables was assigned by the school matron and changed each school term. Except for the Senior IIIs, seating at the tables was mixed so that the girls would meet others in the school. One person each day was assigned the responsibility of allocating equal portions of the food; this practice reinforced the importance of sharing. The standard fare for breakfast was piping hot rice porridge and vegetables. Breakfast was a meal Yuanshuang frequently missed. "My favorite meal was the hot rice porridge in the morning. Huge pots filled with steaming porridge were made and ladled into the serving bowls for each table. But I missed so many of those meals because I could not get up in time for breakfast. I preferred to secretly sleep in and so missed breakfast often that first year particularly." She also skipped the morning calisthenics—which she detested—and was one of the students that Miss Roberts had to "check up on . . . in order to keep the attendance up to the mark."[11]

After breakfast, classes began, and they were scheduled from 8:30 until noon; lunch was served between noon and 1:00. The standard fare for lunch was vegetables with noodle soup or rice. Afternoon classes commenced at 1:15 and ended at 3:30, at which time students were expected to be outdoors in the school yard exercising or relaxing in the fresh air—weather permitting—or performing small tasks. From 3:30 until 5:00 was the only free time during the day when students could do hand laundry, knit, crochet, read novels, eat snacks, or socialize with one another. On inclement days, the classrooms were open for these activities. Dinner was served between 5:00 and 6:30. This meal normally contained some form of protein (most often pork and soy, occasionally beef, chicken, or fish), soup, rice, and vegetables. Eggs were a rarity. "Only the foreigners had eggs regularly and the servants raised chickens that were kept in a coop on the school grounds near the garden." From 6:30 to 7:00 vespers—called Evensong—were held in the chapel. From 7:15 to 9:00, students were expected to work on class assignments. Each weekday evening there were individualized tutoring sessions for students; otherwise, the classrooms were used as study halls where the girls were supervised by one of the teachers. As early as 8:00, students who were ill or on restricted activity and expected to be in bed by 9:00, began preparing for bed. For all other students, they cleaned and washed between 9:00 and 9:55 with a strict lights-out at 10:00. After that time, students were not expected to study or read even though many would sneak under their covers after the final inspection by the room leader was completed and read with the aid of a flashlight. In all, classes were held from Monday morning through Saturday morning.

On Sundays, students followed a different routine; instead of morning classes, they were expected to attend chapel, and subtle, but tremendous, pressure was exerted on non-Christians to participate. Holy Communion was administered at the 8:00 a.m. service followed by another service at 10:30 and then Sunday School. Many of the Christian girls would personally invite their friends and classmates to "keep them company during the service." After registration, the practice of having the girls sit by class was eliminated, and attendance improved because friends could sit with each other. After lunch, a "Young Peoples' Service . . . conducted by the [Christian] girls themselves" was offered in the hopes of attracting the non-Christians.[12] These services tended to be more lively and fun for the girls, and they were responsible for many conversions. The Young Peoples' Service was preferred to the "weekly meeting mainly of an ethical nature with songs and speaking" that was required in lieu of the alternative youth service.[13] All students were expected to take a short rest on Sunday afternoons before their community work in the local "Li" village commenced at 2:00 p.m.[14] Although the girls were expected to nap, Yuanshuang would use that time to knit, read her beloved novels, or chat secretly with her friends. On Sunday evenings, Evensong was a song service presented by the music department that was popular with the students and was better attended than Morning Watch.[15]

While daily life was regimented to produce order, it was rarely that peaceful or disciplined. The students enrolling in St. Hilda's in 1929 arrived at a time when the school was undergoing dramatic changes. Yuanshuang's class was, by many of the students' own admissions, very "naughty" (tiaopi). Because mandatory chapel attendance was no longer required, Yuanshuang and her classmates who were nonbelievers had other ideas about what to do with their time while the others were in the chapel on Sunday.

> My particular class was particularly naughty. The naughtiest . . . The Christian students had to go to the church. There were many of us who were not believers. They did not force you to attend services if you were not a believer; consequently, there was a group of us including [Yuanshuang], naughty ghosts who remained in the classrooms while the others attended church. Believers had to attend services as well as all of the teachers. But a group of us non-believing little ghosts remained in the classroom. While they sang hymns, we would sing the song, "A maid by the name of Wang, repairs a water urn." We would bang on the desks, drum the desk tops with pencils and pens. One of us would watch beside the door, and when we heard the footsteps of one of the teachers, we would immediately stop. We could hear the high heels of the teacher walking down the hallway. She would check the rooms, but did not see anyone. Where did the students go? Where did we go? We were so small that we could hide beneath the desks. If you peered into the classrooms, you could not see us because we hid beneath the desks. We kept very still, and you couldn't see us. The teacher would leave, and we would begin all over.[16]

Yuanshuang became a class leader early on, not only because of innate leadership abilities, but also because she was four years older than her classmates, and she was regarded more as an older sister rather than a peer. The class's basic naughtiness coupled with Yuanshuang's leadership "style" led to a continuous change in the class advisor. Because class discipline was entrusted to each cohort in conjunction with a class advisor, the regular departure of the faculty advisor disrupted any consistent disciplining of the class. Normally, a cohort would have one class advisor for each year, but their teachers did not last a school term much less the entire year. In this state of near-constant flux, the Junior I class took full advantage of its inconsistent supervision.

St. Hilda's itself was undergoing dramatic changes as a result of the political shifts occurring in China. The Northern Expedition and the frequent closing of all the foreign schools from 1926 to 1928 had a dramatic effect upon the student body. Once the Guomindang achieved nominal control over China, missionary schools became a target when the newly established government insisted upon registration of all foreign schools. Mission schools had to either conform to the new regulations or close their doors. Regulations required that all courses had to be taught in Chinese except for English classes; the principal had to be Chinese; and courses on religion and church attendance could no longer be mandatory. The significance of this transformation was not lost on the students—particularly the non-Christians. As one of Yuanshuang's classmates stated:

> We fought wars with foreigners. As a consequence, because China lost, we had to allow missionaries to enter China. [At St. Hilda's], it was an Episcopal church and missionary group. Originally the school was organized by foreigners. All of the courses were taught in English. It was entirely taught by foreigners using English. With the exception of Chinese classes, everything was taught in English. . . . [After the Northern Expedition], all of the schools had to register with the government. . . . This registration demanded that the courses be taught in Chinese. From that time on, the courses, with the exception of English, had to be taught in Chinese.[17]

Even the most politically naive of the girls was exposed to the changing political and social climate in China following the Northern Expedition. Nationalist sentiment was rising, and the loathing of foreign imperialism was intense. "At that time . . . we were of the opinion that foreigners were invading our country. They were invaders who oppressed the Chinese."[18] "The American Episcopalians were accused of invading and penetrating our country using culture; they were accused of cultural imperialism."[19] Their education was seen as "enslaving [the girls] to the foreigners, what they called 'nuhua jiaoyu.' That is, [the foreigners] were using education to enslave you."[20] Yuanshuang was particularly antiforeign because of her family's history with the British; consequently, she fomented nationalist sentiments and championed any cause that appeared to fight against perceived foreign oppression.

Yuanshuang was not alone in fanning nationalist fervor. A Senior I student who was head of the Recreation Club, decided to present a patriotic "movie" on a Sunday afternoon. Sewing together "mosquito nets" and using lights in the background and "flashlights as spotlights," the actors presented a "living movie." When Deaconess Clark learned of the "movie," she sought out Wang Yingan, to discipline her for disregarding "regulations" that forbade "performing or watching plays on Sundays." When confronted by Deaconess Clark, Yingan argued that she had not performed a play but had produced a movie which was not forbidden.

> Deaconess Clark said, "The next time I see your father, I will tell him about this incident." "Fine, you tell him about this incident." So even at that time, we thought that foreigners took advantage of us. Can't do this; can't do that. Actually there were many things that they did that we thought were wrong. But we would not accept what they did. We had patriotic activities that Deaconess Clark did not approve. If the foreigners did something right, we would respect them. But if they oppressed us or did something which we thought was wrong, then we would oppose them. It wasn't just me or just my class. It was this way for others from [post-registration] on.
>
> Later on, [Deaconess Clark] said this about our class. "Individually, everyone in your class is good. But when you get together, you are very strong; no one can manage you."[21]

As nationalistic fervor intensified, so did feelings of oppression and victimization. When a young female teacher, a "Peking [Beiping] University graduate who was carrying the Chinese work in Senior III and II, left in the middle of the [1929] term to take up a more attractive position in Peking," a rumor circulated throughout the student body suggesting that she left because of " 'foreign oppression' at the school."[22] Although the circumstances of her departure had nothing to do with the rumor, suspicion and mistrust still abounded to the extent that many of the foreign teachers lamented that the "Chinese girls . . . excel in poise and self-reliance" but that they were, at times, "independent to the point of being rude," and that "the girls have lost their beautiful Chinese manners."[23] Nevertheless, because the girls were now "considered more and consulted more in matters relating to school affairs so that they too [felt] they [were] making their contribution to the school" relationships between the foreign teachers and the students became better.[24]

Although relationships between the foreign teachers and the pupils improved, distrust still lingered. The foreign teachers lived separately in their "Ladies House," and on rare occasions, a few of the American teachers would join the Chinese teachers at the front tables for meals in the dining hall. As with Yuanshuang, some of the Chinese students were invited to the house, but many students spent their entire school careers without once stepping inside the "Foreigners' House" as the students called it. Like tourists visiting a foreign land, those students who were invited inside would bring back tales of the lavish furnishings and bowls of fresh fruit even in the dead of winter. This social separation and student tales about the Ladies House fed rumors that the foreigners hoarded the best food and water for themselves. When St. Hilda's did not have its own wells, water was hauled in by carts from neighboring mission compounds, from the Yangzi river or from a nearby lake (the Xiao Hu portion of Dong Hu). The water quality, however, was poor and students would develop mouth sores which led to further rumors that the foreigners saved the "sweet water" for themselves.

Beliefs about hoarding persisted because the foreign faculty had their own cook who planted a garden in the spring and summer. The rumor seemed to be confirmed when on Easter night 1930 "ninety odd [Chinese] teachers, men and women, pupils, and servants, men and women," but none of the foreign faculty, came down with a mild case of ptomaine poisoning.[25] "The principal was scared to death that someone would die," and even though there was a nurse at the school, "a doctor from the hospital was summoned to check" on those who had become ill.[26] The largest dormitory room was converted into an infirmary, and "no one could attend classes on Monday."[27] Although "nothing that all had eaten could be found to serve as the cause," and "none were ill for long,"[28] Student Self-Governance Association officers, led by Yuanshuang, went to complain to Deaconess Clark that the food "was not always fresh," and the food "was much better for a long time afterwards."[29]

Prior to registration students were not permitted regular visits home; instead, there were breaks for the Lunar New Year and for the sweltering summer months when the foreign teachers went to the missionaries' mountain retreat in Guling. As one student recalled, "[St. Hilda's was seen as] a convent. It was a boarding school and interaction with outsiders was not permitted. . . . At our school, you could not go home when you liked. We were not allowed to go home even on Sunday. We were only allowed to go home once every five months . . . once a school term. Every year there were two school terms, five months each."[30] Because Wuhan is renowned as one of the three "steamers" of China, the school was closed in July and August. Registration, however, loosened the home visitation restriction, and once a month, on a date selected by their families, students were permitted to go home after Saturday morning classes but they had to return by 7:00 p.m. in the evening. Monthly visits could be accumulated, and after a sufficient number were accrued, students were permitted to spend the night at their home, but once again, students were required to return before Sunday Evensong at 7:00 p.m. Students were issued a pass that had to be presented to the gatekeeper so that the staff could keep track of who was not on campus. "When we left on Saturday, we had to pick up a permission slip from the headmistress and hand it to the gatekeeper. When we returned to St.

Hilda's, we had to pick up the card from the gatekeeper who noted the time we entered and returned it to the headmistress." Such procedures led students to draw an analogy to being in a prison. "We were treated as if we were prisoners being released whenever we went home. We felt oppressed by such measures."[31]

The graduating class of 1933 sought even more home visits. In fall 1932, the eighteen Senior IIIs made a "determined request" to modify the restriction even more, and requested that they be permitted to leave the compound twice a month; Principal Dorothy Tso would only consider the privilege for the second semester, and "then only on condition that they carry on as dormitory proctors through that term." The Senior IIIs rescinded their request "because they hate[d] to be proctors."[32]

Realistically only students who lived in Wuhan could make the monthly visits home; otherwise, they remained at school the entire time. Immediately after morning classes were over at 11:30, rather than eat lunch on campus, Yuanshuang (and later, Yuanquan and their cousin, Yuanlu) would race down to the wharf in a taxicab to catch the small river transports that shuttled passengers to and from Wuchang and Hankou.

It was these home visits that would help make Yuanshuang, Yuanquan, and Yuanlu, popular with their fellow students.[33] They were permitted to invite classmates and schoolmates home during these monthly visits, especially those classmates who could not afford to go home or lived too far from the school. The hour-long trip to Hankou was spent laughing and chatting together. Once the girls arrived at the Yeh mansion, they would bound into the house for food and drink. Dexing graciously accepted any friends that the three girls brought, and they were all treated as if they were family members. The girls and guests alike were treated to large lunches and snacks throughout the afternoons before heading back to the wharf to catch the last possible transport back to Wuchang. Because the Saturday evening curfew was strictly set at 7:00 p.m., arriving tardy would affect their next home visit. Too many tardy arrivals—noted on the permission cards—resulted in forfeiture of a monthly home privilege. As a consequence, upon returning to Wuchang, the girls would hire a taxicab that took only twenty minutes to get to St. Hilda's rather than the normal thirty- to forty-minute ride by rickshaw.

> It only cost twenty "coppers" by rickshaw and the taxi cost two [Chinese] dollars —that was big money in those days. But we were always running late and would always take the taxi in order to arrive at school on time. Besides, there were always at least four of us and the cost of the taxi was worth it. But if a taxi was unavailable, we had no choice but to hire rickshaws. Because the rickshaws could only carry a certain number of us, the first to arrive would plead with the

> gatekeeper to notate all of our permission cards with one time so that those arriving later would not be marked tardy. Some of the gatekeepers were very understanding and would give us all the cards. Our favorite was Gatekeeper Han; he was the best. His daughter was in [Yuanquan's] class. Others, however, would not. They did not want to take the chance of being discharged if they were caught helping us to falsify the entry times.

During school recesses, Yuanshuang, Yuanquan, and Yuanlu would also invite girls whose parents were unable to afford tickets home to vacation with the Yehs. In addition, local wealthy families were permitted to send food every Tuesday. Dexing would have the servants or family relatives deliver large bamboo baskets filled with fresh fruit in season, snacks, and specially prepared dishes and delicacies which Yuanshuang and Yuanquan shared with their friends and classmates. Their generosity was appreciated and formed the foundation of many friendships that would last a lifetime. By the end of the 1929–30 school year, Yuanshuang was voted by every student in her class save one—herself—to be the class leader, a position she was to hold throughout her time at St. Hilda's. She was also consistently elected student body president from 1930 to 1934.

Because St. Hilda's instituted the practice of "sister classes," Yuanshuang was paired with a "big sister" from the Senior I class—none other than her distant relative, Bao Xunyi—during her Junior I year at school. Despite the family connection, Xunyi was diligent and strict. Frequently Xunyi was the proctor responsible for inspecting the junior middle dormitory rooms, and she did not hesitate to disqualify the room because Yuanshuang overslept or because her bed was improperly made. Since the large rooms rarely received any commendations—too many girls in them—Yuanshuang was able to indulge her propensity to sleep in without being detected, but once she graduated into smaller rooms, she was aided by her friends who would warn her of an imminent inspection. "The girl who slept in the bed right next to mine, Zhu Yuying, was in the earlier shift. She served as my scout and when she spotted Xunyi, she would quickly rush in, 'Yuanshuang, get up! Hurry up and get up; I saw Xunyi coming.' I just couldn't get up in the morning—it was so hard! But when I heard that Xunyi was coming, I would jump out of bed, and Yuying would hustle me off to the bathroom; meanwhile she fixed my bed as I washed up." Nevertheless, Yuanshuang was often the cause of deportment infractions.

> I was often the reason why our room was penalized, and it got to the point that the other girls didn't want to share a room with me. They decided upon a warning system to awaken me, but even that didn't always work. Xunyi would deduct points if you left anything on the bed! One day, Zhu Yuying had a pin fastened to her pillowcase, and Xunyi deducted points for that. Yuying was so furious that

she said, "Next time I will fart on the bed to see how many points she will deduct for that!" As I moved into smaller and smaller rooms, I was much better. I did not want to be the reason for our disqualification—too embarrassing.

These feelings of sisterhood became sincere bonds of friendship. Classmates were particularly close; spending virtually all their waking hours in the classroom, eating, sleeping, and socializing with one another bonded the girls together.[34] One classmate recalls, "We became family—like sisters, and in some cases, better than blood relatives. We did everything together from morning until night and we helped one another. Under those circumstances, we had very close bonds with one another."[35] Thus, while Yuan-shuang was being tutored by Miss Tomlin, one or her classmates would hand launder or mend her smaller items of clothes. One time, however, Yuan-shuang decided to wash the coverlet of her quilt and busily tore it apart.

> I remember that I had already torn it [the cotton-padded blanket] apart and decided to wash it myself because it hadn't been washed in two weeks. I tore it all apart and put it in the water. And there it was. I didn't know how to wash it. And furthermore, I didn't know how to wring it out now that it was wet. I was in a panic about what do when [Chen Siyu] showed up and said, "You big family girls don't know how to do anything. Let me in, and I'll take care of it for you." I never saw anyone who could handle a washboard as well as [she did]. In no time, [Siyu] had the blanket washed, wrung, and hung up to dry.

Relationships among the students, however, were not always harmonious. When a series of thefts occurred during the 1931–32 school year, the accusations and suspicions abounded. Although valuables were not permitted in the personal lockers, "one girl broke the rule and had a [gold] ring in her box." When the owner of the ring refused to involve the school administration "because she knew that she was wrong in keeping it at the school," the girls themselves devised a number of ways to have it returned.[36]

> Our first thought was to search every single locker and every single girl's bed, but there were just too many places to hide something as small as a ring. We thought about offering a reward, but decided that stealing should not be rewarded. Finally, we posted a notice in every single dormitory room and made an announcement during the assembly that a "ring had been lost," and if anyone found it, would they place it in the Student Body suggestion box or leave it somewhere that it could be found.

The tactic worked, and the "ring was secretly returned and there was no sure proof of the thief."[37] When a watch was taken, the tactic changed with the girls once again taking action; standing before the others, all the girls in that dormitory room were made to swear: "With a clear conscience, I did not steal the watch."[38] When the watch was still not returned, the lockers, bedrooms, and personal belongings of every single girl were searched. The watch was found in the possession of one of the tuition-paying girls "who came from a very wealthy family. Searching through her personal belongings, we found many things that belonged to other people. These items were not expensive things—pencils, hairpins, combs—nothing expensive, but they did not belong to her because she had hidden them in her things. She had that stealing sickness." The girl was reported to the administration, and the watch and other items were returned to their rightful owners. Shunned by the other students, she left the school abruptly in the middle of the term.[39]

As was the school custom, girls were given English names by the American teachers which were much easier for them to pronounce. These names were not arbitrarily assigned, and Miss Tomlin, after some deliberation during her first year, decided to give Yuanshuang the name of "Judith" because it "was a good pairing with Yeh," and it meant leader. Her friends and classmates, however, rarely used this American name, and when not using her Chinese name or some shortened form of it, they affectionately referred to her as Xiao Pangzi ("Little Fatso").

In Yuanshuang's Junior II year (1930–31), two hundred students enrolled in St. Hilda's, and despite the fact that she was only in junior middle school, her popularity was such that she was elected to be the student body president by all but three votes. The three dissenting votes were cast by Yuanshuang, Yuanquan, and Yuanlu because "I wouldn't vote for myself; and neither did my sisters because I asked them not to vote for me, and they wanted to spare me from the position's responsibilities."[40]

As student body president, Yuanshuang presided over the half-hour weekly Sun Yat-sen memorial assemblies held at 8:30 each Monday morning as mandated by registration. The patriotic assembly consisted of singing the national anthem and:

1. Three bows to the national flags and to the portrait of Dr. Sun Yat-sen
2. Repeating by the whole school of Sun Yat-sen's will
3. Two or three minutes silence for meditation[41]

Important notices were read, announcements made, other school business reported, and students were given a free-speech opportunity. The teachers would also take the opportunity to speak to the students, "telling them how to love their country truly and rightly."[42]

Significant improvements were made on campus in 1930—an electrical plant was built on the school grounds that provided lights for the main campus and all the windows were screened; as a consequence, students were able to study in the individual classrooms rather than gather in the assembly hall. Only the gatekeeper's residence was not electrified (or screened) so kerosene lamps were still used there. After years of requesting money to dig a well on the school grounds, funding was allocated and much needed wells were dug. Complaints about the water and mouth sores decreased as a result.

Curricular changes were made for the 1930–31 school year. In order to obtain an official diploma from the Bureau of Education, all students had to pass government examinations in four subjects: mathematics, history, science, and civics (which included the Three Principles of Sun Yat-sen). Instead of a diploma, St. Hilda's now issued a Certificate of Completion. The examinations were administered at central locations in Wuchang (including Boone) over a period of two days. Failure to pass these examinations required additional work and a retaking of the tests before a diploma would be issued. Additional preparatory classes for the Senior IIIs were created. Also added to the curriculum were more physical education and recreation courses to "counterbalance their heavy review for the various sets of examinations that [the students] were required to take."[43]

As the worldwide Depression worsened, the financial crisis necessitated increased efforts to raise money to continue the "good work" in China. To temper any possible fears surrounding registration and to recruit potential new students, a Parents' Day held in October offered "class-room teaching, an exhibit of all varieties of handiwork, and gymnastic work and a ball game, as well as talks on the purpose and management of the school, and an opportunity on the part of the parents to speak or ask questions" was instituted.[44] Since the target audience was potential tuition-paying parents, one student made the following observation about the interactions between Deaconess Clark and those parents.

> There is one thing that I remember about the headmistress, Deaconess Clark. She was very conscious about money. She would always treat the daughters with money better than those who did not have money. . . . She was supposed to be a Christian, yet she treated the daughters of the Chinese missionaries and preachers far less courteously than those who paid. I never liked that. She would pander to the parents of tuition-paying daughters. Otherwise, she tended to look down upon us.[45]

The financial situation coupled with registration requirements had unanticipated consequences for the students at St. Hilda's. The total isolation of the student population prior to registration was no longer possible. Although some intramural sports were played in physical education classes, intermural team sports were introduced at St. Hilda's because teams were expected to compete "with members of Government Schools in ball games."[46] Physical education uniforms—dark shorts and white blouses—were now required of all students. At its initial competition against the public schools, the team from St. Hilda's created quite a stir because the girls were participating for the first time, and for the sake of modesty, they were wearing pants. Women normally wore dresses or long skirts until about age twenty-five at which time, many began wearing pants; schoolgirls seldom wore pants. For the girls of St. Hilda's, it was also their first time interacting with students—both male and female—from the public schools. To help students prepare for future competitions, Miss Margaret Spurr instituted a school-wide calisthenics competition in April 1931, and a first-ever Field Day that included "marches, drills, relays, and dances" was held in May.[47] At the first Government Tournament in 1931, St. Hilda's sent its basketball team, and Miss Spurr urged Bishop Roots to hire a "Chinese gymnasium teacher." Miss Spurr felt that a full-time, Chinese physical education teacher "could best show [St. Hilda's] friendliness and maintain [the school's] independence," so a graduate from St. Hilda's, Miss Charity Chen, assisted during the year.[48]

To help increase financial support for St. Hilda's, "the first Saturday after Easter of each year [was designed] as Alumnae Day" in 1931. An executive committee was elected and the members would be "active in raising funds toward our much-needed Music Building" as well as "in getting in touch with graduates [of St. Hilda's] in other parts of China."[49]

In fall 1931, the great summer flood delayed the opening of the school for a month, and when classes did resume on October 1, the school building could not easily accommodate all of the 206 students due to water damage on the first floor. Classes were held on the second floor of the school building which was normally used solely as dormitories, and Junior I and II classes were moved to a nearby missionary compound. By day, the dormitory rooms and hallways were converted into makeshift classrooms using the classroom furniture that was rescued by Deaconess Clark, Hazel Gosline, the matron, and Robert Kemp from Boone. The normal daily regimen had to be relaxed out of necessity, and the girls enjoyed the "camping experience." By night, the girls had to double up in their sleeping quarters to accommodate the added classroom furniture, and the scene resembled a huge camp. The school building was screened the year before, and the screens helped prevent the number of malaria cases from increasing; nevertheless, because of the flood waters and the open doors, mosquitos swarmed in the rooms, and those who had mosquito netting, strung them together to pitch giant "tents" throughout the rooms. Fearing the outbreak of malaria, Dexing had purposely packed extra nets when her daughters returned to school, and these were used in the "tent city." Home visits had to be suspended during the month of October because of an outbreak of cholera among the refugees surrounding the school.[50] Despite the conditions, the school maintained a regular routine, and on November 1, all of the students returned to the school grounds. "Daily group meetings for prayer for their country," as well as "First Aid classes," were held, and by mid-November, "most classes report having caught up to within a week of the work that should have been covered, in spite of beginning a full month short."[51]

Relationships between the students and teachers were generally warm, cordial, and deferential, and the girls had their "favorites." The girls tended to be closer to the Chinese women teachers rather than either the foreign faculty or the Chinese male teachers. Although some of the male faculty lived with the gatekeeper, his family, and the male servants in four small rooms on the second floor of the gatehouse, contact with the Chinese male faculty was purposefully kept at a minimum to prevent the possibility of any inappropriate contact. The Chinese women teachers lived with the students in the dormitories, and the foreign faculty lived in their separate "Ladies House." Once the Cox Music Building was completed in 1931, Miss Venetia Cox lived there.

While the students were generally well-behaved, they could also be mischievous and troublesome—particularly to the single, male faculty. Culturally, male teachers did not have much interaction with female students, and it was even more awkward for the young male teachers to discipline girls who were close in age to them. The tuition-paying students tended to be the perpetrators of pranks, "never the girls who were Christians and who were attending the school for free."[52]

The requirement that the Three Principles of Sun Yat-sen must be taught by a Nationalist Party member created a problem at St. Hilda's. Since most of the Chinese female faculty were former students and none of them was a party member, the instructor was going to be a male. In the case of one of these party members, while the girls were not disrespectful, neither were they particularly attentive during his instruction. Yuanshuang recalled, "The classes were boring, so we would just listen but do other things. I would knit in my lap or sometimes, I would read tales of the Monkey King. Other times, we would lift the desktop up to whisper behind them. The Party member would turn around and say, 'I hear voices but I don't see anyone' because we were all hiding behind our desks." Complaints made to Deaconess Clark by the Party member prompted "surprise classroom visits" to not only reestablish order but also to observe what was being taught by him.

Other teachers did not fare as well. Hiring teachers was a chronic problem for all missionary schools, and when a "recent graduate of Shanghai College" backed out of her commitment to come and teach biology in the fall of 1932, a young male teacher was hired "in a hurry." The teacher was taken advantage of by the students "because he [did] not know how to manage the girls and to keep good discipline in his classes."[53] One student recalls what they did to the hapless young man. "There was a teacher who wasn't very good. We took Chinese ink and smeared it all along the end of a desk. It was black Chinese ink. That teacher taught health, hygiene, and biology. As soon as the teacher stood up, he would get the ink all over him. His entire front or back would be covered with Chinese ink."[54]

Although the girls would play pranks on the male teachers, students were also sympathetic to what they considered to be mistreatment of the Chinese male faculty and the servants. In November 1930, Gatekeeper Han, who had always been lenient to late-arriving students, was forced to retire because of illness. Some of the student leaders would take turns visiting him at his new residence. Because Yuanshuang and Yuanquan's family owned the famous Yeh Kai Tai Chinese pharmaceutical company, medicine was sent weekly and the sisters would share a portion of the special food that their mother would send over every Tuesday. He died in January 1931, and after his funeral, which was attended by everyone on campus, the Senior IIIs and other student leaders gathered to meet with Deaconess Clark to protest the living conditions for both the male faculty and the servants.

> We used to have Chinese teachers who worked [at St. Hilda's]. They were taken advantage of. While the foreigners lived very comfortably in the foreigner house, the Chinese [male] teachers and servants lived in terrible quarters. In the winter, it was bitterly cold. The foreigners had heat and were quite nice and warm while the Chinese teachers and servants did not even have a stove. The students in my class banded together and protested that they were taking advantage of the Chinese.

Citing financial difficulties created by the Depression, Deaconess Clark tried to explain the housing conditions for the male teachers and servants. The girls persisted in their demands for better heating and went so far as to allocate monies from their own self-help organizations to help defray the costs for the purchase of stoves. The students "created such a nuisance and such a fuss that eventually stoves were installed for the Chinese teachers and servants as well."[55] Money for the funeral expenses was also raised for the widow and the family through donations and from the Student Self-Governance Association.

As spring and summer approached and the weather became hotter, other complaints about the housing conditions arose. Even though the buildings on campus were screened in 1929, the gatekeeper's house was not. The lack of screens was also an issue for students who, once again, protested the conditions and discussed the living conditions during the Monday assemblies. "In the summer, while the foreigners were away, the servants had to stay at the school. Although we had screens on the [dormitory] windows, the servants' quarters did not, so they were eaten alive by the mosquitos because they had to keep the windows open just to get a breath of fresh air in the stifling heat." Again, financial constraints were cited as the reason why screens for the gatekeeper's residence were not included in the school's budget. When the school building roof and the chapel floor were repainted in 1930, the students grumbled even more. "They had money to paint the roof, but they did not have money to screen the servants' quarters. Roofs were more important than people. It was not right. They were oppressing the servants."[56] Once again, the students raised the issue during the Monday assemblies. "That was always the case. If we felt that an injustice was done, one of the students—usually [Yuanshuang] or one of the other leaders—would call a meeting and we would discuss. Then the entire group would go and see the headmistress and complain."[57]

These incidents involving the assistant principal, Deaconess Julia Clark, served to cement an image of her in the students' minds as someone who did not "really [like] the Chinese very much."[58] Although a Chinese principal was required by government regulation, and one was appointed in 1928—Chen Jiang—the real power was Deaconess Clark. The nominal position of Chen Jiang was a sore point for students who regarded the arrangement as yet another example of how "the foreigners did not have respect for the Chinese." Continuing with her assessment, the student noted: "After St. Hilda's reopened [in 1928], it was supposed to be supervised by the Chinese, [but] it was still Deaconess Clark who was the acting principal. They said she was the acting principal; however, all of the authority was still in her hands. She was supposed to be acting in Deaconess Chen Jiang's place. We had a Chinese Deaconess in charge only for appearance sake. It was one of the regulations. . . . But in reality, Deaconess Clark was the real principal."[59] In fact, Yuanshuang noted, "It was always Deaconess Clark. Everyone knew she had the power. We didn't even see Deaconess Chen Jiang." Although Yuanshuang generally enjoyed a good relationship with her teachers, she frequently had run-ins with Deaconess Clark.

Noted for her "hooking finger," Deaconess Clark would summon students by beckoning them with her index finger, and Yuanshuang was frequently hooked. During class, girls would read novels, knit, or pass notes to one another all to the dismay of Deaconess Clark who would patrol the hallways and check into the classrooms from time to time. While reading novels and passing notes were not easily detectable, knitting was, and Yuanshuang would be hooked and her knitting materials confiscated. Undeterred, she would get more yarn and another set of needles and start anew. During evening study sessions, Yuanshuang would also sneak her favorite novels into her books; these, too, were confiscated in bulk, and they resulted in many visits to the Principal's office.

During the hectic fall term of 1931, however, a more serious confrontation between Deaconess Clark and Yuanshuang occurred. During one of the Three Principles of Sun Yat-sen classes, the girls were informed by the teacher about forthcoming announcements that would be read to them during their regular Monday morning assemblies. When several weeks passed and there were no party announcements whatsoever, Yuanshuang requested that Gao Sifu (Master Gao), one of the workers at the school who cleaned the offices, bring the contents of the wastebaskets to her. Sifting through the trash, Yuanshuang and the other student body officers discovered that the official government announcements were being pitched by Deaconess Clark. The very next Sun Yat-sen memorial assembly, as the student body president, Yuanshuang read the retrieved announcements to all. This action precipitated a hook and an immediate summons to the principal's office where they argued back and forth.

> Deaconess Clark was furious. She said that what we had done was a crime and that all who were responsible would be expelled for being the criminals that we were. I told her that I alone was responsible for what had happened and if anyone should be expelled, I, and I alone, should be the one. I argued that it was my responsibility as the Student Body President to read all government announcements and that she was wrong to just throw them out. She was violating government regulations. Moreover, I told her that I asked the gatekeeper to keep track of all the incoming mail. I was afraid she would destroy the government announcements, and we had a right to hear those announcements. I threatened her that if she continued to toss out the announcements before they were read, I would report it to our politics teacher who would report back to the Party. That news frightened her, but she still threatened to expel me, and I was not permitted to attend classes.

Upon hearing the news of Yuanshuang's confinement to the library and the threat of her possible expulsion, the entire student body engaged in a silent strike against this perceived injustice. Unable to boycott classes for fear of being expelled, what the students chose to do was to attend all classes, but they refused to answer any questions or respond to the teachers. After three days, Deaconess Clark summoned Yuanshuang to the chapel.

> We met in the chapel—after all, I was a sinner and sinners had to confess in church. While I was sitting in the very front row, Deaconess Clark pointed to her eyes. Tears were falling down her cheeks, "Look at my eyes! Look any my eyes! Do you see how what you have done has hurt me so much?" Because of the support the entire school had shown for me, she could not expel me. But the whole school would lose that month's home visit and no one was allowed to receive any food from home the next week as punishment for the silent strike. As for my additional punishment, I was told that I would not be permitted to attend my junior middle school commencement exercises.

Government bulletins from that time on were read each week during the assembly. Use of the assemblies to publicize events and arouse nationalistic spirit was finally curtailed during the second term of 1932 when Dorothy Tso officially became the principal while Deaconess Clark was on home leave. (Dorothy Tso's appointment ended the four-year-long charade that Deaconess Chen Jiang was St. Hilda's principal.) "The students' opportunity for free speech at the Sun Yat-sen Memorial Service was abolished," so that "school announcements" could be made, "because I felt that the students had plenty of opportunity for free speech in other meetings of the student body."[60] In addition, Principal Tso also prohibited secular groups from meeting on Sunday afternoons. Although the secular students protested, these two changes effectively ended the ability of the student leaders to organize protests about conditions at the school; however, since Principal Tso was asked by the student leaders to serve as the faculty adviser for the Student Self-Governmence Association, student concerns were told to her during its regular meetings.

At the end of her third school year, in June 1932, Yuanshuang was sent home early along with a trunk filled with half-knitted items and partially read Monkey King novels. As a disciplinary action, Yuanshuang would not be permitted to participate in her junior middle graduation ceremony. Being a much older student graduating from Junior III, the ceremony meant little to her; food and freedom were far more important. "Although Deaconess Clark thought it was a terrible punishment to be denied the honor of attending my junior middle commencement, I was delighted to go home early where I could sleep in as late as I wanted and to eat my favorite foods!"[61]

But the girls also participated in activities that built qualities such as self-sufficiency and independence—two virtues most often named by the students as characteristic of the ethos of St. Hilda's. The student organizations at school played an important role. There were five religious organizations on campus—"the Choir, Altar Guild, Vestry, Teachers' Christian Fellowship, and the Missionary Service League."[62] Inspired by a stirring lecture by Dr. Stanley Jones in fall 1931, the Teachers' Christian Fellowship was created and met

> every ten days for prayer for our students and discussion of "Christ of the Mount." The Missionary Service League [was] run by the students; all the religious activities [were] of their own initiation, and [were] organized and executed by this League. They divided the work into four groups: praying and reading, teaching Sunday School and Servants' Night School, preaching to the village women, and sewing. They elected their own leaders. They had a prayer Meeting every Friday morning. There were about sixty children coming every Sunday to their Sunday School.[63]

Abilities of any sort were recognized and nurtured by the staff. All the girls participated in the Student Self-Governance Association, where, "aided by a faculty adviser, practically every school activity except the curriculum and class teaching" was conducted.[64] The Student Self-Governance Association was divided into five groups: "the promotion of virtue, editorial, hygiene, civics, and good times; each [had] its own faculty advisor."[65] Students with leadership abilities were encouraged to run for student association offices or were appointed dormitory proctors. Those with athletic ability not only served on the school teams but were made the leaders of the daily calisthenics. Those with scholastic ability were encouraged to mentor their classmates or assist in the study halls.

Self-governance and self-help organizations blossomed. Anyone who required a haircut, laundry washed, shoes repaired, or clothing mended could seek the services provided by the student organization self-help associations. These groups not only provided needed services but they also provided the means by which girls who needed financial assistance could earn money.

While such practices might appear to drive a wedge between the wealthy, tuition-paying girls and the poorer, non-tuition-paying ones, they did not. Rather, they provided an honorable means by which students could earn money by utilizing their talents. Many of the wealthy students were excellent embroiderers because of the training they received at home preparing their trousseaux. Rather than keeping the money, many chose to donate their income to charitable causes or to contribute to the school's student "emergency fund." This was especially the case when the Japanese began their occupation of Manchuria in September 1931, and patriotic feelings welled up within the girls. In a fit of patriotic fervor, Yuanshuang bobbed her hair in support of the government and encouraged others to do the same. Monies generated from the self-help organizations were donated to the "Wounded Soldiers' fund." Clean, old linens and white clothing were torn into strips for bandages, hair was saved from haircuts—including Yuanshuang's—to be used to insulate winter uniforms, and other supplies were gathered for the Chinese Red Cross. Yuanshuang, who was particularly adept in both embroidery and cutting hair, joined the efforts enthusiastically. For twenty-five "coppers," she embroidered the school's name on uniforms or cut hair and contributed the equivalent of one hundred Chinese dollars to the fund.

With each successive southward movement by the Japanese, the girls became even more politically active. When the Japanese invaded Chinese provinces from their puppet state of Manzhouguo in 1933, defeated the Chinese army, advanced on Beiping, and forced the Nationalists to agree to the terms of the Tanggu Truce, which "legitimated" the Japanese occupation of Rehe (Jehol) and parts of Qahar provinces, the girls could no longer remain indifferent.[66] The 1933 incident precipitated an "Anti-Japanese Products Campaign" at St. Hilda's and some of the girls joined student demonstrations to show support for the country.

As president of the student body, Yuanshuang organized the campaign with the other officers. "During the Japanese occupation of Dongbei [the Northeast], there was a great deal of hatred of the Japanese because Chinese men and women were pressed into service and after the work was completed all of the workers were killed." This heightened awareness led to a successful student campaign.

> While we were in St. Hilda's we had several nationalistic campaigns (aiguo yundong). One such campaign was a boycott of all Japanese products.
>
> The officers of the student body association and I would check the luggage of all incoming students and notate what Japanese-made products were in their possession. Each one of these items would be stamped with a chop stating "Japanese good" and the year, 1933. This campaign began in 1933 because the Japanese invaded Dongbei and the country was swept with anti-Japanese sentiment. Each Japanese-made product was stamped with the chop and student was given a certificate. The following year, any products made in Japan that were brought back to school without the necessary chop and date were confiscated and sold.

The "anti-Japanese products" campaign with its accompanying speeches made by Yuanshuang and other student leaders denouncing the Japanese was quite successful, and it was continued during her final two years at the school.

The student body engaged in other good works as well. The girls taught literacy classes for the women servants and their children on the weekends. Some of the male faculty organized classes for the men servants. Each Sunday afternoon the girls who belonged to both the religious and secular student organizations would venture into neighboring "Li" village. There they would teach the peasants about sanitation, cleaning, and health care. They would demonstrate by cleaning the houses and by explaining the importance of hygienic practices. Old and young alike were gathered and read Bible stories. Simple scrapes and cuts were treated by the girls, especially those who were interested in becoming nurses or doctors. More serious wounds and diseases were treated by the school nurse, Miss Li, or a nurse—typically Mary Cabot—from the Church General Hospital who regularly joined the girls on their Sunday sojourns into "Li" village. Yuanshuang loved this work, and rarely missed an opportunity to participate. As an "older sister" to one of the junior middle students, she was finally becoming a positive role model.

One incident was instrumental in helping facilitate the change in Yuanshuang's attitude toward learning. Even though she was not disappointed in missing her junior middle school graduation, she had been thoroughly shamed in one of her classes. Students were assigned summer reading for which they were expected to write a short report and give a presentation when they returned for the fall semester. The ethics teacher, Zhou Yuying—"the teacher we feared the most"—issued Yuanshuang the "perfect book" that would "take just minutes to read and a mere three sentences to write and give a report." Yuanshuang was presented with *The Shining Spirit Smiles Thrice* [*Ling Guan San Shao*]—all three pages of it—in front of the class. Yuanshuang was simultaneously "insulted, ashamed, and indignant." Zhou's strategy, however, accomplished its intent because Yuanshuang "stomped right to the library"—where she ironically worked—and promptly borrowed "several thick volumes to show my teacher that I was not such a lazy student." From that point on, Yuanshuang was a more diligent student.

In June 1934, the girls were involved in the preparations for the wedding of Margaret Spurr to Fred Gilman, the son of the suffragan bishop of Hankou, Alfred A. Gilman. Presided by his father and Bishop Logan H. Roots, the ceremony was held at St. Hilda's chapel. As the President of the student body, Yuanshuang helped coordinate student participation. One of her closest friends, Cai Sumei, was one of the photographers. Members of the Altar Guild helped with the flower arrangements and decorations in the chapel; the choir sang; and student pianists performed throughout the service. For the majority of the student population, including Yuanshuang, it was the first foreign wedding they had ever attended.

Fall 1934 involved the girls in another life event. On August 4, 1934, Eliza McCook Roots, the wife of Bishop Roots, died in Guling where her burial service and internment took place. To commemorate her long years of service to China, a memorial service was held at St. Paul's Cathedral in Hankou on October 14, 1934. Because Mrs. Roots was a teacher at St. Hilda's in 1899, the chapel was filled with wreaths, scrolls, poems, and plaques in honor of her memory. When heavy winds prevented representatives of the school from crossing the river to Hankou for the memorial service, a small service to commemorate the event was held in the chapel instead.[67]

Senior III year for Yuanshuang was both exciting and busy. During Parents' Day in early October, Rongzai stunned Yuanshuang by attending. While preparing for the festivities, one of the teachers found her and stated: "Your father is here to see you." "My father?" Yuanshuang responded, "With so many parents, how do you know he is my father?" The teacher replied: "Just one look, and instantly, I knew he was your father because you look so much alike."

> I did not take [the comment] as a compliment. I was so surprised because I did not know he was coming. My mother never came to the school, and I never wanted my father to come. He was an opium-addict; years of smoking opium made his skin yellow and discolored his teeth and hands. Who wanted to look

> like him? I certainly did not. When I would go home for visits, I had to pay my respects to him, but after that, I avoided him as much as possible. Often, he would be in a drug stupor, and I could escape talking at any length with him. Just a nod, and I was off. Other times, he would question my sister and me about the school. . . .
>
> I went down to the school yard, and there he was standing straight and tall. He was wearing a new gown; his teeth were scrubbed white; his hair was black, shiny, and combed back. He did look handsome, and I was stunned to see him. He smiled when he saw me, and said: "Look. I am wearing a new outfit, new shoes." He showed me his teeth and hands—all scrubbed clean. "I won't be an embarrassment to you, today." He did look good, and he stayed for a while before leaving.

Yuanshuang's relationship with her father improved. On one of the home visits when their mother was away, Yuanshuang, Yuanquan, and their friends dutifully paid their respects when they arrived, but avoided disturbing Rongzai and Concubine Yu when they departed. They left the house quietly, but upon reaching the street,

> My father had opened the shutters and called down rather quietly: "So you are leaving without saying a word?" I said: "We thought you were resting and did not want to disturb you." I tried to avoid seeing him as much as possible. "Just a minute," my father said. A moment later, I saw something fluttering gently down from the window. When it reached the ground, I saw that he had floated down a [Chinese] twenty dollar bill. He didn't return to the window, but we shouted our thanks and went on our way. He didn't dare linger too long or Concubine Yu might have awakened and would have berated him for his action. At that moment I realized that my father did have affection for me.

Joining the foreign faculty and participating in her first Parents' Day was Miss Dorothea Kingsley Wakeman, given the Chinese name of Miss Wei. Although Miss Wakeman came down to St. Hilda's in March of 1934, her first assignment was to teach Junior I and II level English in order to free up the existing foreign faculty to enable them to work with the senior middle school English classes. Ironically, Dorothea was replacing the teacher whose place she was originally supposed to take when she arrived in September 1933—Margaret Spurr. In October, Miss Wei was asked by the Entertainment Committee of the Student Self-Governance Association to serve as their faculty adviser—a position that she gladly accepted. Still active in the Student Self-Governmence Association, Yuanshuang would have brief encounters with Miss Wei. Dorothea also wrote some of the school plays that were performed during that year, and while the two worked together on various projects, Yuanshuang was never her student.

The Senior III class of 1935 decided to present an interpretive play of *The Dream of the Red Chamber (Hung Lu Meng),* written by Cao Xueqin in the mid-nineteenth century. The story revolves around the various members of the wealthy Jia family, particularly the young male protagonist, Baoyu. Because Yuanshuang was so familiar with the story and her own life story paralleled that of the Jia family, she played the role of the beautiful maiden, Ling Daiyu, the love interest of Jia Baoyu. The play was such an enormous success that additional dates were added to the schedule, and outside guests were invited to attend. A respectable fund was generated from the admission price that was given to the Student Self-Governance Association. Seeing the play inspired Dorothea to read the novel in English, and it would become her favorite work of Chinese literature; the production also inspired her to write adaptations of American stories and tales for the Chinese.

During her Senior III year, Yuanshuang remained the class leader, but she was no longer the student body president because studying for the national examinations was considered too important and too time-consuming. During the 1934–35 school year, for the first time, Yuanshuang worked diligently on her course materials. She had neither the patience nor the desire to take supplemental courses or to delay her graduation. Much to her classmates' frustration and amazement, Yuanshuang was able to pass her courses by reading their class notes or by joining their cram sessions.

> Because I was so involved with school activities, my classmates were very good to me. Although I never missed class—you could not miss class without an excuse—I did not always take the best notes; my classmates would lend me theirs. Some refused like Auntie Yin because she was always such a good student and did not want to encourage my bad habits. Others refused, especially if I did better than they did on the tests! But others lent me theirs to read; they wanted me to pass. We would get up early on the mornings of the tests and study underneath the cross by the chapel or in the covered walkways. They would ask me questions about the material to prepare me. That is how I passed some of the classes. I was good in mathematics, and in return, I would help some of my classmates who had trouble. We helped each other.

No such help from classmates and friends was possible for passing the national examinations, however. Although the examinations were proctored, because there were hundreds of students from all over the city taking the tests, cheating was rampant, but students from St. Hilda's refused to cheat.

> Some of the other students from the public schools would ask us for answers but we never gave them, and we did not cheat. We were a Christian school, and

> cheating was not allowed. We would sit together and not pay attention to any of the other students; we just did our own work. Because we were wearing our white uniforms, the students from the public schools could easily identify us and would accuse us of being brainwashed because we would not give them answers. In fact, we rarely spoke to any other students besides our classmates.[68]

The two days of testing were grueling, but for once, Yuanshuang knew the materials and her correct answers were not merely the result of lucky guesses.

In 1934, the religious reformer Yangchu "Jimmy" Yen was in Wuchang, and Yuanshuang wished to hear him speak. Yen was a dynamic speaker who never failed to inspire. Although Yuanshuang had always opted to select ethics courses instead of taking the classes in religious knowledge, she wished to hear Jimmy Yen. Yen had launched an adult literacy program throughout China based on his World War I experiences working in Europe as a member of the Chinese Labor Corps, and he had gained a great deal of fame throughout the world as a result.[69] On this occasion, the entire school went to hear him speak not only about his literacy efforts but also about his agricultural and medical efforts in the countryside. But it was Yen's description of his work in the countryside that captured Yuanshuang's interest. She admired how Yen's Christian values served as a motive force behind his dedication to the poor. His lecture piqued her interest further, and Yuanshuang began to see a connection between Christianity's teachings and their practical application in the community work she did on Sundays. In her Senior III year, much to the surprise of many of her classmates and teachers, Yuanshuang decided to convert and be baptized.

On one of her many return visits to St. Hilda's from Yichang, Deaconess Julia Clark learned of Yuanshuang's decision to convert and be baptized, and sent for her. "Deaconess Clark was so happy. 'I have been praying for this day for many years,' she told me. I had to take religion classes before I could be baptized, but I could take them with the minister and teachers whom I liked. I enjoyed the classes and discussions."

Thus by the time she graduated, Yuanshuang's ethos had been miraculously transformed through her exposure to the Social Gospel at St. Hilda's. The previously indifferent student had passed the national exams and was looking forward to going to college; the strong antiforeign critic had become a Christian; and the student who was totally unconcerned about her junior middle school graduation proudly became a St. Hilda's alumna.

Although her father did not attend her graduation, he surprised her once again by attending "Class Day"—the day before commencement. Instituted first in 1930, Class Day was "a less formal day, full of good times, to which former teachers and members of the class were invited,"[70] and was the day that Senior IIIs were permitted to wear their finest outfits instead of their uniforms. It was the "occasion [where] special guests, brothers, cousins and friends of the male sex [were] allowed for the first time,"[71] and that evening, the Music Department performed its final concert for the school year. Yuanshuang's only regret was that her "mother never came to the school. Not once. She did not want to interact with foreigners; she was not comfortable with foreigners." With her St. Hilda's Certificate of Completion in hand, Yuanshuang, who was accepted to Wuhan University based on her high scores on the national examinations, was ready to commence study in social work beginning in September 1935.

Principal Dorothy Tso and St. Hilda's Student Self-Governance Association Board Members, 1934–35. Top row, left to right: Yeh Yuanquan, Liu Defu, Wu Anzhen. Middle row, left to right: Zhang Meiyu, Ma Biling, Xiong Yuqing, Zhou Zizhen. Bottom row, left to right: Yeh Yuanshuang, Cai Sumei, Principal Dorothy Tso (Zuo Dezhen), Wang Minying, Wei Ana.

Yeh Yuanshuang, Senior Middle School Diploma, 1935.

Dorothea, UCLA Graduation, 1929. Courtesy Catherine Howe Collato, Private Collection of Dorothea Wakeman Howe.

5

Dorothea and the "Saints"

ON THE EVENING OF MARCH 27, 1934, DOROTHEA ENTERED THROUGH THE gates of St. Hilda's and into another world. After accepting the position, Dorothea's temporary one-year position was changed to a regular appointment, and she would spend the next three years teaching in Wuhan. At St. Hilda's Dorothea would be initially working closely with four other women. Describing them in a letter to her parents, Dorothea wrote:

> Venetia Cox you know visited in Peiping. She teaches the music here at St. Hilda's. I don't know how old she is but imagine about 35. She's also full of pep. Well they all are. . . .
>
> There is Hazel Gosline, 33 yrs. old, a little fat, a keen sport, and just as dear and good hearted thro and thro as she can be.
>
> But the very sweetest of them all is Olive Tomlin. Peggy [Margaret Spurr] calls her Aunt Tommy. She doesn't look any older than 35 at the most but she says that Judy [Julia] Clark has only been out four years longer than she has so she must be older than she looks. She is most lovable and very loving. She has the very kindest twinkle in her eyes all the time and is always thinking about the rest of us. She is a regular mother. The whole bunch of them are full of pep. . . .
>
> Peggy Spurr—an awfully cute little Canadian girl whose place I'm taking next fall. . . . Peggy Spurr is about 25 and has suddenly announced her engagement to Fred Gilman, bishop's son and will be married to him in June instead of going home to marry a man she's been engaged to for some time. Well now you have met my co-workers.[1]

After a "delicious dinner," Dorothea was given her first tour of what would be home for the next two and one-half years.[2] That evening, she began what would become her evening routine. One of the servants, Li Sifu (Master Li), filled her large tin tub with boiling water so that Dorothea could take her evening bath; it thrilled her to remember that the very tin tub in which she was about to bathe was the reason she was now in China. The story told by her friend, Julia Clark, about the great flood of 1931 at St. Hilda's and how the tin tubs were strapped together to serve as a boat to paddle around the flooded compound in salvage missions inspired Dorothea to apply. Dorothea slipped into her bed, where the "covers were already turned back and a hot water bottle within," and fell asleep listening to the howling wind and pouring rain.[3]

Bright sunshine and blue skies greeted Dorothea the next morning, and she was initiated into her morning ritual. Before she awoke, one of the male servants would quietly enter the room, build a fire if the weather was cold, and place large, tin watering cans filled with hot water in her bathroom. As early as 6 a.m., a Western breakfast such as eggs, toast with butter and jams, cereal, pancakes, ham, French toast, and fresh fruit was served. Joining Dorothea on that first morning was Frances Roots, daughter of Bishop Logan H. Roots, who stopped by to introduce herself to Dorothea and to take her to see the Boone compound. "Very pretty and talented and only 23 years old"; Frances would become a lifelong friend.[4] Together with Venetia Cox, the three walked up and down hillocks on the dirt road to acquaint Dorothea with the local environs around St. Hilda's, "all green and fresh, sloping hills and charming little vegetable garden plots with occasional groves of trees and intermingling rivulets."[5] Reveling in the sun reflecting in the pools of water that collected in small ruts in the road, Dorothea never "felt so alive."[6]

Dorothea was about to encounter Chinese rural life. Although Wuchang was an ancient city, St. Hilda's was located in a predominantly agricultural area outside of what was once the eastern wall of the city, near the Little East Gate. Once the compound was established in the early 1900s, streets "made of flag stones, rough and hard going and not very wide, with store fronts or houses on either side which open wide and hiding nothing, right onto the street," gradually sprung up beside St. Hilda's so that it resembled a small village.[7] After the siege of Wuchang, the city streets were electrified and joined with the main part of the former walled fortress. South of the compound was a large Daoist monastery. Immediately west of St. Hilda's were the Wuchang-Changsha-Guangzhou railroad tracks, and a little further west was Serpent Hill so named because the old city walls once twisted and curved around the contours of the landscape.[8] From its upper ridge one could enjoy a panoramic view of the area that spanned all the way to the Yangzi River.

> It is a narrow knife edge with steep green slopes on either side. This razor-back path undulates steeply as the wall climbs up and down over hills. On the highest point, there is the rusty old remains of a great cannon—the greatest one—they say—in the siege of 1926. At the foot of the slope is a great grave mound where the many dead (Chinese soldiers) of that little skirmish were hastily interred above. The besieging army was in our own St. Hilda's compound at the time, until they decided it was too low a vantage point and moved to higher ground. The wall and hill were honey-combed with tunnels, dug thro by maneuvering armies. They say that you could watch the shells bursting in the air all day long, right over the city. Exciting![9]

Many a picnic was held on Serpent Hill, and during the Lunar New Year, Dorothea and her friends would climb atop to view the various villages celebrating with their dragon dances and firework displays. The dirt road to the Boone compound wound through a countryside composed of neatly terraced rice paddies and crop fields punctuated by an occasional small village; Dorothea noticed the differences between the North and the South immediately. Besides the types of crops being grown, one striking difference was the rooflines, which were more pronounced in the South: "they all sweep sky ward at the corners most decidedly." Designed to thwart "the devils and bad spirits . . . a bad spirit descending suddenly over the roof of a house like this would find himself sadly foiled and gnashing his teeth, would be forced to leave the house unmolested."[10] Small but elaborate miniature temples dedicated to local gods dotted the countryside. Erected by the peasants, and adorned with flowers, incense, and food, these gods were entreated to bring rain, good weather, bountiful crops, and good health. Dorothea would often travel the one-mile trek to Boone, or to the British Wesleyan compound located between the two, either by foot or by bicycle on regular visits with her friends or to attend functions.

Dorothea's living quarters were a two-story, Western-style residence referred to by the Chinese as the "foreigners' house" or the "Ladies House" by its residents. The south-facing exterior door opened into a tiled porch that extended to a screened porch on the east side and the main entrance. The front door led into an entry hall with "oriental rugs and furniture and a large mirror at the end."[11] A living room with piano and French doors, a study/library with piano, the dining room, and a small conservatory with piano were on the west side of the residence. Olive Tomlin's study, Dorothea's study, supply and pantry rooms, laundry and servant's bathroom, and stairwell to the second floor were on the north side. Upstairs were the bedrooms. Peggy Spurr's study, Dorothea's bedroom suite, and a guest suite were located in the west wing; Hazel Gosline's bedroom, bathroom, and study, and Olive Tomlin's bedroom suite were in the east wing. Peggy Spurr's bed was located in the upstairs screened porch that also housed five birdcages and large potted plants. Throughout the house and in each bedroom and study were fireplaces. In keeping with Chinese tradition, the kitchen was in a separate building located adjacent to the house on the north side and connected to the house with a screened hallway. A large vegetable and flower garden and the chicken coop were on the north side as well.[12]

Three servants—two men and one woman—worked at the house and were essential individuals in the smooth functioning of the household; Li Da Sifu (elder Master Li) was primarily the cook and handled the food and purchased supplies while Li Sifu (Master Li) did most of the heavier manual labor (such as hauling firewood and water in and out of the bathrooms and kitchen) required around the house and garden. With no refrigeration, food was purchased daily at the local market places. On their daily forays into the city, Li Da Sifu and Li Sifu scouted for the best deals in fruits, vegetables, and meat for the rest of the compound and made arrangements for delivery. They would also negotiate a better price for goods purchased in greater quantity. For that service, they would "squeeze" a portion of the purchases for their own use.

In accordance to Chinese custom that dictated male servants have limited personal interactions with the women of the household, the wife of Li Sifu—referred to as "Amah"[13]—was responsible for cleaning the women's rooms, sewing, mending, laundering the women's personal items, and keeping an eye on the house. Although each woman had her own bathroom, there was no flush toilet but a "throne-like" seat with a hole that was directly above a large bucket; indoor water pipes had been installed in 1932, and although hot water was available, the servants continued to carry the water up to "save the trouble of running the tap until [hot water] comes."[14] Several times each day, the amah and her young daughter checked and cleaned the "honey pots."

Although servants were prevalent at the College of Chinese Studies in Beiping, they were much less visible; their constant presence at the Ladies House was something new for Dorothea. Shopping in Beiping was something that Dorothea and her friends enjoyed but locating items in Wuchang was not convenient. Although Wuchang was developed centuries before Hankou and served as "the Center of the whole Empire" during dynastic times, Hankou was the great inland port where commodities from all over the world could be found, and it was the place where most foreigners and wealthy Chinese preferred to shop.[15] Hankou was called the "Chicago of China" by the American expatriates, "because it [was] more or less the transportation and commercial crossroads of the country. Waterways, airways, high ways, railways branch out in all directions of the country."[16] A Chinese tailor visited regularly to create outfits with material and designs provided by the customer at the rate of one dollar and twenty cents per day (less than forty cents gold), and Dorothea designed the clothing she had made.[17] During her first week in Wuchang, unfamiliar with the location of markets, Dorothea encountered her first instance where purchasing items common in the United States would not be as simple a task in the areas surrounding St. Hilda's.

> I gave one of our servants a couple of dollars to go out and buy me some kind of white shoe cleaner. I didn't know what kind might be available, so on a slip of paper, I wrote: "Universal Shoe Cleaner, Shu milk, or Peachie." I explained that I wanted something to clean my shoes with and that any one of the three was sufficient. At the end of the day, what was my amazement—to find a can of Del Monte sliced peaches and a can of Borden's evaporated milk and a hand-

ful of change upon my dresser. It took me a minute to figure it out and then how I laughed. I told the rest of the house and we all howled. I'm afraid that poor Lee Se Fu (the servant) heard us because it wasn't very long before he came up to ask if it was right. He said "I went in this store and in that store and all over town. And they all told me that it was peaches and milk that you wanted. I knew that wasn't right but Tien Yueng [the store] says you can return it if it isn't." Poor Lee Se Fu. He had spent a whole day searching the stores for a foreign concoction that might bear one of those funny names! We explained the situation to him tho, and he laughed with us.[18]

Because Dorothea's arrival coincided with Easter, she was formally introduced to all of the Chinese faculty at an Easter Sunday dinner held in her honor. The following Tuesday,

all of the foreigners of Hankow and Wuchang were invited to meet the "newly arrived little miss." It was most exciting. Getting the place ready before hand reminded me absolutely of sorority days getting ready for our rush teas. This house is so beautiful any way and then they were all so dear running around getting flowers thro out the halls and rooms. Soon the people began to stream thro our little front gate house; our servants, all in white uniforms for the occasion, simply bustled about serving coffees, tea, sandwiches and mountains of cakes. The house buzzed with enjoyment. Oh such perfectly nice people! I adore them all! How could a whole group of people be so perfectly lovable.[19]

Although the spring term was well in session when Dorothea arrived in late March, she immediately went to work in the junior middle school teaching four courses a week. She was asked to be the English Club adviser, and in May, the girls presented Dorothea's first play, *Gifts for China.*[20] During her spare time, Dorothea continued her Chinese language speaking, reading, and writing lessons with a male Chinese teacher (a standard practice for all foreign teachers). For her own enrichment, Dorothea took music lessons at Boone.

During the month of May 1934, Dorothea was gradually woven into a social fabric quite different from her colleagues. Her friendship with Mary Richards, the secretary to Bishop Roots, and especially his daughter, Frances, opened doors for Dorothea to meet people from different social circles. Frances was a renowned social butterfly and famous for the parties she threw for the younger set where she whipped up her " 'Bishop's cocktail'—lovely concoctions of fruit juices and ginger ales."[21] It was on one of these occasions that Dorothea attended her first meeting of the Oxford Group.[22] She was somewhat ambivalent about what she heard:

Now a Group meeting means nothing less than Buchmanism or Oxford Group, but the members of this particular group are very level headed and not at all extreme. In fact most of them are people who want more to know and learn about the Oxford Group. . . . Guests for the evening were Venetia [Cox], Tommy [Olive Tomlin], and me. . . . The subject of the evening was [God's] Guidance and how we can get it. Well I simply object to all their terms. I have never doubted that God was very close to our thots and actions . . . so I don't exactly see why they should make such a fuss over it and call it by definite names and think that no one outside the group can know the same joy and happiness that they do. I do think that the Oxford Group has been a wonderful influence on some people. It has wrought changes that were miraculous by showing the doubting or unbelieving soul, a Way. And we certainly all derived a great deal of good out of the meeting.[23]

On May 30, Dorothea was invited to her first Hankou's American Woman's Club garden luncheon held at one of the homes located in the Jardine Estates—an exclusive residential area for foreigners only. There she was introduced to young men who worked for foreign banking firms, business enterprises or were diplomats.[24] Such introductions led to a future whirlwind of "chits"—invitations for dates to social functions in Hankou—that placed Dorothea in a race to keep pace with the activities. Her family would refer to her socializing as the "Galloping Horse Latitudes."[25] These invitations catapulted Dorothea into even higher circles than she would have enjoyed in the United States. Her socializing and dates distinguished her from the "Saints"—the appellation coined by other missionaries for the older women teachers at St. Hilda's. Being younger and so much more social and gregarious, Dorothea was not included as one of the "Saints." Instead, the other missionaries began referring to the "unspoken for" residents of the Ladies House as the "Saints and Dorothea," a distinction that amused even Dorothea. The "Saints" (Cox, Gosline, Tomlin) were women who were imbued with the spirit of the Social Gospel. With the Social Gospel falling out of favor following World War I and America, in general, suffering from a "religious depression," one of the few avenues left for ardent adherents to the Social Gospel was foreign missionary service.[26] Dorothea, by contrast, came to St. Hilda's as a temporary teacher as a way to distance herself from her father's overwhelming desire to control her life. While deeply religious, Dorothea was not as committed to Social Gospel praxis as the "Saints" were. The "Saints" had a calling and came to serve; whereas, Dorothea came to serve and possibly find a calling. The difference in missionary zeal affected how Dorothea and the "Saints" interacted toward Wuhan's foreign community: Dorothea interacted socially within a wide circle of friends and acquaintances; the "Saints" interacted religiously within a narrow circle of like-minded individuals. In essence, the "Saints" felt that they served a purpose larger than themselves, and evidently the missionary community felt Dorothea did not have the same level of religious dedication because they were the ones who made the distinction between the "Saints and Dorothea."

Shortly after St. Hilda's June commencement ceremony, a mass exodus from Wuhan occurred when substantial numbers of the foreign population boarded riverboats headed downstream for cooler environs. As part of their contract, foreign missionaries were given a two-month, paid vacation, and those in the inland China missions congregated in the mountains around Lushan, Jiangxi Province, to escape the sweltering summers. It was also the favorite summer haunt of the wealthy foreign business class and wealthy Chinese. Generalissimo Chiang Kai-shek summered there as well. At the port of Jiujiang, vehicles transported the passengers south to the foot of the mountains where they either climbed the "stairs going straight up the mountainside" including the steep "Thousand Steps" or hired sedan chairs for the ascent. All baggage "was taken up on the shoulders of coolies" and the servants.[27] At the top was a thriving town, Guling [Kuling], referred to as "The Gap" because of its location between the mountains. Because of the large foreign population that summered there, the services and stores catered to their tastes and whimsies by carrying an impressive array of imported products.

There on the narrow, winding, cobblestone streets one could purchase ice cream, sodas, candies from around the world, cheeses, tins of meats, fish, fruits, and vegetables all toted up the mountain by laborers who suspended the goods on bamboo poles. Local peasants provided the fresh vegetables, pork, and poultry at a daily open market. The area surrounding the town also boasted its own hospital; restaurants and cafes; tailor shops; clubs; schools; churches; concert and assembly halls; swimming pools; badminton, basketball, and tennis courts; baseball fields; children's playgrounds; and recreational facilities—all designed to provide a resortlike atmosphere for its foreign residents.

Once comfortably settled into "Number 9"—one of the many row cottages owned and built by the mission—days were whiled away being tended to by the house servants who accompanied St. Hilda's foreign faculty. In the cooler altitude of the area's beautiful mountains, Dorothea described how the younger set spent their days by

> either having guests in for dinner or else trudging up a little hill in your best dress with your best shoes in a bag under your arm, going someplace else to dinner. You spend the whole day either hiking up to the post office and places or lying with the gang in the sun by the swimming pool. The swimming pool is a grand place. All the young people practically spend the day there, and there are very few Chinese in it. (That sounds snotty but a wise precaution after all.) To get a membership in the place you have to go thro a whole rig-a-marole of get-

ting the committee to pass upon you and then plunk down eight bucks. So you see that eliminates any undesirables. I'm getting glorious tan but protecting my face from it. My lungs are becoming husky with all the extensive walking.[28]

In mid-July, Dorothea once again experienced pain in her abdomen, and doctors at the local hospital determined that her appendix had to be removed immediately. This was not Dorothea's first bout with appendicitis. When Dorothea was eighteen, her family physician recommended an appendectomy but her father resisted and had insisted upon additional consultations.

> The long and short of it is that, when one doctor said I should have my appendix out, my father said he would wait until he had three opinions on it. So, we had a visiting missionary who just happened to be a doctor, but not of medicine. He had the missionary come up and take a look at me. And here I was supposed to go and have my appendix out by one doctor. And this missionary, looking so embarrassed about being pressed into giving an opinion. And, of course, Daddy was used to having what he said, observed. Why he forced the man to say that I shouldn't have my appendix out, I don't know. This man was no more a practicing doctor than Daddy; he had a Ph.D. in religion! But he reluctantly agreed with my father that I certainly did not *look* like I needed the operation. And that was that.[29]

Dorothea had another attack in Wuchang "last Spring just like the one Dr. Nelson wanted to go after," but Dorothea chose to ignore it.[30] In Guling, after the third attack, Dr. Barrie—a well-regarded English surgeon who was vacationing from Shanghai—insisted that the surgery be performed without delay and served as her surgeon. After her surgery, Dorothea wrote home to tell her parents and "was scolded out there in China by letter from my father for having had my appendix out. Imagine, trying to justify having an operation that we were told to have by the doctors on the spot."[31]

While she was recuperating, Dorothea learned that on August 4, 1934, Mrs. Eliza Roots, wife of Bishop Logan Roots, died. Funeral services were held in Guling where she was buried per her wishes in the foreigners' cemetery with its "sweeping magnificent and peaceful view of mountain slopes and sunsets and plains below."[32] Heavy storms and fog prevented the private plane carrying Madame Chiang Kai-shek (Song Meiling) and Bishop Roots from landing in Jiujiang; consequently, the funeral was postponed from Friday noon until Sunday evening.

> The Bishop and his sons arrived during the early morning hours [Sunday]. The plane circled round several times over our valley to let us know that they had [arrived]. The plane couldn't land up here of course so the little party was on its way up the mountain side from Kiukiang [Jiujiang]. We spent the morning mak-

ing wreaths and sheaves of flowers, lovely lilies brought in from the mountain sides by the coolies. We made some very beautiful things.

At five we went to even-song at the Church of the Ascension and from thence over to the cemetery. All of Kuling gathered there silently, by the open grave. It was a beautiful service. In front of us, dimmed by sweeping mists, were the long slopes of hills. Far below we could see the undulating hills and valleys that finally reached the level plain and the Yangtze. It was very peaceful and beautiful and God seemed very close.[33]

Dorothea spent the day with Frances and her brothers, John and Logan, who suffered comments from others that they were "inappropriate in their mourning." They gave the impression of being "tremendously exalted" about their mother's death because, unlike the other mourners, they "believed that death was just a beautiful step to the promised land and acted exalted. But others [in the church community] thought they looked too happy, and it led to talk about them."[34] Sharing the same beliefs and defiant of others' opinions, Dorothea stood by her friends.

In late August, the entire group descended from their retreat and returned to a still-sweltering Wuhan. When classes began in September, Dorothea's new schedule allowed for free afternoons:

I have a pretty good schedule. I get up at 6:15 and practice [piano] from 6:30 to 7:15. Then I go over to the chapel for morning watch from 7:15 to 7:30 (and longer if you want to stay.) We have breakfast at 7:45. We're thru by 8:15 and I use the time until school starts to either practice or get my lessons ready. I teach three periods [of English] every A.M. which leaves me one free period in which to correct papers. And the whole afternoon free except for two hours of Chinese study. That's the sum total.[35]

All faculty taught a half day on Saturdays, and social gatherings were planned for the afternoons. Other missionaries from Boone, the British Wesleyan compound, or Hankou might come over for a picnic; to sail on Xiao Hu (Little Lake), the lake immediately to the east of St. Hilda's; or to take day-trips by foot, bicycle, sampan, or riverboat.

The expatriate community was close-knit and tightly bonded to one another, sharing resources whenever needed. For years while St. Hilda's did not have its own water source, it would send water carts to the Wesleyan compound. When there were foreign teacher shortages, faculty from other schools would help one another interchangeably. Visitors from other missions around the world would also volunteer their services teaching English classes and thereby freeing up the "Saints" to teach the other classes where Chinese was required. Saturdays were also the times when Dorothea would dash off to Hankou for her social engagements. Unlike the "Saints," she attended functions at the exclusive foreigners' Race Club, complete with "golf course, polo grounds, tennis courts, swimming pool, [and] innumerable ball rooms in the club."[36]

Returning to Wuchang for the fall term, "chits" awaited Dorothea for social events in Hankou. In addition to the usual shopping, tiffin dates,[37] movies, plays, and concerts, there were also invitations to attend speciality balls. There were dinner and dancing dates at "The Cathay"; dancing at "The Little Club"; galas such as the Halloween Costume Ball at the Race Club; the Scots' Ball held on St. Andrew's Day; Guy Fawkes Day;[38] the Thanksgiving Ball; the Christmas Extravaganza; New Year's parties; the St. Valentine's Day Sweetheart Ball; the Washington's Birthday Ball; St. Patrick's Day; the Spring Festival; Easter egg hunts; and May Day celebrations. Dorothea spent so much time in Hankou that she frequently spent the night staying with friends or other members of the mission community which also made her behavior distinct from the "Saints."[39]

Such overnight stays in Hankou gave the appearance that Dorothea was rarely at the Ladies House on weekends, so much so that "the 'Family' seemed surprised to see [her] return home again. . . . and the favorite topic of conversation among the mission for awhile was 'how Dorothea is saving on laundry bills, not sleeping in her own bed enough to need clean sheets.' "[40] Dorothea often attended church services on the Hankou side before ferrying over to Wuchang. Even if she remained in Wuchang, she spent the Saturday afternoons out visiting friends to play cards, sing, dance, discuss works of literature, listen to records, and attend Bible study in the other compounds.

Her love of dance prompted St. Hilda's students to create a dance club with Dorothea as the faculty adviser. Dorothea added tap dance lessons for both students and interested Chinese women faculty to her preclass morning schedule. On the Hankou side, the YWCA requested she teach an occasional dance class, and Dorothea eagerly agreed. Bolstered by the demand, Dorothea began choreographing dance numbers to accompany the plays she was writing.

In January 1935, Madame Zhang Xueliang requested Dorothea give her English lessons. In the previous May, Olive Tomlin was hired by Marshal Zhang Xueliang (the son of Zhang Zuolin who was the warlord of Manchuria from 1919 to 1928) to teach his wife English "an hour and a half every day" for which the mission would receive a hundred dollars.[41] When Zhang Zuolin was killed after his private railcar was bombed by the Japanese in 1928, his son Zhang Xueliang succeeded him, and after several runins with the Japanese himself, he left Manchuria. As Dorothea explained to her parents:

> Have you heard of Chang Hsueh Liang [Zhang Xueliang]? He is properly referred to here in Wuchang as "the Marshal." His father was one time war lord

of Manchuria. He was assassinated about ten years ago and this son succeeded him. During the recent trouble, the Japanese came in and took his Manchuguo. I don't understand it all yet but the Japanese expected him to give them the place without a struggle and Marshal Chang felt it necessary and best for his health to leave the country. Hence he has been in England and just returned [to Wuchang]. They say that he may be assassinated by the Japanese any day. Also that the fact that he has suddenly and unexpectedly returned to China, indicates that there must be something "in the air."[42]

While Olive Tomlin was on furlough, Dorothea replaced her. On the appointed day of the lesson, a large black limousine was sent to the school to transport Dorothea to the Marshal's home that was located five miles away in a "well-concealed area." During the lesson, Dorothea was treated to tea and delicacies. Because of this connection, Dorothea was invited to other exclusive events at the foreigner's Race Club hosted by Marshal and Mrs. Zhang who were its only Chinese members.[43]

On April 27, 1935, St. Hilda's hosted its annual Field Day where "all of the girls and teachers wore white. Each class wore a different colored badge or insignia of the class colors, upon her white dress. [The girls paraded onto the field by class, and those who were competing then changed into their team uniforms.] The lawns were all a bright green, gayly marked with the white lime lines for races and various other events." As a referee, Dorothea had to "see who came in fourth every time they had a race. I had to measure the distance of the base ball throw."[44] Families were invited to attend, and the "girls sold cakes, bottled drinks, 'chocluts' and chewing gum out under the big trees."[45] As Dorothea surveyed the crowd, she observed:

Two old grandfathers, seemingly quite alone, wandered about that day. You are not entitled to wear a beard in China until you are a grandfather. Finally they got together—those two old grandfathers witnessing this amazing display of New China—and sat together under the same black umbrella. They watched with solemn eyes. One had a little red button on the top of his cap instead of the usual black one. That means that he is very happy. No one has died in his family. It must have been an amazing sight to those old bearded patriarchs, to see the young woman hood of China bouncing around on light airy feet—racing, jumping, making baskets, etc. and clothed in shorts, shirts, and socks, bobbed hair flying. However, they are all having to grow their hair as I suppose you have read. New order of the New Life Movement[46]—Chinese women are not to cut, or curl their hair. And officials of any kind can not marry women who disobey these rules and edicts.[47]

After graduation, the foreign faculty once again packed up to summer in Guling on June 28.[48] There Dorothea spent another summer lounging by the pool, hiking into the mountains, swimming in the clear, clean, crisp mountain streams and pools, and attending the usual round of dinners, dancing, concerts, and games with mission friends. Her expanded social network led to invitations to social functions from other foreign legations as well.

While in Guling, another flood struck Hankou. After a severe drought in 1934, flooding followed in 1935. To protect the Hankou Bund, huge cement gates were slid into place to serve as a temporary dike. Rising water levels caused alarm, and "all the Chinese who had anything to do with the building of the dike have fled the country to escape execution. In reality, the dike is holding very well according to the foreigners, but the Chinese must make an example of somebody so as to appear law enforcing and efficient. A man was executed right on the dike the other day [in July] because he had had something to do with its building."[49] The dike did hold, and Wuchang was also spared the flooding that engulfed St. Hilda's in 1931. By the end of August, tanned, well-rested, and reinvigorated, Dorothea returned to Wuchang for the start of her second full year at St. Hilda's.

On Sundays, some of the teachers accompanied the girls who regularly went to the local village of "Li,"[50] but one of the nurses from the Church General Hospital, which was located next to the Boone compound, would travel by bicycle to outlying villages. On a regularly scheduled village visitation in September, Dorothea decided to accompany nurse Nina Johnson —"Johnnie." Traveling over an hour by bicycle, they arrived at their destination.

> It was certainly interesting to suddenly arrive in a little village, so remote (not dangerously remote because the whole Chinese military head quarters is very close [as is] the flying field . . .). But they are away from any people but their own as far as they are concerned. They would never venture off their farms to investigate the flying field. They live for generations, a few families together like a single family. At least they don't marry within those villages. Goodness knows what would be the outcome if they did. A bride always goes off in her bright red satin chao tze [sedan chair] to another village.
>
> How glad they were to see Johnnie. They came swarming, one after another, with boils, abscesses, bad ears and eyes, everything imaginable. Babies cried and were pacified by the ever available breast, even tho that breast were abscessed. . . . Johnnie is a jewel with those country people.[51]

After a quick bite to eat, "we decided that my place was not in the clinic but since I love playing with the children so, that would be the biggest help possible. So I decided to organize the children in games to keep them out of Johnnie's way."[52] Dorothea was so taken by the village clinic that she and several other friends joined Johnnie the following week. On that trip, Dorothea once again organized games for the children—"Drop the handkerchief" and "crack the whip."[53] Her love of village work would be an impetus for Dorothea to continue going out as often as possible.

Fall term, Dorothea assumed the responsibility of "house manager." While Dorothea enjoyed cooking, the kitchen arrangements at the Ladies House precluded her from doing any actual cooking because Li Da Sifu did not wish to cede any control over his kitchen; however, when Dorothea expressed an interest in designing the menus, the role of house manager was quickly ceded to her by the "Saints." Not a role that the other women relished, they gladly relinquished the position to Dorothea who immediately wrote home requesting new and interesting recipes to prepare. Menus were negotiated between Li Da Sifu and the house manager because, except for Thursdays which was "Cook's Choice" and the menu was Chinese style, all of the meals were Western style. Ingredients for some of the recipes were not readily available; consequently, new Western recipes had to be explained to Li Da Sifu who was "a genius in cooking and could figure out anything we asked him to cook."[54]

Serving as the house manager required both finesse and cultural understanding as Dorothea quickly learned the delicate balancing act between "saving face" and getting the "squeeze." For Christmas, her family, acting on her request, sent a number of cookbooks as gifts, and Dorothea enlisted Li Da Sifu's assistance in creating these new dishes. Not only did Li Da Sifu purchase the food, he also presented the house manager with the weekly expenditures. During one of the first of these accounting sessions, Dorothea began questioning an item on the statement.

> The only thing that really showed my ignorance of the way things should be done was when I decided that [Li Da Sifu] was getting far too much salt when shopping, you know, he would give me the expenditures he had made and all that. And there was always such a tremendous amount of salt. And, so I asked him about it, and I had decided that I had caught him in some kind of squeeze which afterwards—my house mates didn't, they didn't warn me about not doing that. But finally, they told me that I shouldn't do that. I made the cook lose face by [questioning him]. And it was just a legitimate squeeze. But they just let me learn my lesson. I felt sorry about that in years afterwards because I said, "Well, where is all this salt?" And the poor cook went just into a kind of a scattered brain way, he was sort of opening cupboards and looking for it. And then the last I saw of him on that discussion, he just went out of the house and went running down the pathway to go home. I, I don't know whether he brought salt back or what, but I was being very picayunish about the salt.[55]

Dorothea's experiences as house manager, however, provided her with a working knowledge of household economics and making the most of a limited budget—something her father would admonish her about not "appreciating the value of money" and even "blowing up" at her for spending so much.[56]

> Daddy seems to think that we have a gold mine or something out here from the way he expressed disgust at my not saving money. Tell him to holler at Mr. Roosevelt. If the present trend in financial legislation continues, it will be worse. You must remember that my salary is only $67 gold and with the exchange now at 2.5 and less at intervals, it means that I get around $170. or less Mex. a month if I'm lucky. Now while it takes much less in gold when the exchange is good out here to live and you hear all this about "how cheap it is to live in the Orient", when you figure in Mex things are more expensive than at home. Just examine the postage on my letters home. What would you think if you had to put a half dollar on a letter to me! It costs me over a dollar for a roll of film, 80 cents for a bottle of ink, and so it goes. Translated back into gold it isn't very much but just the same it eats up things out here. Oh yes, it cost me anywhere from $10 to $20 to get a pair of shoes. Just paid eighteen for my silver slippers which was the cheapest it could be done anywhere in town. (Don't start sending them because you'd pay that much gold and have duty and postage besides.) No one is able to do any saving now and these are the people that were getting an exchange of five to one a couple of years ago and buying rugs, mandarin coats, and having a glorious time. I'm not complaining and am having a wonderful time but please be patient for a little and I will be as careful as I can and do wonders one of these days.[57]

Money was an issue for the Wakeman family that year because Gwen, Dorothea's sister, was getting married on November 10. In her mind's eye, Dorothea conjured up the entire ceremony.

> I started imagining the swell of the organ as Mr. Hallett—dear Mr. Hallett—sits there playing as I've seen him play most of my life. I can just see his kind loving face and a glint of light on his glasses. . . . Then I can see queenly Jerry looking as magnificent as a picture. I try to imagine the color she's wearing. Precious red headed Norman in his tux. I can just see him and long to give him a kiss above those white bushy eyebrows of his. And then Gwen-gwen!!! You precious. I can't imagine lovely enough how beautiful you'll be. You'll be a veritable Dream Bride—your golden curls capped with a filmy veil, clinging to our precious Punkin's arm as you progress down the aisle of dear old All Saints. And in front, down at the end of that aisle will be our dear Dr. Learned waiting, and dear little Mommy close at hand. For some reason or other, every time I think of little Mommy there, I cry cuz some how that's what I'm afraid she'll be doing. In fact I can realize now just how they all cried over the wedding in Little Women. I could never understand it before, at all! What on earth makes us cry at a wedding—because I'm really at this wedding you know. I don't know why I feel this way about it but I feel as tho I could really see it all only I'm being there all day long so it is lasting longer than the "eight minutes" for me and I'm getting more for my money.[58]

As wedding gifts, Dorothea sent an embroidered bedspread, embroidered place mats, and bamboo name card holders.[59]

The relatively brief period of peace that reigned in China was about to end. In November 1935, the Japanese, who had established a base in Rehe (Jehol) Province, began to move south of the Great Wall into Hebei Province in violation of the Tanggu Truce.[60] Despite Nationalist efforts to suppress protests over further Japanese incursion, thousands of students in Beiping began demonstrating on December 9. Demonstrations quickly spread throughout the country. At first, the Wuchang Education Bureau sought to suppress such demonstrations, but it finally acquiesced and permitted students around Wuchang to demonstrate on December 20, "thinking it better physchology to have them doing it with permission since the demonstration had become inevitable. The government has stopped all ferrys to Hankow however so that the students are confined to this place. Tension is great."[61]

Dorothea optimistically wrote home:

> The Chinese are "sensationalists" as we love to say in our family. About a month and a half ago [November], the girls in school began making elaborate plans to start first aid and nursing courses in the school. They were going to give up regular classes to do it. From the big eyes and plans you would have thot that war was already raging. It was only with great difficulty that we persuaded the Chinese teachers and students that it would be better to wait for orders to such an effect from the government. If we should try a stunt like that on our own hook, we might find our selves a target for "idly" passing Japanese planes as did the Becks and their school at Yochow [Yueyang, Hunan Province]. That was caused because of some student activity that the Japs concluded indicated the school was anti Japanese. At least so the story goes. Of nothing can anyone be certain.[62]

At St. Hilda's, Dorothea busily prepared for her Christmas extravaganza. Not only did she write the play, "a night before Christmas idea with toys which came to life and did a dance," but she choreographed the dances, designed the costumes and sets, and worked with Venetia on the music. The play was written "all in rhyme. There was a jumping jack dance, skaters who jumped out of boxes the same as I did once and did a dance to the Skaters Waltz, tin soldiers, two Chinese dolls and a French doll. There were numerous other characters who did no dancing."[63] The play was a hit and attendance was high despite the demonstrations occurring throughout Wuhan. The play was a culmination of confidence-building successes for Dorothea in 1935 when she also began writing entries on St. Hilda's for the *Hankow Newsletter*, an English-language publication.[64]

On December 30, 1935, another demonstration was scheduled. Martial law was declared, and no one was permitted in the streets from "midnite to six in the A.M. because the demonstrations have been excuse for other perpetrations."[65] An emergency faculty meeting was convened.

> And we had our meeting in the grey dawn, trying to decide whether it was better to try to get the children home while the goin was good, or to wait and let them go home in an unsensational manner Tues. afternoon as tho nothing had happened and they were simply observing New Years.
>
> We have had absolutely no feeling among our girls so knew there would be no trouble from within and hated to admit to them that we had seen any from without. We decided to go right on with school, in the end. We didn't feel any too comfortable however as we heard tales of other schools where the children had gone on strike and refused to leave as well as to attend classes. They had threatened to cut telephone wires and other insidious things if any attempt were made on the part of the faculty to get in communication with their homes to send them home. The ferries were commandeered by the government and turned over to the students as a peace offering. The students were having a glorious time. It got so bad out at Wuhan University the President feeling himself able no longer to cope with the situation, resigned. Posters every where showed Chinese dressed in foreign clothes "thinking only of their own pleasure." A large kitchen knife was suspended over the entrance to the university and threatened to kill all those who weren't patriotic. Quite a mess to be sure. . . . Well everything went as smoothly as usual here. No pickets arrived but by Tues. morning, we decided we had tempted fate long enough. It would be terrible if anything did happen to arouse spirit among our girls. The spirit here has always been so beautiful and Christian like here that it would be shame to have a blot on that memory.[66]

Fearing that student demonstrators from the government school might come to St. Hilda's, the faculty notified the students' parents to "come after them for the New Year Holiday" and that "the holiday would not be over until February 1st at the earliest." With no fuss or bother, the "lambs got peacefully and happily and quietly home."[67]

Once the students were safely at home, Dorothea and three of her friends embarked on a two-week riverboat vacation to Sichuan Province on January 11, 1936. Given the recent unrest, the foursome "consulted both British and American Consulate generals (since half our party is Canadian and the other American). They say it is O.K. and believe me they take no chances because when people walk into any kind of trouble, the consulates have to dig them out." Permission was sought and granted by both Bishops Roots and Gilman, and they were instructed to "keep them informed of our where abouts by telegram."[68] As the boat steamed its way westward, one of their first stops was at Yichang to visit Julia Clark where she spent most of her time working with the Bible women now that she was no longer at St. Hilda's. Despite the cold winter weather, and clothed in warm winter wear borrowed from the "Saints," Dorothea "had a simply wonderful time." The trip served to strengthen her confidence and her resolve to visit Beiping in the summer, "no matter what," given its proximity to the Japanese-occupied areas in Hebei.[69]

Unlike the Fall 1935 school term, the spring 1936 term was relatively uneventful. News from the United States about the flooding of the Mississippi River prompted a response from the girls. All too familiar with the devastation flooding brings, "the first thing our chaplain said was that he thot [St. Hilda's] should send something" and the Student Self-Governance Association responded to the call.[70] Fifteen dollars was sent with "a large amount of sympathy and love and understanding for the poor people who are suffering from flood."[71] With the success of her Christmas musical and bolstered by her mother's letters raving about her plays, Dorothea was inspired to compose an operetta that was performed on May 16 with "the money proceeds to go for our Self-support fund." A portion of the admission fees was the source of an additional fifty-dollar donation to the flood relief fund in America.[72]

The theme of the operetta was "A Midnight Fantasy." As the program stated, "A little girl longs to be able to talk with dolls, especially the ones she has seen in a toy shop nearby. Her wish is fu[l]filled when the fireflies, on the strength of their own invitation from the Fairy Queen, manage to get her into the birthday party for the Toy Shop Grandfather Clock."[73]

> Well darlings, the place was packed. The auditorium holds one thousand and all seats were taken and the entire space around the sides filled. Zenith's studio in Hankow sent over a photographer unbeknownst to us and he took flash light pictures all thru it and the two of the entire cast assembled at the end. Can hardly wait to see those. Will try to color some of them and send to you together with the play. Golly, I can hardly wait to begin the next production. . . .
>
> The Chinese teachers are terribly thrilled and said that our reputation is made now and anything of the kinds we have again we'll be able to ask any price. The Chinese were terribly thrilled over the dancing—you see anything like that is so foreign to them. They see it in the movies and never dream that they themselves could do it. The soldiers made the hit of the whole afternoon. They are really splendid—did a tap dance and keep the rhythm perfectly. At the end they went back up their flight of stairs (especially built for this performance) and did a tap step up and down the stairs and back again. The people clapped that tremendously and it really was awfully good. I gave tickets to our Lee Se Fu and his family because he helped me so much cleaning up dye messes after me and running around findings pieces of wire, bamboo or what have you. He told Venetia very proudly that we gained a whole lot of face Saturday. He said that all the people around him were talking and talking about it and that he said to them "It was our Wei shao chi [Miss Wei] did all that work." (That is my name in case you didn't recognize it.)[74]

Triumphant, Dorothea exclaimed, "Everybody thinks I should be tired. Golly whizz NO! I never felt better in my life. Guess when I get back to

California I'll join up with Gilmore Brown."[75] It was the first mention she made of future plans for herself that involved more than marriage or a teaching position that her father wanted. Determined to continue to build upon her successes, Dorothea "heard that all I have to do is to write to the Church periodical club in New York and they will send me practically anything [in terms of dance books] I want. I'm writing immediately for a whole scad of marvelous dancing books and *will* we have a dancing department next year."[76]

The *Hankow Newsletter* further fueled Dorothea's desires when it published a rave review. "In the first place, [Miss Wakeman] manufactured the play itself, getting songs, and dances from many different sources and stringing them together into a story with a conversation of her own inventing. . . . In fact when the curtain was drawn on the final tableau the audience could not tell whether to praise most Miss Cox's success in her training of the singing, Miss Wakeman's in the planning of the whole and the training of the dancing, or the costumers' in their most charming effects."[77] The operetta also spurred an interest in Chinese opera, and Dorothea began collecting as much information on it as possible and planned to attend operas in Beiping during her vacation.

That summer, with another round of permissions from both Bishops Roots and Gilman, Dorothea headed north by train to Beiping to reconnect with her friend Caroline Schulz Service and to meet her husband, Jack, for the first time. Dorothea went despite entreaties from her father to not go as "Peiping is not safe." To quell his fears, Dorothea provided her own somewhat incorrect assessment of the situation:

> The Chinese are too preoccupied with their civil war difficulties and the Japanese are so decidedly un ready to fight that they are doing everything in their power to intimidate the Chinese so that they won't dare make a false and rash move to precipitate a war. I think every one is sure that Japan is not ready for war and fears that in the event of war, Russia would jump on her back. The Japanese are certainly infuriating tho aren't they. They have staged two or three military demonstrations in the city of Peiping since I've been here. They paraded great tanks thru the city streets, truck loads of soldiers with fixed bayonets, and what not. Their tanks tore up the beautiful new roads that the Chinese government had just been at great expense to have built. They say the damage is estimated at many thousands of dollars—and the wild thing about it—the Chinese simply *take* it. They can't do anything else.[78]

With the start of the 1936–37 school year, Dorothea was preparing for her final year at St. Hilda's. During the summer, she worked on her operetta—one with a gypsy theme—for its December debut, gatherings bits and pieces of materials wherever she went to construct the costumes and props. Dorothea also prepared for her furlough. From the moment Dorothea signed her teaching contract, Dorothea's parents, especially her father, made every effort to insure she did not reenlist for another term. Ever fearful that Dorothea had given up on marriage after her broken engagement with Merrill, Earl would make suggestion after suggestion as to her future once she returned so that she would not remain overseas.

> Poor Daddy said he didn't see why we couldn't be happy together and we can and I'm not going to stay in China. Not by a long shot. May I reiterate, this is part of my education. This will be a background and polish and finish that I would never have gotten in Puente or any other place in the U.S.A. Really and truly isn't that the truth? I will be much more interesting to talk to than if I had even been in the Pasadena Junior College as Daddy so magnificently pipe dreams, teaching English. Daddy forgets perhaps that for three solid years, I had been pestering Mr. Blair and any other influential people and fairly knew the Pasadena school board by their first names, I haunted the place so often and they wouldn't even say "Perhaps later." I took the Pasadena teachers exams every year to keep up to date on that. Do you remember? Probably not. Now eventually I might have won out but if I had had to wait three years more for results and let Daddy and Mommie support me in the mean time, you might not have been so sorry to see me go to China. At least I'm not stagnating and getting sour.[79]
>
> Now as to coming home, I'll probably be making reservations to sail next June but don't start counting the days. I'm entitled to come home and can do it with full expenses paid and salary of $67.50 for a few months thereafter but I'm not sure that I want to light out that fast, specially if I'm not coming back again. I've rather gotten won over Daddy's side that there is nothing like being with one's own precious family and have decided that I don't want to sign myself up for another term. It would be all right if it didn't mean that it would be five years (barring war) before I could come home again.[80]

Complications arose because Olive Tomlin was also scheduled for a furlough at the same time. It would be difficult for both to take furloughs simultaneously "because it would limit the English dept too much." However, Earl wrote "desperate letters," filled with "mania about getting [Dorothea] home immediately" to such an extent that even Olive Tomlin concluded, "I see where I don't go home next June. Dorothea's Daddy will never stand her staying out here another year." Dorothea proposed a solution, "Well, I have thot of an excellent alternative. Tommy could go home in June and she would be back the end of January in time for the new term. I could leave in January at the beginning of the Winter vacation. That would be about the 10th. How does that sound?"[81]

Not only did Dorothea suggest extending her stay for six months, but she also had another "new inspiration" during her visit to Beiping. "I think I shall put in applications for the various American Schools out here before leaving—Peiping, Tientsin, or Shanghai or Kuling. You only have to stay three years at one of them. Might even teach in one of the British schools. They always have one American teacher on the staff. I'll also try England and Scotland on the way thru."[82]

Dorothea began exerting her own will to counter suggestions made by her father. Once Dorothea decided upon writing another operetta with a gypsy theme, Earl sent her recommendations to which Dorothea replied,

> No, I'm not worrying about another operetta in the near future. But Daddy is wrong on the idea of writing a Chinese folk lore based play. He's not often wrong but here he is. You see, I had the same idea. I was going to have this last one Chinese in atmosphere. The Chinese vetoed it and then again I suggested for next year having a kind of pageant of the year bringing in all the Chinese festivals and celebrations. They all say that is next to impossible to do because in the first place, the Chinese are horribly critical of anything of their own. Everything is built on tradition and anything Chinese must adhere to certain traditional standards and some of those are too subtle for the foreigner to catch. The most difficult things in the world would be an attempt of that kind and the most foolish. The Chinese would ridicule it if not walk out in disgust. I would shed tears for my pains. I *will* write something of the kind to present at home however. Foreigners are the only ones who would appreciate it and such an entertainment I am sure would go over big at home.[83]

During the first weeks of the new 1936–37 school term, Dorothea was stricken with malaria that required her to rest and take "it very easy" especially during the fever stage.[84] The time off allowed her to complete a book review for the prestigious *T'ien Hsia (Tian Xia) Monthly* in Shanghai, "a high class magazine," that was the "Atlantic Monthly or Harper's of China and only prints the most top notch stuff."[85] When her review was accepted for publication, it not only bolstered her confidence in her writing ability, but it was also a source of tremendous pride for Dorothea.

Changes were occurring in China as well. In December 1936, Dorothea wrote about "the latest affliction which has befallen China"—namely the capture of Chiang Kai-shek in the city of Xi'an, Shaanxi Province.[86] "Marshal Chang Hsueh Liang (whose wife I used to teach) has turned traitor and captured the Generalissimo Chiang Kai Shek. A great many of the official classes here in China feel that Chiang has been murdered and that the Nanking authorities also feel so, or else they wouldn't have proceeded so brashly to disempower the young Marshal and send troops against him."[87] After complex negotiations that involved U.S. mediators, Chiang was released on Christmas night after a two-week confinement. Echoing the sentiments of many in China and the United States, Dorothea exclaimed, "Chiang has certainly done a magnificent job of unifying the country. Never before in this huge scattered country lacking the unifying medium of communications of any sort has a leader succeeded in holding so consistently and constructively, the support of the entire country. He has plenty of worries goodness only knows but comparatively speaking, he is amazingly victorious." On the eve Chiang reemerged:

> It was certainly thrilling the nite he was released. It was Christmas nite. We came out of the movies (The Great Ziegfield) to hear a blaze of fire works from every direction, and people yelling. Right in front of the theatre stood a stolid figure of a coolie supporting a hastily scrawled poster proclaiming in English that Chiang had been released and was in Loyang [Luoyang, Henan Province]. Another placard said the same in Chinese. (All courtesy of the Herald). When we got to the ferry, we were just in time to miss one but got a big thrill of seeing it swing out into the river with a fireworks blazing out in every direction from her stern. I didn't realize the Chinese had so much national spirit. It was marvelous.[88]

The remainder of Dorothea's appointment was spent in Hankou where she lived in the bishop's house and taught English at the elementary school, St. Lois's. Living with Frances, her sister, Beth, and two other women who had "been brought up in China," Dorothea spent the last five months in an endless round of parties arranged by Frances.[89] Dorothea's teaching load of four periods of English to be taught on Monday, Tuesday, and Thursday left her entirely free on Wednesday, Friday, and Saturday. Because Frances also had a horse stabled at the riding school, Dorothea, an accomplished equestrian herself, was encouraged by Frances to ride the horse "at least once a week." The prospect thrilled Dorothea who managed to pack a riding habit along with other necessities when coming to China, and when weather permitted, she rode whenever possible.[90]

Beginning in March 1937, despite a period of relative calm between China and Japan, preparations for war began throughout Wuhan. In anticipation of air raids, the first nighttime drill was conducted.

> We had marital law most of yesterday. All rickshaws were relegated to the shore side of the Bund, all streets kept *clear* of people or vehicles of any kind. Warning sirens shrieked across the city "warning" of the approaching "enemy planes." Then the most magnificent bombers winged their graceful curving flight over the city, dropping brilliant white and green and red flares. It was lovely, really. At 9:30 the warning sirens shrieked. A few minutes later, the entire city was plunged in darkness by a single pull of the switch at the Hankow Light and Power Co. We ran out to our front gate to watch. The city was so very silent and so black it didn't seem real. Police patrolled constantly to make sure no candle shone from any window or any pedestrian ventured forth. Everyone spoke in whispers. Search lights from the harbor gunboats began to play upon the sky—searching out the approaching planes. And then they came—with a roar out of the sky. They dropped their flares, illuminating the city weirdly.[91]

Amid these events, while preparing for her operetta with dress rehearsals open to the public on May 15 and 26, Dorothea received a lengthy letter from her father outlining his view on what awaited Dorothea if she remained an unmarried woman: "Now I wake up in the night and imagine you sitting alone on my grave, no husband, no child, no father and mother, no one who wants you, beating the tombstones in the night with your fists."[92] Never dreaming that Dorothea "would not be married within a year or at most two after going to China" because "being away from the love of home would drive" Dorothea "to it out of sheer lonliness," Earl reiterated Harriett's admonishment to never return home until she was married. Earl explained that they were fearful that Merrill "would be calling up," if she returned home still single.[93] Fearing, however, that Dorothea might be swept up in the romance of Europe, Earl then wrote to caution her against marrying inappropriately. Caught between her father's entreaties on the importance of being married, but only if her prospective husband was suitable, Dorothea continued her rehearsals.

Opening night was held in the new St. Lois's auditorium on May 29. Originally the operetta was envisioned to have a "gypsy" flavor, but in the end, numerous suggestions and pressures from her father notwithstanding, Dorothea decided upon a "Dutch" theme.

> I have had my operetta and it was lovely. It was a thrill to stand on the side lines and watch the whole performance go thru and realize it was all <u>my creation</u>! There is a thrill in creation which is tremendous. Nothing in the world <u>like</u> it. The lines, the songs and each little step of the dances. It is a strange feeling to see a chorus of twelve or so going thru a routine absolutely together and remember the moments I worked each step out in my mind & on paper & then in execution. Then to realize the power of having my plans carried out just as I once merely visualized them. It is wonderful!! I have never felt it as tremendously as lately.[94]

Following the opening-night performance, Dorothea had "my first call for 'Author' and went out to bow and receive my flowers. <u>That</u> was a new experience. All in all a thrilling evening."[95]

The eve of the first dress rehearsal performance was also the time for a monumental decision. In a letter written that night in response to her father's letter, Dorothea laid out her own plans for the future, thinking that "I won't have time to get an answer from this letter now will I?"

> Do you know, I have been thinking and it seems to me that it would be happier all around if I didn't plan to stay in Southern California. One thing, I am not married and for some reason or other, it seems to me that home is no place for me unmarried. It would bother me and I think it might bother you. I will get married as soon as I can manage it and until then, try not to be too unhappy

about it. I am less anxious to lead a single life than you are to have me so you can rest assured that I am not simply saying to myself that there is plenty of time to do the getting married. I know better. But I don't think that any of us would prefer my being married to be being unmarried if it meant what many marriages mean in the way of unhappiness. This is not an excuse and I don't use it for rationalizing my state into an ideal one. Quite the contrary! But I thot that that thot might help you a bit. Try to relax and hope for the best. At any rate, I have outgrown the nest and dearly as I love you all, I can't imagine that it would be good for any of us for me to come crowding back in. I will try to get settled down in southern California near you some time but not until I am married! If the mission will have me back, I think I shall return in January. It is doubtfull that they will however, in which case, I am going to try to get a job someplace in Europe. That ought to make you happy because I could do a lot of "seeing England and Scotland" at any rate. So much for that.[96]

Dorothea continued:

Well I shall not give you some more accounts of my "froth and bubble" as I know my life out here must seem to you. And at this point I should like to deliver a little sermon to dear darling Daddy which may make him very wroth but I am not there to see him explode so it will only be hard on Mommie. As for my happiness or anyone else's happiness including you own, remember that happiness comes where you least expect it. . . . Your love has been so unselfish that it is an ever present treasure deep in my heart. I love you so darlings! And now that we are grown and there are some things that you can't give us—things that we simply have to get for ourselves, if we don't get them, you suffer cruelly. Oh if there were only some way that I could keep you from suffering those things. . . . All I can do is pray that dear little Mommie won't scold Daddy and say she thinks he has been making "dear little Dorothea" unhappy and that Daddy won't get wild and say he doesn't know why all his children have to be so everlastingly sacrificial—"hasn't enough of that been done already in this family?" Will you please get as much good out of this little admonition of mine as possible and worry about something else. . . . Mother has been through far more, catering to your moods and tempests. Why don't you stop Daddy dear and think about your days. Is there ever a day which goes by that every one feels quite at ease around you? On the contrary, any one within hearing distance of you as long as I can remember, has had all the calm assurance of those risking a peek into the crater of a seething volcano. Now when you think of 365 days to the year and thirty or so years that mother has been watching you like a thermometer, trying to ward off remarks from "the children" which might aggravate the ever ready to explode volcano and trying to sooth the outbursts, then worrying about money and worrying because I am not married. . . . If I am not happy, it is no one's fault but my own and try not to worry. Happiness lies within one self in the philosophy of one's heart moreover. Adopt a philosophy my darling! Did you ever think of that. In the meantime, I shall try to improve mine and get a husband! Let me assure you all that I am as happy as a lark and in no manner disturbed by the fact that you wish I were married other than to bewail the fact that you must suffer over it. You are all darlings and deserve much more happiness than you ever seem to get. So much for that and now to the threatened "froth and bubble."[97]

But there was time for a reply, and much to Dorothea's relief, her father "was an angel" about her admonitions. "I know when you scold you are doing it for my own happiness. I have long since learned to realize that. But it always gives me two or three heart aches instead of one. In the first place my heart hurts to think how you have suffered to such outbursts forth coming. Next I suffer for the strain it all is on Mommie, and lastly feel a little miserable in self pity on my own account. But you say you are going to be good for a little while now and let me get married or not as I please."[98]

No longer was Dorothea "out on a lark in China"; she was now a woman who wanted to return to China to do more. "I have no idea in the world why I love the Chinese the way I do darlings, but I simply do," she wrote her parents. "My heart almost hurts sometimes it is so full. I have tried to analyze the joy that comes from our little conversations and good times together or the most casual contacts in daily life as the smile of the rickshaw coolie when you pay him a few coppers extra or just his exceeding good will in trying to find an address for you. The spirit in these people is wonderful."[99] She was determined to return to China.

With that spirit of love and determination, Dorothea left Hankou's Bund for the last time on June 19, 1937. Her journey began with a riverboat trip to Shanghai. After a few days in Shanghai, Dorothea set sail on June 25 aboard the SS *Scharnhorst* with ports of call in Hong Kong, Manila, Singapore, through the Suez Canal to Port Said, and finally to Genoa.[100] From there, Dorothea would wend her way through Europe before returning to the United States. While sailing from Singapore to Port Said, the ship's intercom announced that on July 7, 1937, an incident at the Marco Polo Bridge (Lugouqiao)—ten miles west of Beiping—had occurred; officially war between Japan and China had begun, and many lives and dreams would be changed. Upon hearing the news, Dorothea stood on the deck facing China and wept.

Guling, Jiangxi Province, 1935.

Dorothea and Yuanshung, 1998.

6

Into the West

St. Hilda's School for Girls

The years between 1932 and 1937 were a period of relative calm at St. Hilda's, but following the Marco Polo Bridge Incident on July 7, 1937, the War of Resistance Against the Japanese officially began. Despite the Japanese invasion, St. Hilda's opened on September 10, 1937, to what would become "a hectic troubled year with air raids any time of day or night."[1] In an article for the *Hankow Newsletter,* Olive B. Tomlin wrote, "St. Hilda's opened for registration . . . with a full quota of Chinese staff" and "Miss Christina Li . . . as student advisor." Joining Olive Tomlin and Margaret Sherman were "Miss Althea Bremer of Saint Faith's School, Yangchow [Yangzhou, Jiangsu Province], and Miss Catharine Barnaby of Saint Mary's, Shanghai." Both were "refugeeing" at St. Hilda's where they would be "an invaluable help in the English Department."[2]

Jarred into action by "listening in" to events of the war on a radio given by Bishop Alfred Gilman in loving memory of his wife, Gertrude, the entire school organized itself in a "Service League to help in war activities." "On Saturday afternoons some girls go to the various hospitals in the city and write letters for the soldiers or entertain them by singing to them. At school some girls are sewing making gowns and cloth shoes which we hear are very much needed at the front. The women teachers are meeting once a week to sew. The staff has promised to be responsible for four months for the disinfection of dressing materials for the wounded in one of the city hospitals." In preparation for Japanese air raids, church architect, Mr. John Bergamini, supervised the construction of "dug-outs . . . large enough to hold 309. These are 6 feet deep, covered, and have benches along the sides, in case we are confined [i]n them for two or three hours." Air-raid drills were held "so that teachers and students [would] know what they are expected to do."[3]

As air raids continued, St. Hilda's closed on December 18 for two months before moving to the " 'First District' of the Boone compound" and reopening with a decreased enrollment of "153 students."[4] The "Boy Scout headquarters" housed "nearly 100 of [the students] in dormitory space, six women teachers and the nurse, and . . . two classrooms. In the Brotherhood Hall and Infirmary, [were] offices and four more classrooms, while in still another building [was the] Assembly Room and singing classes." Sharing of teachers with Boone made it possible for the school to continue since "eight teachers did not return" to St. Hilda's as a result of the war.[5]

Although the St. Hilda's campus was closed to its students, it nonetheless served as a refugee camp and refugee school. "Our number of 106 during January has grown to 237." With "our kindergarten of over twenty children" and "more than sixty children of school age . . . it may be necessary to have grades from one to six" at the refugee school.[6] Medical care and the general health of the refugees was provided from "Miss Ts'en So-lan, who [was] a Saint Hilda's graduate and a graduate from Saint Elizabeth's Hospital Nurses' Training School. Several times a week, a doctor from the Seventh Day Adventist Sanatorium [came] to care for the sick and to take those who need[ed] treatment out to the lovely new hospital situated on the shore of East Lake [Dong Hu]."[7] Another St. Hilda's graduate, "Miss Lieo Teh-wei lived here and gave generously and untiringly of her time and energy to the running of the camp and the problems of the individuals . . . Some Central China College students and Saint Hilda's graduates . . . living in the city, [came] regularly to help with classes for men and women and for evenings of entertainment for the refugees."[8]

Alfred A. Gilman succeeded Logan H. Roots as bishop of Hankou in March 1938, and Gilman began reporting on the war that came ever closer to Wuhan. In his heartfelt "An Appeal to the Government and People of Japan," which he signed, "An American resident in Central China for thirty-six years, and the intimate friend of many fine Japanese people," Bishop Gilman wrote of the great Japanese contribution to the Chinese. "But a great mystery has appeared. This beneficent, artistic, ingenious people have taken our money, gladly given to them, and with it have purchased aeroplanes, tanks, and bombs, and now instead of giving us those things which we enjoy, they only rain death upon us? Why? Do the people of Japan think that slaves are better customers than free devoted friends?"[9] "Before it is too late," he pleaded "I appeal to Japan to desist from making enemies for hundreds of years to come, and instead to return to her place of beneficent service to mankind."[10] Of course, his plea was futile.

The battle for the new Nationalist capital of Wuhan[11] began on June 12, 1938, and when two bombs struck St. Hilda's gatehouse in July 1938, the decision was made to move St. Hilda's, Boone High School, and Huazhong Daxue as far away as possible from the fighting—southwestern China—an area where Diocesan scouts found a suitable location.[12] St. Hilda's, Boone, and "two Junior High Schools from Hankow"—St. Paul's and St. Lois's—joined together to form the "refugeeing amalgamation" known as the "Hankow Diocesan Union School [Lian Zhong]."[13] "Students, faculty, members of their families, and as much equipment" as could be possibly packed, took the railroad to "Chuan Hsien [Chuanxian]" in "Kwangsi [Guangxi Province]."[14] There, a large pawnshop's warehouse was rented to house the Diocesan Union School people. Since structurally safe bomb shelters could not be built because railroad tracks ran in front of the building and a river ran behind it, students and teachers would arise early in the morning to walk to their hiding place "in the hills" which became an "open-air school," even in the "freezing cold winter days."[15]

This bad situation became worse, and six months later, the entire school population walked twenty-five miles and arrived "weary and footsore and sunburned" at a more remote area known as Gold Dragon Mountain in the Guangxi/Hunan Province border region.[16] As one Union School student recalls, the area was "spectacularly beautiful" with nothing but a small village surrounded by rice paddies, but "it was so desolate and at night, when the moon was full, all you could see were the trees and hear barking dogs way in the distance."[17] The isolation was too extreme since the nearest semblance of civilization—a post office—was in Chuanxian, and thievery was rife; consequently, in June 1939, the Union School moved once again after scouts found another location in Yunnan Province. Forced to leave most of their equipment behind, the school embarked on a difficult "four or five day" journey aboard trucks to "the French Indo-China border."[18] The school "moved in three groups—the first group left May 10—the second group May 19 and the third group left the country on May 26. There were boys and girls and families in each group and a teacher in charge of each group. The third group was the largest requiring 5 trucks but the first and second moved in 4 trucks each group—13 truck loads of boxes and bedding and human cargo!"[19] At the southern coast, people and possessions were transferred to boats for the trip to Haiphong. Once in Vietnam the groups encountered French Customs where many of the meager items in their possession were confiscated. Then the groups crowded onto trains that transported them on their three-hour journey to Hanoi. During their stay in Hanoi, students witnessed people being "openly robbed in broad daylight."[20] From Hanoi, the group traveled three days by train to Kunming, Yunnan, where they rode buses for 145 miles on the narrow, unpaved, twisting, and turning Burma Road to the town of "Chennan [Zhenan]"[21] in a Miao minority group area. The site was chosen specifically "for its very smallness and unimportance" to avoid any possible danger of bombing.[22] The school was housed in a Chinese inn built with mud brick walls and dirt floors on the ground level and "rough boards with wide cracks between them on the second storey."[23] Desks and benches were fashioned by laying planks across mud bricks held "together by a heavy coat of white plaster."[24]

Although the peasants of Gold Dragon Mountain were poor, their level of poverty was nothing comparable to the poverty in Zhenan where the farmers were so destitute that malnutrition was the norm. "Goiter," "malaria and typhus," as well as "intestinal troubles" were rampant.[25] Children wore no pants in the summer and crotchless pants in the winter.[26] The well water was so filthy that using it to wash hair was tantamount to wasting time, and students resorted to the more traditional means of bobbing their hair and brushing thoroughly twice a day.[27]

Since the school was situated in the midst of "farm homes," "water buffaloes, and donkeys [were] numerous, as well as pigs and chickens." Lice, fleas, mosquitos, and flies plagued the people.[28] To this inventory of vermin were added "stinging caterpillars" that resided in the roof tiles and stinging and biting "rice bugs" that emerged in the summer.[29] Most of the students had head and body lice that required rubbing gasoline into their hair and wrapping it to kill the larvae. Students would comb each other's hair to remove the debris and to check for a new infestation. Bowls of water were placed underneath their beds to attract mosquitos and "a slapping chorus could be heard everywhere" at night.[30] But it was the lice and fleas that ate the students and teachers alive and tortured them with the itching—"we looked like we all had measles because we were covered from head to toe with huge, red, swollen welts." In the evenings, the students would groom each other carefully in desperate attempts to capture the lice and fleas and deftly use their fingernails to snap them in two.[31] The boys would plead with the girls to "save" them, "it was the few times that the girls were permitted to stay with the boys. We had fingernails, and they were so pathetic! All you could hear was 'snap, snap, snap.' "[32] A gift of U.S. one hundred dollars from Dr. John W. Wood enabled not only Chinese mosquito netting to be purchased and screens made for all of the dormitories, but the "exchange [rate] was so favorable it did one more thing,—namely, built a room over our kitchen for storing rice" thereby eliminating the rice bugs that had made Venetia Cox's and Hazel Gosline's lives miserable as they were sleeping in the rice storage room.[33]

The Diocesan Union School remained at Zhenan for three years until 1942 when the school was forced to move because Japanese forces captured Burma and closed the Burma Road; consequently, the school and its "refugees" fled to Kunming. From there, the school relocated to "Tsingchen, [Qingzhen]" in "Kweichow [Guizhou Province], where the school was set up in a temple"—the "Phoenix Nest Monastery."[34] From 1942 to 1946, the school remained at Qingzhen, and a regular school schedule was maintained. Students attended four classes from 8:00 a.m. until noon at which time they ate lunch. The remaining three classes resumed beginning at 1:30 p.m. and ended three hours later. A two-hour study hall during the evening was conducted by the light of kerosene lamps. On weekends, the boys would do odd jobs in the community in exchange for food for the

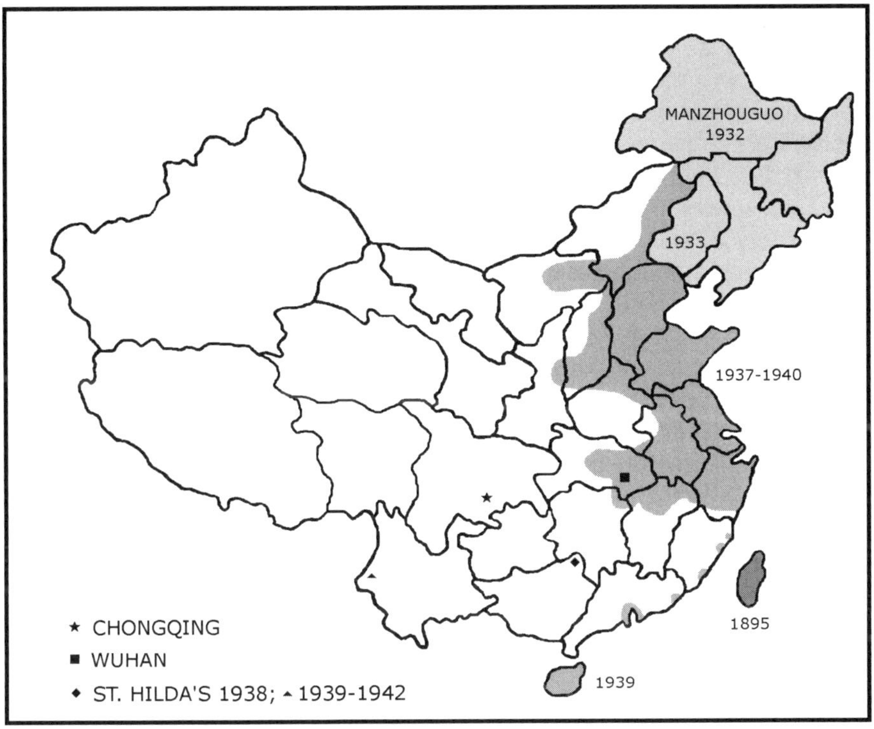

Japanese Occupation, 1940. Adapted from USMA online map: http://www.dean.usma.edu/history/web03/atlases/china%20civil%20war/chinese%20civil%20war%20pages/chinese%20civil%20war%20map%2004.htm.

school; on Sunday afternoons, the students ventured into the local village and conducted their community service.[35]

In 1944, the Japanese launched their final offensive in Chinese territory—Operation ICHIGO. The offensive was initially successful with the Japanese occupying portions of Hunan, Guangdong, and Guangxi Provinces in the south. Further, it was feared that the Japanese would also invade Guizhou. As such, contingency plans were made for relocating the school once again. Because the drive stalled, the school did not have to move from Qingzhen.

When the St. Hilda's faculty returned to Wuchang in early 1946, they arrived at a campus where the buildings were completely gutted.[36] Every fixture, all of the furniture, doors, cabinets, floors, even walls had been torn down in all of the buildings and burned as fuel—as evidenced by the blackened walls and fire pits located throughout the campus and within the school building. The Ladies House was gutted including the porch, stairway to the second floor, and most of the second-story flooring. Gaining possession of St. Hilda's was quite a task. "Six thousand . . . young patriotic boys" of the "Youth Army of China" were tempted to take over the St. Hilda's campus for their use; however, Gwendolyn Seng "marshalled her army of students, Seniors 1 & 2 and a few Junior girls . . . raced over to the school compound —60 in number" and they managed to secure the campus.[37] While carpenters were hired to rebuild the interiors, students and faculty alike worked on restoring St. Hilda's—washing, scrubbing, and whitewashing walls.[38] Hazel Gosline, who left in 1942 on her furlough, was requested by Bishop Gilman, and she rejoined the faculty in September 1946.[39]

St. Hilda's reopened in September 1946 but on the Boone campus; it would take a full two years before the repairs to the St. Hilda's campus were completed.[40] Wuhan was "liberated" by the Communists on May 16, 1949, with little destruction or resistance, and the entire St. Hilda's campus was

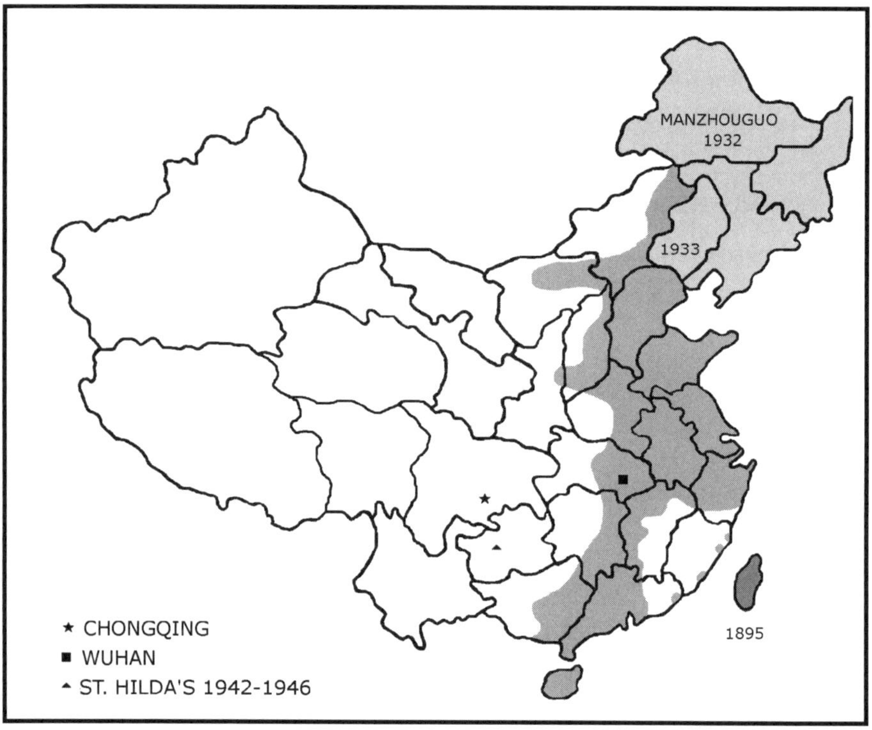

Japanese Occupation, 1945. Adapted from USMA online map: http://www.dean.usma.edu/history/web03/atlases/china%20civil%20war/chinese%20civil%20war%20pages/chinese%20civil%20war%map%2005.htm.

temporarily occupied by People's Liberation Army troops with no incidents. "They brought or paid for their own food and did not commandeer or steal food as the Guomindang troops did."[41] While foreign missions attempted to work with the Communist government, the attempt was futile—all foreign mission workers were ordered to leave China. Writing as much as she could about the changing tide in China, Hazel Gosline wrote, "There is one word that covers the whole situation—persecution," as the Chinese administrators were systematically the "subject of attack—Gwendolyn [Seng, the principal] is punished for the time being—the Dean will be next and so on."[42] Leaving St. Hilda's under the direction of Gwendolyn Seng, Hazel Gosline and Carman Wolff from St. Hilda's were joined by Olive Bird Tomlin (who was working at Boone), and the three left on the evening of September 1, 1950, surrounded by "at least eighty well-wishers" and they arrived three days later in Hong Kong.[43] Olive Tomlin set sail for her new assignment in Sagada, Philippines, on September 28, 1950, while Hazel and Carman took their freighter bound for Europe on October 2, 1950.[44]

Once the Communist government nationalized all the foreign schools, St. Hilda's School for Girls ceased being a private school, and it was renamed Wuchang Number 25 Middle School, which continues to this day. The school building, the Ladies House, the music rooms, and the chapel were being used into the mid-1980s when a fire destroyed most of the school, but the chapel building still remains.[45]

Journey to the West

Yeh Yuanshuang

After graduating from St. Hilda's in 1935, Yuanshuang attended one semester at Wuhan University but left when, through a family friend, she was hired as the director of the Students' Bureau and as the director of membership in Hankou's Young Women's Christian Association (YWCA). The salary was far too attractive to forgo. Earning a monthly salary of one hundred American dollars paid in silver coin, Yuanshuang helped provide for her family during the unsettled times of the late 1930s. Yeh Fengchi's death that year also placed more financial burdens on Rongzai's shoulders. Each week, Yuanshuang would arrive home to be greeted as a returning "empress." With her wages, Yuanshuang brought special treats for the entire household but especially for Tai and her mother—oranges and fresh fruit in season, roasted meats, and snacks—everything her mother delighted in eating. When Tai died in 1936, Yuanshuang helped with funeral expenses to honor her as a grandmother she respected and loved. With her earnings,

Yuanshuang helped send Yuanquan—upon her graduation from St. Hilda's in 1936—to nursing school in Shanghai, and her younger brother, Yuanli, to an art institute in Hangzhou.

Given the transformation in her ethos from her St. Hilda's education, it was a "natural" step for Yuanshuang to take a job at the YWCA. The YM/WCAs, unlike the vast majority of Christian institutions in China, were highly "indigenized." Most of their employees were Chinese who were imbued with the spirit of the Social Gospel and were desirous of making the world a better place.[46] Unlike the individualistic nature found in most Protestantism, the Social Gospel believed that substantive social change was both possible and necessary for improving the lives of people in this world. This view resonated with the nationalist beliefs held by many Chinese, regardless of whether or not they believed in Christianity. The Social Gospel advocated many of the same social changes that the Communists did. The major difference between the two movements was on their focus: the Communists, under Mao Zedong, professed that their ideas "bubbled up" from the rural masses; whereas, the YM/WCAs' Social Gospel beliefs "trickled down" to the masses from its urban middle-class base. In essence, one movement sought revolutionary social change; the other sought evolutionary social change. Civil war would dictate which approach would be more successful in China.

In June 1938, the Japanese commenced bombing Wuhan, forcing thousands of residents to flee from approaching Japanese troops. At first, Yuanshuang and Yuanquan joined their parents, cousins, servants, and Concubine Yu in their Guling summer home high in the Lushan mountains. This was the same general area where the Episcopal Mission Board maintained bungalows and where some missionaries also fled initially.[47] While there, a wealthy Chinese officer's wife opened a school, and Yuanshuang, once the most indifferent of students, was hired at the rate of twenty American dollars per month to teach English, mathematics, Mandarin, history, and geography—all the required educational courses.

When it became apparent that the Japanese would overrun the area in the late summer of 1938, for their safety, Dexing urged Yuanshuang and Yuanquan to leave immediately. Dexing, whose bound feet were not conducive to her being a refugee, remained in Guling for a short time longer, but she insisted her daughters leave immediately. Rongzai, accompanied by Concubine Yu, had previously gone to Hankou in order to keep Yeh Kai Tai in business. To help Yuanshuang and Yuanquan blend more with the refugees fleeing the ever-advancing Japanese, Dexing dressed them in the simplest of peasant garments in which she sewed silver coins in the hems. Dexing also hid pearls and jade jewelry in typical peasant fare of hard buns and wrapped the food in old, clean, cloth napkins. Accompanying Yuanshuang and Yuanquan were a number of young Christian students they were to escort to Nanchang, Jiangxi Province, a city south of Guling.

During the trek down Lushan to the nearest train station at De'an, Yuanshuang contracted dysentery which slowed down her party's progress. The only open road was dangerous "because it led near the front lines and planes were constantly flying over machine gunning moving groups," forcing any travel to be conducted at night.[48] What normally would have been a twelve-hour trip became an ordeal. Although Yuanshuang begged Yuanquan and the others to leave her, they refused, taking four days to arrive at the train station where Yuanshuang was propped against a railcar while the others searched for food and water. While the group was scavenging, a Japanese air raid occurred. After the aerial bombing and strafing, the crowd searched for survivors, hastily buried casualties in makeshift graves, and cleared rubble from the tracks. Yuanquan and other members of their party clawed through the rubble and searched among the dead only to find Yuanshuang completely buried in debris and surrounded by dead bodies but totally at peace and, miraculously, unharmed. Protected by the railcar where she had been left, Yuanshuang drifted in and out of consciousness during the entire raid that killed hundreds, but she suffered no effects of the raid. With the assistance of the group, she was shoved aboard the train when it finally arrived two days later. Although the De'an station was totally leveled, the tracks were intact, and hundreds of refugees clamored aboard every inch of the train creating a human encasement. The group took turns tending to Yuanshuang, sitting and standing for the duration of what became a two-day trip as the train inched its way along its route; further, the train could only travel by daylight. The group managed to reach Nanchang safely where Yuanshuang was provided medical care. Upon Yuanshuang's recovery, she and Yuanquan were unable to obtain any work there, and with nowhere else to go, they returned to Hankou.

By the time they arrived in Hankou, Dexing had already returned home, but, fearing for her daughters' safety once again, she insisted that Yuanshuang and Yuanquan leave Hankou for Sichuan Province where thousands of refugees were fleeing the coming Japanese onslaught. After a two-month stay in the city awaiting the river's water level to rise, the two sisters once again departed at Dexing's insistence and went upriver in early fall 1938. It would be the last time that Yuanshuang and Yuanquan would see their mother alive. A few weeks later, on October 25, 1938, the Japanese captured Wuhan, and it became an occupied city.

Upon their arrival in Chongqing, the Nationalists' latest provisional capital, Yuanshuang and Yuanquan stayed with one of their St. Hilda's schoolmates. Through the St. Hilda's network of graduates and friends living and working in the city, Yuanshuang obtained a position as a teacher/governess caring for the children of an official in the Nationalist government's Ministry of Economic Affairs, Dr. He Lian. From late fall 1938 until March 1941, Yuanshuang lived on Huang Shan, a mountain resort situated above Chongqing.[49]

In January 1939, Yuanshuang along with five other governesses created a school that operated in the spacious home of Cai Zhenxing, president of one of Sichuan Province's largest banks. At the makeshift school, Yuanshuang taught history and geography. Inspired by the enterprising women, Dr. Wang Daixi, a prominent Chongqing physician, decided to build a primary school. Construction commenced, and Yuanshuang was invited to be the principal upon its completion in 1941.

At a party hosted by the Wangs in late 1940, Yuanshuang was introduced to Brigadier General Liu Xianjie who was an instructor at the New Army Officers' Academy which was located in the mountains outside of Chongqing. The only son of the well-known, warlord from Gongxian (Gongyi) in northern Henan Province, Liu Zhenhua (born Liu Maoye),[50] Xianjie had a doctorate in mathematics and physics from the Technische Hochschule in Hannover, Germany. He was also schooled in the Chinese classics. The introduction was arranged in part by Mrs. He and her friends who hoped to find a suitable mate for Yuanshuang. After a pleasant evening of conversation, much to Yuanshuang's shock, Xianjie proposed marriage citing their ages and the wartime situation as the reasons for such a brash offer. Yuanshuang refused on the grounds that she scarcely knew him and she would not consider the offer without more knowledge about him. When a letter from Brigadier General Liu arrived for Yuanshuang three days later, the courtship began in earnest. Every weekend from that time forth, Xianjie would travel from the military academy to Huang Shan, stay with the Wang family, and woo Yuanshuang.

The completion of the primary school in January 1941 posed a problem for Yuanshuang who wanted the position, but she was under tremendous pressure by Xianjie to marry. Given the circumstances and the uncertainty precipitated by the war, Yuanshuang finally relented to Xianjie's persistent courtship, and the two were engaged in early January after a mere six weeks of courtship. (It was Yuanshuang's destiny to marry the son of a warlord after all.) On March 1, 1941, at age forty, Xianjie and Yuanshuang, at age twenty-seven, were married at the Chongqing Hotel with Dr. Wang and Dr. He serving as their witnesses. Gao Dehua (one of Dexing's nieces who was raised in the Yeh household) as well as Yuanquan and Yuanlu (both married themselves) represented Yuanshuang's side of the family.

During their honeymoon at the New Army Officers' Academy, Yuanshuang learned of Xianjie's past which included a divorce from his first wife who bore him five children—three girls and two boys. The marriage was arranged by his father before Xianjie was born. Xianjie was married in 1918 when he was seventeen prior to his departure with his new wife to study in Germany. Wealthy Chinese families sent their children to study abroad, and Xianjie was sent to Germany to study mathematics, physics, and the "art of war."[51]

Summoned by his father to return to China following the Japanese annexation of Manchuria in 1931, Xianjie met his second wife aboard ship while he and his family were returning to China, and upon their arrival in Shanghai, Xianjie posted a notice in the newspaper stating that he was divorcing his first wife. This public humiliation and scandal led to Xianjie being disowned by his father for this disgraceful loss of face. After a meeting with his father where he refused to rescind the divorce, Xianjie set sail for Germany, and he and his second wife were married aboard ship by the captain. There was no direct contact between Xianjie and his family until he was recalled to China when the Japanese invaded China in 1937. By this time, Zhenhua was seriously ill. Xianjie and his second wife returned to China, but they were still estranged from the Liu family so Xianjie joined the Nationalist army. With the family's connections, he was commissioned a brigadier general. When his second wife died of throat cancer in 1940, the family placed enormous pressure upon Xianjie to remarry his first wife who, with her five children, had continued to live with the Liu family. Having no desire to do so, Xianjie was desperate to find a suitable match; hence, his haste in courting and marrying Yuanshuang.

Xianjie and Yuanshuang lived at the academy from March 1941 until the winter of 1942 when Xianjie was summoned by his father's younger brother, Lieutenant General Liu Maoen, the commander in chief of China's Fourteenth Army Group, to help protect Henan's northern borders against Japanese forces.[52] Pregnant with their first child, Yuanshuang did not wish to risk travel during the bitter winter weather, but when a vice-commander was dispatched to retrieve the reluctant Xianjie, the couple had no other choice but to travel to Xi'an to meet up with eight other families in the Liu clan. Introduced to the Lius for the first time, Yuanshuang was warmly received by the clan thus mending the family rift. With Liu-led military forces defending the border region of Henan, Shanxi, and Shaanxi Provinces, Yuanshuang returned to the Liu family ancestral home in Gongxian to give birth. On January 29, 1943, a son—Jiazhang—was born. Yuanshuang's only regret was that her beloved mother, Dexing, had suffered a major stroke in 1942, and died before Jiazhang was born. Routing a letter through Hong Kong, Yuanshuang wrote her mother that year about her pregnancy. When her brother, Yuanli, informed her about Dexing's death, Yuanshuang was devastated. She was comforted, however, by the fact that her mother died peacefully knowing of her pregnancy and that Dexing had been well cared for by faithful family servants and Yuanli.

When the Japanese launched Operation ICHIGO in 1944, the Liu clan was forced to evacuate westward into Shaanxi Province. Xianjie was deployed to the Luoyang area in northwestern Henan Province where the fighting between Chinese and Japanese troops was particularly fierce. When the Japanese overwhelmed the area and no word of Xianjie was heard, he was presumed dead. In escaping the Japanese, Xianjie swam under a less-than-pristine river which caused severe ear infections. As a result, Xianjie sustained a total hearing loss when a high fever associated with the ear infections resulted in his tympanic membranes bursting. Weeks later, the few survivors of Xianjie's troops managed to get word to Lieutenant General Liu Maoen, and the small band of soldiers was rescued. Despite his defeat and his hearing loss, Xianjie was promoted to major general, made head of the Army's Sixty-fourth Division,[53] and deployed to the front south of Kaifeng as soon as he recovered.

When the Japanese surrendered in 1945, the War of Resistance ended, but soon the Civil War re-erupted between the Nationalists and the Communists. Aligned with the Nationalists, Xianjie was deployed to help protect the border between Shaanxi and Henan Provinces. During this time, a second child was conceived and another son, Jiaxing, was born in Kaifeng on September 20, 1946. As the tide slowly turned against the Nationalists and with an increasing dissatisfaction with Generalissimo Chiang Kai-shek's prosecution of the war, Xianjie decided in 1948 that it would be a good time to consult hearing specialists outside of China. At first, the decision was that Xianjie would travel alone to the United States. Pregnant with their third child whose birth was imminent, Yuanshuang was reluctant to travel anywhere much less journey to the West. Their friend Liu Binyi, joint owner of a Shanghai-American airline, persuasively argued that Yuanshuang had to accompany the deaf and non-English speaking Xianjie, and he made the necessary arrangements to obtain passage on his airline—a feat in and of itself—given the extraordinary demand for flights to destinations outside the country. Leaving their two sons with family members, the two embarked on their trip to the United States. She bid her father, Concubine Yu, and her brothers and sister farewell. It would be the last time she would see all but one of them alive.

Armed only with the name of an audiologist in New York, Yuanshuang and Xianjie boarded a fifteen-passenger airplane destined for San Francisco. The five-day, four-night journey with multiple fueling stops was enough to induce contractions. During a refueling stop in Hawaii, the flight crew refused to allow Yuanshuang to continue and ordered her and Xianjie off the plane. Insisting that she had experience with two previous pregnancies, Yuanshuang argued that she would be able to "hold on" until they reached the States. Only after a telegraph message was sent and a response obtained from Liu Binyi giving his full authorization were Yuanshuang and Xianjie allowed to continue. And hold on she did. As soon as they arrived in San Francisco, Yuanshuang insisted on having her first Chinese meal of hot pepper and rice dishes in five days. After the meal Xianjie hailed a cab, Yuanshuang pointed to her very swollen, but sated, belly, and two hours later, she delivered another son in San Francisco's Chinese Hospital on July

24, 1948. Commemorating his birth in America, he was named Jiamei by incorporating part of the Chinese word for the United States—Meiguo—into his name.

Yuanshuang and Xianjie eventually arrived in New York in late 1948 where they sought out the audiologist recommended by their friends in China. When the specialist suggested treatments that could restore some of his hearing, they continued to see him until they could no longer afford the doctor's visits. Yuanshuang and Xianjie sought out other specialists for many months, but the diagnosis was always the same—that his tympanic membranes were ruptured and nothing could be done. Finally, with the triumph of the Communist Revolution and the declaration of the People's Republic of China in October 1949, Yuanshuang and Xianjie could not return to China. Their sons, Jiazhang and Jiaxing, were taken by family members and Xianjie's military aides to Taiwan. In order to support themselves and the family in Taiwan once the money they brought with them from China was largely exhausted, Yuanshuang used her limited English and her exposure to American culture and values that she had obtained from her St. Hilda's education to get a job despite being pregnant with her fourth child. I was born in Brooklyn on April 8, 1950, named, Judith, after my mother, and given a name selected by my paternal grandfather in one of his more lucid moments—Mengbai—to commemorate the fact that I was born near Washington, D.C. When combined with the Jia character in my brothers' names, my name translates to "Dream of the White House."

America afforded a level of freedom that Yuanshuang would never have been allowed had she remained in China or gone to Taiwan where women of prominent families continued to have control over household affairs but little else. Yuanshuang, however, had been coached by Dexing and Tai to be independent and her St. Hilda's education taught her to be self-sufficient and self-reliant. As a person who had a "good head for numbers," Yuanshuang began taking evening accounting courses and learned how to use a comptometer. She became both the first non-Ashkenazim and the first Chinese woman to work for the manufacturing firm Weiss and Klau, beginning in 1955. Because of her stellar work ethic, Yuanshuang paved the way for three more St. Hilda's graduates to obtain positions at the company.

In 1955, Jiazhang (Frederich Wolfgang, a.k.a Fred) and Jiaxing (Wilhelm Hans, a.k.a William) were reunited with their parents and introduced to their younger siblings, John (Jiamei) and Judith (Mengbai), in New York.

The New York-based St. Hilda's alumnae community was close. Once a month, a group of five St. Hilda's graduates (three of whom also worked at Weiss and Klau), their husbands, and families would get together on a rotating basis to eat and play mah-jongg. Although there was no active St. Hilda's alumnae association, there was, nonetheless, a worldwide network of graduates. In addition, a number of St. Hilda's graduates (especially the daughters of Christian church workers) attended Ginling College in Nanjing. As the first Chinese college to offer baccalaureate degrees to women, it had a worldwide alumnae association that held regional reunions. In addition to the Ginling Alumnae Association, each summer a group of Chinese Christians would gather at a birthday celebration for the former bishop of Hankou, Alfred A. Gilman, at his home in New Jersey. Hundreds of Chinese Christians and their families would gather for the reunion with former American missionaries who were stationed in China. These reunions continued until Bishop Gilman's death in September 1966.

In June 1966, the Liu family moved to Los Angeles, where Yuanshuang obtained employment as an accountant at Traveler's Insurance through the wife of a childhood acquaintance of Xianjie. Again, through the St. Hilda's network, Yuanshuang reconnected with other graduates in the Los Angeles area, and they socialized regularly.

The Yeh Family

Following President Richard Nixon's visit to the People's Republic of China in 1972, Yuanshuang returned to China in 1973 where she was able to reconnect with the only surviving member of her immediate family—her younger brother, Yuanli. From him, she learned of her family's fate. Rongzai was persecuted to death during the 1955 Anti-Rightist Campaign as a opium-addicted, feudalistic oppressor. Workers from Yeh Kai Tai refused to denounce Rongzai and secretly sent him food; upon his death, Concubine Yu—who had continued to live with him—was evicted by the Communists, and with no financial means and with no family to support her, reports were that she eventually starved to death.

Yuanshuang's older brother, Yuanfù, died in 1959 during the Great Leap Forward. Although a graduate of Shanghai's prestigious St. John's College, as an individual classified by the Communists as a "person with a bad family background"—the son of a feudalistic oppressor, having overseas connections, and possessing a Western education—he died of starvation in a remote area of Hubei after he was sent to the countryside to be "reformed through labor." Yuanshuang's sister, Yuanquan, was able to join the Nationalist exodus to Taiwan with her husband, Yuan Xingyi, who was an army officer, and their five children. She died in Taipei in 1951. Yuanshuang's cousin Yuanlu also married a Nationalist army officer, Du Jingzhen, and fled to Taiwan in 1949 as well. Yuanshuang visited her in Taipei in 1972, 1982, and 1990; Yuanlu died in 2000. Yuanshuang maintained contact with and supported Yuanli from 1973 until he died in Ningpo, Zhejiang Province, in 1996.

After Yuanshuang retired in 1979, she accompanied me on two research trips to China in 1982 and 1990. During those trips, she reconnected with graduates from St. Hilda's. In city after city, we would meet with former classmates and schoolmates. Inspired by their reunions and reminiscences about their school days, I began to interview them. The quotations and information about their experiences at St. Hilda's are from these interviews. Yuanshuang returned to China in 2008 so that she could bring Xianjie's ashes home to Gongxian and in 2009 so that she could see the "new" Beijing and visit with three of Yuanquan's children, two of whom now live on the mainland.

Yeh Yuanshuang (Judith Yeh Liu) lives in Irvine, California.

Return to the West

Dorothea Kingsley Wakeman

When the SS *Scharnhorst* docked in Genoa in July 1937, Dorothea embarked upon another journey her parents always dreamed of doing as well. Armed with a movie camera sent to her in China by her parents, Dorothea filmed parts of her journey. Traveling with Bishop Huntington and the Arthur J. Allens,[54] China missionaries who were also making their way stateside, the group made their way through Italy. Dorothea would visit a continent whose political landscape would soon be changed by World War II, and the atmosphere crackled with political tensions. From Genoa, the group traveled to Rome, Florence, and Venice before Dorothea departed on her own to Oberhofen, Switzerland, where she would stay with her China friend, Elita Smith, who lived there.[55] From Oberhofen, Dorothea went to Bern and Basel before she crossed the border into Germany. In honor of the "victrola record, 'The Hunt in the Black Forest,' " played in her youth, Dorothea spent an evening in Heidelberg in order to visit the Black Forest before journeying to Berlin on August 13.[56] Sternly cautioned by her father to eschew discussing politics at all costs, Dorothea wrote how she met people who were "kind and good" along the way, and who "all took it as a personal responsibility to see that I got off at the right place & understood perfectly how to make connections."[57] Dorothea loved Germany regardless of "what the world says about a Dictator."[58]

From Germany, Dorothea traveled to Sweden to stay with Vivian and Mons Hallberg whom she had also befriended in China. From Sweden, Dorothea traveled south and west through Denmark, northern Germany, the Netherlands, and France, before reaching England. All told, during Dorothea's "round the world cruise," she was in "eleven different countries other than the United States and in the capital city of each to say nothing of some of the island possessions of some and our own."[59] From London, Dorothea set sail for New York on September 22 aboard the "3,000 passenger" SS *Europa,* "third class."[60]

Prior to leaving China, Dorothea wrote to a New York employment agency seeking a teaching position, but a letter forwarded to her in London indicated that "there was very slight possibility of . . . getting a teaching position if [she] didn't get back to America earlier."[61] Letters from her parents informing her that she could visit other friends and would not have to "camp on the Hammonds," who were her mother's relations "while job hunting in the East," helped to strengthen her resolve to stay on the East Coast instead of returning home to California.[62]

Upon Dorothea's arrival in New York, one of her first tasks was to visit the Park Avenue headquarters of the Department of Foreign Missions to inquire about returning to China following her furlough. Never far from her mind, she was "sick" with the "sad state of affairs in China," so much so that Dorothea had "a hard time to keep from crying every time [she] read the newspaper."[63] As she had feared, no missionaries—new or returning—would be allowed to travel to China for the time being, and Dorothea set about finding employment. Dorothea held firm to her "declaration of independence" proclaimed in her letter of May 15, 1937. Because of her excellent typing skills and her missionary contacts, Dorothea was able to obtain temporary work as a secretary "to the editor of the national magazine of the YWCA,"[64] where she "typed and corrected [manuscripts] for them for two months."[65] Dorothea also joined New York's Industrial Arts Cooperative Service—"an association of teachers, club leaders and others interested in a more dynamic type of education" that emphasized "the arts and their place in education."[66] Through "scouring the want ads of newspapers," Dorothea learned of a teaching position advertised for the Cathedral School in Washington, D.C.[67] When she contacted the employment agency about the job, they were confident that she would "get the job" because Dorothea possessed the "subject matter they valued having there." Dorothea's candid responses to questions posed during the interview, however, cost her the job. When the headmistress inquired about her future plans, Dorothea replied, "I hope to be back in China in a couple of years. And I was very emphatic about how I wanted to get back to China as soon as possible."[68] Following the interview, Dorothea was admonished by the agency that while "honesty [was] a good trait," telling potential employers about her plans was not "because they don't want somebody who is just going to be there for a little time."[69]

On December 1, 1937, Dorothea began teaching the fourth grade at the New Canaan Country School in Connecticut, "an extremely progressive & stimulating school in an intensely wide awake, sophisticated & intelligent community. My class all have I.Q's of 7th & 8th graders according to all the well known standard tests. Their parents are all famous people encompassing presidents of railroads, popular writers & temporarily returned from abroad diplomats & engineers."[70] In 1938, Henry Wells, "an old China hand" who was the former director of the American School in Shanghai, became the new headmaster. Delighted to have a fellow missionary on staff, they spent many hours "mostly talking about China and possible mutual acquaintances"[71]

The New Canaan Country School was housed in a magnificent old mansion in an excellent neighborhood, and Dorothea soon became involved with the very things she loved doing in China—writing and producing plays. Near the school was her residence—the Melba Inn—which was within walking distance of the Silvermine Artists' Colony. After work, Dorothea would spend time at the colony where, as "an aspiring artist," she could nurture her desire to write and paint.[72] Her ultimate ambition was to write about her experiences in China and to continue writing plays. One of her first productions at New Canaan was a Greek play which contained historical information she learned from resources obtained from the Industrial Arts Cooperative Service.[73]

In 1940, Dorothea returned to California to "straighten out her teaching credential."[74] Dorothea inquired about positions in California, and with her teaching experience, she was offered a principal's position that paid a much higher salary than the New Canaan Country School did. With considerable parental pressure to remain in California, Dorothea decided against the principal's position but to accept, instead, a position at Garfield Elementary School in Long Beach teaching underprivileged students. Needing to recover from a failed romance, Dorothea returned to the same social situation she so wanted to escape in the first place. At Garfield, Dorothea plunged herself into work teaching sixth graders who were divided into six different reading groups with some students who "could not even read the primer."[75] Far from being daunted by the situation, Dorothea rose to the challenge and developed ways of teaching reading using her talents writing poetry, plays, stories, and using music to pique the students' interest. She would "mesmerize" the students with her China adventures, pictures, and garments.

At her brother, Norman, and Deborah's wedding in June 1940, Dorothea was introduced to a young man—Robert Howe. A friend of Dorothea's sister, Gwen, and her husband, Joe, they frequently talked of Dorothea and her adventures in China, so much so that Bob looked forward to meeting Dorothea because she "sounded fascinating, and the two had so much in common."[76] A Stanford graduate who obtained his advanced degree from the Harvard Business School in accounting, Bob was also an avid sailor; the two did have much in common and soon were seeing each other seriously. Earl "approved" of this young man who was both polished and poised.[77] After a summer courtship, the two became engaged and were married at All Saints in December 1941, two weeks after the bombing of Pearl Harbor. Dorothea continued teaching at Garfield until her fifth month of pregnancy, and on October 11, 1942, she gave birth to their first son, Mark, in Pasadena's Huntington Hospital.

Having served in the Stanford Army ROTC and continuing in the army reserves for a decade following his graduation from Stanford, once war was declared, Bob's reserve unit was called into active duty. Bob, commissioned a captain, served four years in the Pacific theater, and faithfully wrote lengthy letters home. Dorothea assembled the letters, pictures, and artifacts he sent home into a series of scrapbooks just as her mother had done for her while she was in China. When Bob returned home, his hair was "completely white . . . from his experiences in the Pacific," and he rarely spoke of the horrors he witnessed.[78] Bob obtained a position at American Smelting and Refining Company as a controller. Following the war, two other children were born. A daughter, Catherine, was born on September 14, 1946, and a son, Dean, was born on August 5, 1949, both in Huntington Hospital. When Earl and Harriett decided to move to Altadena, California, they purchased three adjoining lots on Sinaloa Avenue, and two of their daughters—Geraldine Wakeman Bowlus in 1948 and Dorothea Wakeman Howe in 1949—and their families moved into the Wakeman family "compound."[79] In many ways, Dorothea's independence was predicated on her separation from her family. Once she returned to California, Earl's patriarchal controls were able to be reasserted. Fortunately, she now had a "good" husband—the fulfillment of her parents' dreams—to serve as a buffer between her and her parents.

Harriett was the first to die in May 1958; Earl followed two years later in April 1960. Gwendolyn died in 1954; Norman died in 2001. Geraldine, the youngest, is still living.[80]

Dorothea was able to return to China but as a tourist. She and Bob embarked on a nineteen-day trip to Beijing, Xi'an, Yichang, Wushan, Wanxian, Chongqing, and Shanghai in April 1987. She regaled fellow travelers with stories about her student days in old "Beiping" and teaching in Wuchang. Although she was "thrilled to be back," it just "wasn't the China" she remembered, and she was "disappointed" in how much it had changed.[81]

The "Saints"

From the moment Dorothea arrived in New York, she began corresponding with the "Saints" and her other friends from China. First, she wrote letters to her friends in Europe—especially to those with whom she had spent time. She maintained an ongoing correspondence with Vivian and Mons Hallberg who were in Sweden during World War II. Dorothea wrote and received long letters from the "Saints"—Tommy, Hazel, and Venetia, as well as from Julia Clark, who wrote of their experiences during the war and the various relocations of St. Hilda's from Guangxi Province to Yunnan

Province near the "Burma Road" to Guizhou Province and back to Wuchang. Frances Roots married Richard Hadden, and the two were renowned pianists with whom Dorothea maintained contact until the day she died, keeping a file of their concerts including their "Peking Premiere" as the "first American concert pianists to perform in China since 1949 and the first concert of Western music in China since the Cultural Revolution (1966)" on October 3, 1972.[82] It was the first time that Frances had returned to China, and her excitement inspired Dorothea to consider returning herself.

When the Communists confiscated all foreign schools in 1950, all the foreign teachers were expelled from the country. Julia A. Clark was the first to die of bronchial pneumonia with heart complications in Pasadena, California where she lived with her married sister. She died in 1951—four months after leaving China. Years in the China field had taken its toll on her health, and upon the death of her beloved brother, Bishop Stephen Clark, just prior to her return, she was "heartbroken and her faithful heart just gave up."[83] Venetia Cox died in a Greenville, North Carolina, nursing home in 1979 at age eighty-six.[84] Hazel Gosline eventually retired to a Washington, D.C., nursing home and died in 1988 at age eighty-eight.[85] Olive Bird Tomlin retired to Winter Park, Florida, where she died in 1984 just two months shy of her ninety-fourth birthday.

Dorothea reconnected with graduates from St. Hilda's through a chance encounter. While shopping at the Fedco Store in Pasadena, she overheard two women conversing in Mandarin. Drawn to the Chinese, Dorothea surprised the two when she spoke a few words of Chinese to them and they struck up a conversation. When they learned of Dorothea's teaching experience, one of the women exclaimed: "My mother went to St. Hilda's!" Within a few days, Dorothea was contacted by a number of women who had not only attended St. Hilda's but who were also some of her students.[86] A reunion was held at the Howe residence on Sinaloa Avenue in 1973. Ironically, Yuanshuang, who lived just a few miles away in Monterey Park, did not attend because she was in China at the time visiting family. Dorothea and Bob moved to Ocean Hills Country Club—a senior residential community—in Vista, California, to be closer to their children and grandchildren. When Bob died in 1994, Dorothea moved a year later to a senior residential facility, La Vida Del Mar in Solana Beach, California, near her daughter Cathy's home.

In a twist of serendipity, in March 1997, as part of a University of San Diego-sponsored public lecture series, I gave a presentation on St. Hilda's in San Diego. In the audience was Dorothea Wakeman Howe who was drawn to the lecture when a friend alerted her about the topic. Sixty-two years after Yuanshuang graduated from St. Hilda's, she was reunited with Dorothea. I began interviewing Dorothea when she was living at La Vida Del Mar, and Yuanshuang made visits to see Dorothea. The two spent hours reminiscing about their lives, much of which served as the basis for this book. Dorothea and I remained friends until her death at age ninety-three on February 17, 2001.

This study of St. Hilda's School for Girls in Wuchang between the years 1929 and 1937 affords a glimpse at the importance of female education; however, the experiences of Yeh Yuanshuang and Dorothea Kingsley Wakeman are unusual. Both were educated far beyond the average woman of that era: Yuanshuang represents a small proportion of Chinese women who received at least a middle school education; whereas, Dorothea represents the small proportion of American women who received postbaccalaureate educations. While the reasons for them receiving their educations may differ, the results highlight the position of women in their respective cultures.

Yeh Yuanshuang's mother, Gao Dexing, was a prisoner of her times. Born into dynastic China, she embodied the most pernicious aspects of that era: she was illiterate with bound feet, and by the time of the Northern Expedition, she had been kept away from interacting with non-familial Chinese society for most of her life. Her culturally mandated ignorance and isolation made her particularly vulnerable to China's ongoing social changes; yet, she was forced by historical circumstances to deal with those changes in order to protect the members of her household. Her feelings of vulnerability made her determined that her daughters would never be as powerless as she was. As such, she recognized that the only way that Yuanshuang and Yuanquan could avoid her fate was for them to be educated, because only by being educated could they possibly become knowledgeable and independent women in a country that had historically valued neither of those two traits. Dexing was able to envision a different life for her daughters because the Revolution of 1912 created cracks in the wall of Chinese patriarchy, and it was through these cracks that Dexing sought to push her daughters into a world where women would no longer be valued for the "trained incapacity" inherent in their pedigree but would be valued for the knowledge gained by their academic degrees. Thus, she made it possible for them to be able to interact within Chinese society because her behind-the-scenes maneuvering permitted Yuanshuang and Yuanquan to escape the odious tradition of foot binding. She also realized that it was necessary for her daughters to be formally educated and used her own money to pay for their tuition. The stage was set for Yuanshuang and Yuanquan to play roles in the New China.

Earl and Harriett Wakeman, too, were caught up in historical circumstances that were beyond their complete control. They saw the value of education; yet, it appears that value was not to be used as a means for Dorothea to establish her independence in the world, but rather, it was to be used as a means to make her a more "marketable" potential wife and mother. There was no doubt that Dorothea would receive a college education and become a teacher, but this was to be a temporary situation that would permit her to meet "suitable," upwardly mobile young men. In essence, Earl and Harriett maintained a view of the world that was somewhat at odds with the Zeitgeist of the Roaring Twenties. They held a much more Victorian view of gender than their daughter did. As such, Dorothea sought more independence than they thought she should have, and in order to escape from behind the patriarchal wall of her parents' constraints, she became a foreign, educational missionary, the very role that her parents had so wanted to have in their younger years. It was through this act of rebellion that Dorothea was able to be more autonomous than she had ever been.

Within the walls of St. Hilda's compound, both Yuanshuang and Dorothea flourished in an environment that was neither totally American nor totally Chinese. The school provided an environment that mitigated extant gender expectations for the girls and for their teachers. Both groups experienced a degree of freedom that was not possible in their respective cultures. This freedom was only possible, however, because of changes occurring outside the school. Government-mandated registration diminished the foreignness of the school by making it more Chinese. This, in turn, made it possible for the students to become acutely aware of the cultural, social, and political events happening outside the walls of the school. While school registration caused consternation within the larger missionary community, it only increased the Social Gospel educational components that the American teachers so fervently wished to impart upon their students. These educational goals were furthered by the fact that this period of Nationalist rule was the only time of relative peace between the Revolution and the founding of the People's Republic of China in 1949. Thus, the cohort of girls who attended St. Hilda's between 1929 and 1937 received the best education the school was able to provide in its entire history. In Yuanshuang's case, she was able to attend St. Hilda's when it was no longer a cloistered environment. The trips between the school and home as well as the social service work in Li village were the first instances where she could encounter Chinese society directly. She, too, was no longer cloistered by her family. This era of social stability also helped the teachers as well. In Dorothea's case, she was able to write, choreograph, and direct plays which provided her with a sense of self-worth that transcended anything she would have experienced had she remained in California.

Moreover, this study shows how significant culture is in shaping one's life. The independence that a St. Hilda's education gave Yuanshuang and the knowledge that education provided her about American culture and society made it possible for Yuanshuang to succeed when she and Liu Xianjie involuntarily emigrated to the United States in 1948. Yuanshuang realized that she would only remain "free" as long as she remained in the United States. Had she returned to Taiwan to be with the rest of the Nationalists who fled the mainland, she would have had to conform to the gender expectations incumbent upon the wife of an army general. Her mother's gender-defined experiences and her education made it such that she chose to rebel against conventional Chinese expectations for a high-status wife and mother, and she chose to stay in the United States where her foreignness placed her outside the confines of America's gender ideology.

Dorothea maintained her independence for as long as she remained away from California and her parents. Once she returned to the intimacy of the family, she no longer had the benefit of distance to mitigate her parents' expectations for her, and her life settled into being more closely aligned with her parents' desires. Unlike the "Saints," Dorothea, despite all her good works, never had a calling that permitted her to openly challenge traditional gender roles. Once she returned to the social and cultural milieu against which she had so fervently rebelled, the pressure on her to conform became irresistible.

Ultimately, a few points are salient from this small, ethnographic study. First, the value of educating girls for the good of the society, in general, and for the girls, in particular, cannot be overstated. Education provides people the possibility of visualizing alternatives to the arbitrary social constructions of their worlds. That is, extant gender expectations do not have to be destiny. Second, we are all caught up in structures where cultural beliefs, social practices, and historical circumstances "conspire" to maintain walls built upon a bedrock of conformity. It is only when cracks develop within these walls that some form of social change becomes possible. Thus, the collapse of the Qing dynasty in China and the displacement of Victorian mores in the United States weakened existing gender constructs in both countries. Lastly, the experiences of Yuanshuang and Dorothea show that it is much easier to question the gender ideology in another culture than in one's own.[87]

Appendix A: A Chinese Context

ON OCTOBER 10, 1911, THE UNINTENDED EXPLOSION OF A BOMB IN THE Russian concession of Hankou began the revolution that overthrew the Qing dynasty. When police discovered a secret society's membership list at the site of the explosion, the surviving members feared for their lives, and decided to rebel against the dynasty. Ironically, the rebels were part of the Qing's New Army in Hubei. Needing a recognized leader, the rebels chose a commander, Li Yuanhung, who, fearing he would be shot by the rebels if he declined their "offer," reluctantly became the leader of the revolution. As the battle raged in Hankou between the rebellious New Army troops and loyal Qing forces, five provinces seceded, and as the revolutionary fight crossed the Han River into Hanyang, ten more provinces abandoned the dynasty. While Hankou and Hanyang were severely damaged in the fighting, by February 12, 1912, the revolution was over as the last Qing emperor, Puyi, abdicated. What led a three-hundred-year-old dynasty to collapse within months of the start of an "accidental revolution," and what followed its fall?

By 1900 the Qing state was tottering as external aggression, as evidenced by the Opium Wars, and internal chaos, as evidenced by the various rebellions that occurred throughout the empire, demonstrated how weak Qing authority had become in China. This situation produced a conundrum: The power of Western countries was predicated on their being nation-states, but China was ruled by Manchus which violated the first principle governing the myth of nation-states. That is, the Qing may have controlled the state, but they were not part of the Han nation no matter how "Chinese" they had become. This was evidenced in the Qing military which was composed of two distinct armies—the hereditary Manchu Banner and the Chinese Green Standard forces. While the Banner forces may have been tied to the Qing state through shared nationality and while the Green Standard forces had been developed upon "more impersonal, bureaucratic organizational features that would normally be considered more 'modern' and hence more, effective,"[1] they proved themselves to be totally ineffective in dealing with the Taiping Rebellion (1850–64) because the Banner forces had become indolent and the Green Standard forces corrupt.[2] The Taipings were defeated by regional armies (yongying) that were "bound together by a chain of consciously promoted personal loyalties and local ties."[3]

Li Hongzhang, the leader of the yongying, Huai Army, was assigned the task of transforming the Qing dynasty's military into a single, cohesive organization. Thus, the Beiyang Navy and the Beiyang Army were created.[4] Yet, these Qing-initiated reforms were limited to North China's military, and their effectiveness was put to the test during the First Sino-Japanese War (1894–95) which was fought for suzerainty over Korea. Both Korea and Japan had traditionally been tributary states of China, but the modernized military forces of Meiji Japan destroyed the Beiyang Navy and defeated the Beiyang Army.[5] Nonetheless, the Beiyang Army remained the strongest military force in China; however, the Boxer Rebellion (1900–1901) and the Russo-Japanese War (1904–5), which was fought on Chinese territory, forced the Qing government to make some tangible reforms that, through unintended consequences, would hasten its collapse.

Transforming China's educational "system" became the first priority, but the full ramifications of this reform could not have been anticipated. For centuries the study of the Confucian classics had been the glue that bound Chinese society and government together. Unlike Europe, China did not practice primogeniture—all sons inherited the family's land equally. This meant that unless a family had some means to increase its holdings, a successful family could be driven to destitution within a few generations. Further, the most rational way for a family to increase its wealth, and hence its landholdings, was through business, but the prevailing Confucian social structure, which was based upon the contribution of productive labor a particular social group made to the overall society, placed merchants at the bottom of the social hierarchy because they produced nothing tangible. The only way out of this situation was through the nonhereditary mandarinate. Entrance into the governmental bureaucracy was based, in theory, upon a meritocratic system that was predicated upon one's knowledge of the Confucian classics. One progressed up the bureaucratic hierarchy by passing exams at the local, provincial, and "national" levels. Even those who failed at the lowest level were educated men who could read and write in a country where illiteracy was the norm, and as such, they served as local leaders. This educationally derived gentry "thus constituted the administrative connection between the localities and the national bureaucracy, and in that fashion served, like the bureaucracy itself, as a component of territorial integration."[6] Because of the gentry's political and social roles, Chinese society could be held together despite overwhelming differences between and among the various regions.

This mythologically meritocratic system began to change, however. As the Qing dynasty started its inevitable decay and as Western influence became more and more prevalent, membership in the gentry expanded "to include those who controlled wealth, troops, new learning, businesses and business organizations such as chambers of commerce, and professional men."[7] The educational and social system that had worked well for centuries was coming under increased pressure for several reasons. First, the Confucian educational/examination system was developed for a rural agrarian society. Admittedly, China was still predominantly rural and agrarian, but wealth and power were migrating to the urban centers, particularly the treaty ports. Second, those Chinese who were desirous of China becoming a true nation-state were inclined to view a Confucian-centered educational system as an impediment to China's ability to modernize. As the Chinese became more perceptually aware of the country's humiliations at the hands of Japan and the West, the Qing finally acquiesced to the inevitable, and the Confucian examination system was abolished in 1905.

With the abolition of the Confucian examination system, China was sailing in uncharted waters. The examination system was the compass that guided dynastic Chinese society for centuries, but its attractiveness to the society was gone. What would the role of education be in the New China? The answer for many educated young men was the New Army that arose to replace the Manchu Banner and Green Standard forces as a complement to the Beiyang Army. If the defunct examination system had served a political role by uniting the country, then the New Army unwittingly became a politicized social institution as well—only its politicization fostered Han nationalism at the expense of Manchu rule.

However as Lucien Pye has noted, Chinese nationalism existed (and continues to exist) in "a relatively contentless form."[8] The reason for this stems from the fact that historically nationalism is a component of the modern nation-state that arose in western Europe concomitantly with modernization and industrialization through the self-serving efforts of the bourgeoisie. In China the bourgeoisie was marginalized by its association with Western imperialism or by its position within the traditional Confucian social hierarchy. Whether the bourgeoisie aided the West by being a comprador class or produced for the domestic market by being a "national bourgeoisie" did not matter. The bourgeoisie's social situation was complicated by the fact that it was associated with the foreign treaty ports which, from the standpoint of the bourgeoisie, "created islands of relative security and order"[9] "where the merchants moved to escape the arbitrary interference and exactions of the Chinese authorities,"[10] but this self-induced social segregation did not help the bourgeoisie's overall social status. Thus whatever nationalistic impulse the bourgeoisie may have held, this impulse was always viewed suspiciously by the greater society because of (1) the Chinese bourgeoisie's intimate association with foreign "devils"; (2) the sense of "national" humiliation that the quasi-imperialistic, treaty port system engendered in the Chinese; and (3) the fact that the bourgeoisie chose to use this system because it benefited them economically. As Pye notes: "The roots of the tension about nationalism in China can thus be largely traced back to the treaty port system which helped create the division between the enclave cultures of coastal China, which gave dynamism to the country's modernization, and an interior China, with its claim of being the authentic China."[11] Yet for this nascent Chinese nationalism to succeed, two things had to occur: (1) China had to cease to be a Manchu colony, and (2) China had to end the imperialist enclaves created by the treaty port system.

From this brief discussion, it can be seen that Chinese nationalism was dissimilar to the form of nationalism that arose in the West. This archetypal nationalism favored democracy (as opposed to absolute monarchy); championed the country's vernacular language (as opposed to the Latin liturgy); stressed public education (as opposed to elite education); and was bourgeois in its ideology (as opposed to authoritarian, whether religious or aristocratic). Chinese nationalism, however, emphasized "anti-imperialism, which meant concentration on recovery of Chinese sovereignty, and statism, which meant the search for unity and a new state orthodoxy."[12] In a sense, western nationalism was the product of evolutionary social processes, but given its foreign origins, the ideology driving Chinese nationalism had the potential for fomenting revolutionary social change.

When the Qing dynasty fell, the Chinese faced a dilemma: What form of government would provide this "new state orthodoxy?" The decision by the nominal leaders of the revolution was that China would become a republic. The person who embodied the revolution was Sun Yat-sen who had been agitating for a revolution for decades, but while he was the acknowledged leader of the movement, he did not command enough authority to actually lead the country. Further, he believed that his Nationalist Party, the Guomindang (GMD), would provide the leadership necessary for transforming China into a liberal democracy in the future; however for the present, it was ill-prepared to control the political chaos following the loss of central authority. Consequently, Sun realized that the only person who could lead the country was Yuan Shikai, the commander of the Beiyang Army. The new provisional government agreed, and Yuan was offered the office of provisional president of the Chinese Republic in 1912.

Sun's recommendation of Yuan was predicated on three conditions: "First, Nanking [Nanjing] was to be the capital of the Republic. Second, Yuan was to come to Nanking to assume the presidency. Third, Yuan was to observe the Provisional Constitution then being drafted by the Provisional Parliament."[13] Yuan accepted the presidency, and promptly abided by none of the conditions as the Provisional Parliament voted that Yuan could be inaugurated in Beijing, the seat of Yuan's power, and that Beijing would remain the capital. This seemingly pusillanimous acquiescence on the part of the Provisional Parliament is understandable since it had little actual power to oppose the northern China based Beiyang Army, and the revolutionaries (who came primarily from southern China) saw that making Yuan the president could unify the country by joining the militaristic North to the revolutionary South.

Be careful for what you wish. Within a year, Yuan dissolved the GMD, suspended parliament, and became, in essence, the "military dictator" of China.[14] When Yuan sought to solidify his position by removing the governors of several provinces, the Second Revolution of 1913 began. In quick fashion, Yuan quelled the rebellion. "The Second Revolution therefore marked a crucial step in the militarization of politics—that is, the application of military power to achieve political ends."[15]

Yuan sought to legitimize his military dictatorship by making himself the new Chinese emperor in December 1915; however, he had misjudged his actual strength. The time for an absolute monarchy had passed, and the Anti-Monarchical War began. While Yuan's political "reforms" had changed the structure of provincial government by making the military governors more powerful than their civilian counterparts, this overturning of the republic was too much even for them. This usurpation of the government was not well received in the South and by portions of the army as well. When the Anti-Monarchical War is placed within the context of Yuan's perceived mishandling of Japan's Twenty-one Demands,[16] it can be seen that he was in an increasingly untenable position. Yuan's defeat by southern militarists forced him to abdicate in March 1916; cost the Beijing government control of Guangxi, Guangdong, Sichuan, and Hunan Provinces; and it began to lose control of Fengtian and Heilongjiang Provinces as well.[17] The Anti-Monarchical War showed that the Beiyang Army was not an invincible force, and the failure of Yuan's rule began China's devolution into warlordism.

China remained intact despite itself when in mid-1917 an attempt was made to return the last Manchu emperor, Puyi, to the throne. He "ruled" for less than two weeks, but the inherent tensions in the country reached a crisis level when the GMD-dominated parliament that was elected in 1912 refused to accept the Beijing government's desire for a new parliamentary election in 1918. Consequently, Sun formed a rival government in Guangzhou in mid-1917, and the North-South War began. While the result was inconclusive, it forced the premier to resign and caused a rift in the military cliques that had emerged within the Beiyang Army structure between those who favored a military unification of the country (the Anhui faction) and those who favored a more peaceful reunification of the country (the Zhili faction).[18] In this turmoil the strongest militarist in Manchuria,[19] Zhang Zuolin, formed, with Japanese aid, a third clique, the Fengtian faction.

The continual breakdown of political authority was not the only transformation occurring in China. The final provisions of the 1919 Paris Peace Conference humiliated the Chinese. China entered World War I on the side of the Allies in 1917 with the tacit understanding that changes in the relationship between China and the West would be forthcoming; however, this hope was dashed during the conference. Chinese concerns were, on the whole, ignored, and when Japan's seizure of the German concessions in Shandong was legitimated by the victors, the fire of social reform in China—the May Fourth Movement—was ignited.[20] As the flames of social reform spread, China was caught in an intellectual firestorm which stressed the importance of accepting "Western ideas of science and democracy" while "traditional Chinese ethics, customs, literature, history, philosophy, religion, and social and political institutions were fiercely attacked."[21] Further, the study of Western philosophical, social, and political thought was encouraged; a new, vernacular-based, mythic high culture (the "glue" that held western nation-states together) was envisioned; and the Confucian social system was attacked as an impediment to modernization and gender equality. Educational reform was seen as the key for unlocking the necessary structural changes in Chinese society because schooling is the means by which future people are socialized into a given culture and the way in which a desired corpus of knowledge is inculcated into future generations. For these reasons, nationalizing foreign schools was seen by the May Fourth generation as a crucial stage in China's quest to modernize, but the political system, by being divided into petty warlord satrapies, was incapable of fostering educational reform on a countrywide basis.

In 1920, while the May Fourth Movement was raging, warfare began between the Anhui faction and the Zhili/Fengtian factions. The Anhui faction was defeated, and it became a minor player in the ensuing warlord years. In 1922 the Zhili and Fengtian factions fought with Zhili the victor. By this time the various factions were becoming identified with their putative leaders: Fengtian was led by Zhang Zuolin and Zhili was led by Cao Kun. The Fengtian faction retreated to Manchuria and in 1924 the Second Zhi-Feng War began, but this time the result would be different. At a critical juncture the Zhili forces were betrayed by the "Christian Warlord" of northwest China, Feng Yuxiang, who occupied Beijing with his Guominjun (National People's Army) forces. A unified Zhili faction was broken in two when Cao Kun was captured. The forces of Zhili's prime military strategist, Wu Peifu, occupied Hebei and Hunan Provinces, and the forces of Zhili's other renowned militarist, Sun Chuanfang, occupied the five eastern provinces located around the lower Yangzi River. Thus, by 1926, northern China was ruled by several prominent warlords: Feng in the northwest, Zhili, and Beijing; Sun in the east; Wu in central China; Zhang in Manchuria; and Yan Xishan in Shanxi Province.[22]

Saying that warlords ruled specific provinces is not entirely accurate. Analogous to all occupation forces throughout history, warlords had direct control over cities and transportation lines, but they were not in complete control of any province. Within the provinces smaller warlords and bandits would operate within progressively smaller spheres of influence.[23] Without a central authority to monopolize the legitimate forms of "state-sanctioned" violence, the average Chinese peasant was constantly at the mercy of brigands who, regardless of the size of their forces, were always finding ways to extract money—licitly in the form of taxes and illicitly in the form of extortion—from those peasants. Further the peasants could be forced into growing cash crops, particularly opium, instead of subsistence crops in order to appease their various military overlords.[24] The rise of the warlords altered the countryside's social structure. Warlords needed money to maintain their armies, and they pressured the landlords for more; the landlords pressured the peasants, and "the traditional relationship between landlords and their tenants, which had often saddled the former with a certain degree of Confucian obligations, was overwhelmed by the new one between landlords and the military."[25]

China's increased militarization placed the GMD at a decided disadvantage. The GMD was initially a civilian political organization that grew out of Sun Yat-sen's anti-Qing organization, the Zhongguo Tongmenghui (the United League of China),[26] in 1912. Thus, by 1920, China was no longer being ruled by civilian provincial governors; rather, it was being ruled by military governors (duban) who "simply assumed top executive positions in national and provincial governments and worked through the civil administrations they inherited."[27] In this way, warlords were able to free "themselves from outside restraints on their authority."[28] With the political system inextricably linked to military might, the GMD, if it was to have any impact upon national (or regional) politics, had to become a military organization as well. In 1924 the GMD opened the Whampoa Military Academy (Huangpu Junxiao) so that the GMD could compete militarily with the warlord factions.[29] Unlike warlord armies, the GMD combined military training with political indoctrination so that the leaders of its army would be, in theory, ardent nationalists, first and militarists, second. Interestingly as the GMD sought to become a Leninist, party-led organization where its civilian elements would exercise control over its military ones, two of the remaining warlord factions sought to legitimate themselves as political organizations. Thus, Zhang Zuolin's Fengtian faction morphed into the Anguojun (the Pacify the Country Army) in late 1926 when he became the leader of the government in Beijing,[30] and Feng Yuxiang's organization became the Guominjun (the Nationalist Army) when Feng turned on the Zhili faction in 1924. Interestingly, Feng was a supporter of the aims of the GMD and this partially explains his use of

"Guomin" when naming his organization. What is noteworthy is that even as Feng and Zhang tried to legitimate their organizations as legitimate political entities, they were unable to avoid using the word "army" when renaming their factions.

As a consequence of these changes in how warlord factions "wished" to be perceived, two major alliances were formed: the Guomindang and the Guominjun versus the Anguojun and the two remaining Zhili factions. The two alliances were further separated by their ideological differences. On the one hand, the Guomindang/Guominjun alliance believed that the present state of militarized politics was "fundamentally feudalistic"; this situation was "an anachronism not to be tolerated in the age of nationalism and modernization."[31] On the other hand, the Anguojun/Zhili alliance felt that the modernizers were the "destroyers of traditional values."[32] This is how the country stood as the GMD began its Northern Expedition in 1926.

The Northern Expedition was the GMD's attempt to unify China politically by ending the social chaos wrought by warlord rule. Unlike the warlords, the GMD had an ideology and its military arm—the Nationalist Revolutionary Army (NRA) commanded by Chiang Kai-shek—was controlled, in theory, by civilian personnel. Also, the GMD was aided by a collaboration with the Chinese Communist Party (CCP) in the so-called United Front. This collaboration was never entirely successful because the CCP and the left wing of the GMD controlled the party apparatus through its Central Executive Committee (CEC), but the right wing of the GMD controlled the military.[33] Initially all went well, however. Wu Peifu's Zhili faction was defeated in its Hunan/Hubei base, and the GMD's political arm decided that Wuhan should become the new capital of China. This move was strategic on several fronts. It gave the GMD (1) "distance" from its association solely with Guangdong and Guangxi Provinces; (2) "a chance to link with revolutionary ally Feng Yuxiang in the north"; (3) "dominance over the rich middle Yangzi region"; and (4) "ready access to Beijing."[34] Its military arm decided that it would go after the provinces controlled by the remaining Zhili faction commander, Sun Chuanfang. This, too, was accomplished, and by 1927 the GMD controlled, when coupled with the areas under Guominjun rule, most of China. At this point the inherent contradictions in the relationship between the CEC and the NRA became seriously strained.

The strain ruptured on April 12, 1927, when NRA members, aided by members of Shanghai's underworld, destroyed the political power of the CCP and its labor union supporters through murder and terror.[35] This army-led assault on the United Front caused the Wuhan government to brand Chiang a counterrevolutionary and strip him of his offices.[36] Chiang's response: he set up an alternative government in Nanjing on April 18. At this point the GMD had three separate governments in existence: (1) the left-

GMD, CEC-led government of Wang Jingwei in Wuhan; (2) the right-GMD, Chiang-led government in Nanjing; and (3) "the extreme right-wing Western Hills faction" in Shanghai.[37]

At this point the CEC decided to continue the Northern Expedition by sending its best troops toward Beijing in May. The Wuhan GMD's fight with the remnants of Wu Peifu's army and the Anguojun was fierce, and the fighting reached its decisive juncture at Zhengzhou, Henan Province, the "critical railway junction and gateway to the north."[38] At this point, Feng Yuxiang did to the Wuhan forces what he had done to Wu Peifu's forces in 1924: he sold them out when he sided with Chiang's Nanjing government by "suggesting" to the Wuhan government that its "Russian advisers be sent home, and that those Wuhan leaders who wished to go abroad for a rest should do so."[39] By mid-June, all were in agreement—Feng, and the governments in Wuhan, Nanjing, and Shanghai—"the workers, peasants, and Communists had to be crushed."[40]

With the United Front destroyed, the NRA began its move north against the remaining forces of Sun Chuanfang and the Anguojun. The campaign was a military disaster, and Chiang, instead of strengthening his position, was forced to resign as head of the NRA in August. He then went to Shanghai for some rest and recuperation, and thence to Japan where he became engaged to Song Meiling.[41] Thus in September, representatives from the three competing GMD governments met and "established a new, supposedly unified, Nationalist government at Nanjing."[42] But this government was far from united as the head of the Wuhan CEC-led government, Wang Jingwei, and the founder of the Nanjing right-GMD-led government, Chiang Kai-shek, were not included in it. By excluding the most important political figure and the most important military figure in the GMD, the government was inherently unstable, and it collapsed in January 1928. In February Chiang was recalled from his forced retirement, was named the new chairman of the CEC, and was reinstalled as the commander of the NRA. In October he became the chairman of the State Council. "He now controlled all three legs of the Nationalists' triad of power—the party, government, and military."[43] At this point, Nationalist China began to become a military dictatorship. Reinvigorated under Chiang's unchallenged leadership, the Northern Expedition recommenced and Beijing was captured in June. Its name was changed to Beiping since Nanjing was to be the one and only capital of China. The Northern Expedition ended in December 1928 when the Anguojun, under the leadership of Zhang Xueliang, the son of Zhang Zuolin, ceded control of Manchuria's foreign relations to the Nanjing government. For the first time since the government of Yuan Shikai, China was nominally reunited.[44]

China was not as united as the perceived success of the Northern Expedition would seem to indicate. With the exception of the Zhili faction warlords, Wu Peifu and Sun Chuanfang, and Zhang Zongchang, the military governor of Shandong, most of the other pre-Northern Expedition warlords remained in power because they had sworn allegiance to Chiang's Nationalist government in one form or another. As a consequence China was still ruled by five major warlords. First, Chiang controlled the provinces of Zhejiang, Anhui, Jiangsu, and Jiangxi. Second, Feng Yuxiang controlled the provinces of Gansu, Henan, and Shaanxi. Third, Yan Xishan continued to control Shanxi as well as Suiyuan and Zhili. Fourth, Zhang Xueliang controlled the Manchurian provinces of Heilongjiang, Fengtian, and Jilin (Kirin).[45] Fifth, the Guangxi faction controlled Guangxi, Guangdong, and large portions of Hunan and Hubei Provinces.[46] Since these warlords had little to lose from joining the government and much to lose by not joining the government, it is hard to say whether the Nationalist Revolution coopted the warlords or the warlords coopted the Nationalist Revolution. In the end, China had a new, Nanjing-based government that was recognized as legitimate by the rest of the world and the government was more unified than it had ever been since the founding of the republic in 1912. All it took was the advent of a military dictatorship; however, "the regime remained weak and unstable" due to the fact that it lacked a direct link to the greater society.[47] Chiang's Nationalist Party came to power by being "the champion of anti-warlordism, anti-imperialism, nationalism, responsible government, and the people's livelihood." [48]

Chiang's government would be judged on how well it delivered on the principles it championed. It was not an auspicious beginning for Chiang's rule since residual warlordism continued, even if its status had been transformed from being "illicit" into being "licit," and foreign imperialism remained.[49] Regionalism still trumped nationalism. Hence if the Nationalists were going to have any measure of success, then they needed to create an honest government and improve the lives of the average Chinese peasant. These two goals would not be easy to accomplish because graft was endemic to Chinese politics and the GMD's lack of a social base meant that its authority did not extend down to the local level.

Nevertheless, the new Nationalist government began on a high anti-imperialist note. Foreign-run schools would become part of the emerging Nationalist education system. China would no longer have two separate educational systems—the state-run public schools and the foreign-run missionary schools. This was more of a psychological boost for China's self-image than it was a blow to foreign imperialism because missionary schools were easy targets. The government never considered challenging foreign control of the treaty ports or challenging the status quo in the countryside. If the initial successes of the CCP in organizing the peasants during the United Front were any indication of the level of peasant discontent in the countryside, then this fact was irrelevant to Chiang's Nationalist government.[50]

The Nationalists' inability to deal with problems of land tenure was only one of many issues they failed to address. The GMD's principal failing involved corruption because party "membership carried privileges rather than obligations."[51] Joining the government bureaucracy in order to "line one's pockets" has a long history in China, but with the Nationalists speaking about anti-imperialism and modernization, the government was not supposed to perpetuate the level of graft that pervaded dynastic China. At a certain level it is hard to separate the ends desired by governmental functionaries from the self-serving means they employed. Policies would be formulated; yet, nothing would happen save an increase in the wealth of the government's bureaucrats. In the end, the government reflected Chiang's rule where he was "hegemonial, but not all-powerful, and to maintain and increase his hegemony he used the same combination of violence and manipulation that other warlord leaders had employed."[52]

By 1929 Chiang's government was in trouble. By not eliminating warlords during the Northern Expedition, the same problems that plagued the government during the republic continued to exist. Thus, in 1930, Feng Yuxiang and Yan Xishan went to war against the government in the Central Plains War when Chiang tried to accomplish what the Northern Expedition had failed to do—limit their power. The war lasted almost a year, resulted in more than a quarter of a million casualties, and bankrupted the Nationalist government. It only ended when the last of the great warlords, Zhang Xueliang, threw his support to the Nationalist government. The government was still in disarray when disgruntled members of the GMD tried to establish an alternative government in Guangdong in 1931. A civil war was averted when the Japanese invaded Manchuria following the September Eighteenth Incident (the Mukden Incident) where putative Chinese terrorists were accused of dynamiting a section of Japan's South Manchurian Railway. Who was ultimately responsible for the action may never be known, but using it as their justification for invasion was a strategic move by the Japanese since most of Zhang's forces were still outside Manchuria due to their participation in the Central Plains War.[53] For Chiang the result was the same as it had been in 1927: he was forced into retirement due to his handling of the war, but just as his earlier retirement had been short-lived, this one was, too, as he was brought back into the government in January 1932. The new, civilian-led government was headed by Chiang's old GMD adversary, Wang Jingwei, but given the seriousness of China's situation vis-à-vis Japan, actual power was vested in Chiang as head of the Military Affairs Commission.[54]

Chiang used his forced retirement to draw some serious conclusions about governing China. First and foremost, he came to the realization that China needed a supreme leader. Chiang made his view manifest in 1933 when he stated: "The most important point of fascism is absolute trust in a sagely, able leader. Aside from complete trust in one person, there is no other leader or ism."[55] Further, China would emulate the Brown Shirts of Hitler and the Black Shirts of Mussolini by establishing its own group of Blue Shirts as Chiang sought to militarize Chinese society from top to bottom.[56] While Sun Yat-sen believed the Nationalist Party should be the paramount group in Chinese society, Chiang gave supremacy to the army.[57] He was also intent upon modifying the structure of Chinese society to fit his new fascist tendencies by promulgating the New Life Movement.

The New Life Movement was an attempt to forge an amalgam out of several disparate elements. Confucianism would be a critical element because if one wanted to find "the means of insuring social stability and popular discipline . . . [then] Confucianism was the most effective and cheapest means ever devised by man for this purpose."[58] The May Fourth Movement may have sought to destroy Confucianism as a vestige of China's premodern past, but it is very difficult to undo a centuries-old philosophy that has at its core an unconditional acceptance of authority. While Sun had proposed the Sanmin Zhuyi, Chiang devised four equally vague Confucian-like virtues for the New Life Movement: *li* (propriety); *yi* (justice); *lian* (honesty); and *chi* (sense of self-respect).[59] Christianity would also be part of the New Life Movement, but it appears that Chiang's Christianity was heavily influenced by somewhat bastardized Calvinist principles. Thus, he "was convinced that immorality was the cause of economic poverty rather than vice versa,"[60] and as a consequence, why should the state seek to ameliorate the social conditions confronting the poor? For all its Christian-tinged moral preachments, for all its attempts to fuse Chinese Confucianism to western fascism, and for all its professed desire to modernize China, the New Life Movement failed to address China's most pressing social condition—the economic plight of the peasantry. Further, it continued China's long historical antipathy toward its mercantile class—the one class that had modernizing tendencies.[61]

Following the destruction of its urban base in Shanghai, the CCP retreated into the countryside where it had great success in mobilizing with the peasants. Thus, there was a clear distinction between the approaches taken by the GMD and the CCP for politically organizing the country. Chiang's GMD increasingly held the line of "one faith, one party, one will";[62] Mao's CCP adhered to the same type of philosophy but with two major differences. The first difference dealt with political ideology: fascism versus communism; the second difference dealt with organizing principles: top down versus bottom up.[63] Thus, the two parties took decidedly different perspectives on dealing with the peasantry. Further, Chiang's fixation with eradicating the CCP also affected his rule. Focusing on the CCP meant that the Nationalist government was less concerned about Japanese incursions into Chinese territory than any true nation-state would ever countenance. This lack of concern belied the party's supposed "nationalist" aspirations.

In some ways the invasion of Manchuria in 1931 and the creation of Manzhouguo in 1932 can be understood by the fact that China's Northeast was not considered an integral part of Han China. When Japan invaded Rehe Province and part of Hebei Province in 1933, the same sort of justification could have been used. After all, these areas were north of the Great Wall—the dividing line used by the first Chinese emperor to separate the civilized Han from the barbarian Xiongnu tribes. Nonetheless, the Nationalist government fought against the better armed and trained Japanese Guandong Army.[64] Defeat was inevitable, and the subsequent Tanggu Truce again made the Great Wall the dividing line between the Tungusic North, Manzhouguo, and the Han South, China.

The increasing intrusions toward Han-occupied territory make Chiang's fixation on eradicating the CCP seem somewhat misplaced. After its decimation in Shanghai, its abandonment by the left GMD, and its pariah standing within Chinese political circles, the CCP retreated to Jiangxi Province where it established the Jiangxi Soviet, nominally modeled along Bolshevik lines. Beginning in 1930 Chiang sought to eliminate the "communist menace" through the first of a series of encirclement campaigns where the Nationalist Army attempted to surround the Jiangxi Soviet before crushing it. This method was also attempted from the second through fourth encirclement campaigns of 1931–32. Beginning in 1933, a new encirclement technique was employed that used the building of blockhouses around the Communist positions. When these were in place, a new smaller ring of blockhouses was then constructed. The process was long and expensive but as 1934 drew to a close, the Communists were on the verge of defeat. While Mao favored having the army slip out of the encirclement in small groups, the consensus view was that the Communists should fight their way out. The breakout was successful, but it occurred at a tremendous cost in men and matériel. Thus, the famed Long March from the Jiangxi Soviet to Yan'an in Shaanxi Province began.[65]

The small remnant of the CCP that finally reached Yan'an in October 1935 was still being pursued by the GMD. Soon after its arrival in Yan'an, Chiang sent his Northwest Army under Yang Hucheng and his Northeast Army under Zhang Xueliang to eradicate them once and for all. Ironically, Yang and Zhang were impressed by the tenacity of the Communists, and they concluded that joining with the CCP to fight the Japanese was a far wiser position for the GMD to take. When Chiang went to Xi'an, Shanxi Province, in December 1936 to find out why the military campaign had not succeeded, Zhang and Yang kidnapped him and forced him into agreeing to form a Second United Front with the Communists.[66]

Forming a Second United Front was becoming a matter of necessity. Japan was not content having a singular puppet regime in Manzhouguo. Japan also tried to foment rebellion and secession in the Mongol-majority areas of North China. Thus, the Guandong Army occupied eastern Qahar in 1935 and annexed it to Manzhouguo. It "encouraged and helped secession-minded Mongol princes to establish a North Chahar-based government claiming sovereignty over Chahar [Qahar], Suiyuan, and [Ningxia] (1936); and sponsored, equipped, and officered a full-scale military expedition into Suiyuan (1936)."[67] Again, these were not Han-majority areas where the Japanese were exercising their military superiority, but this situation was about to end.

On July 7, 1937, the Marco Polo Bridge (Lugouqiao) Incident began the War of Resistance Against the Japanese. The war highlighted all of the problems that Chiang's leadership entailed. China's conscript army was ill-prepared for war. Soldiers were badly trained and treated worse. Chiang favored graduates of the Whampoa Military Academy to officers who had been trained elsewhere. Corruption was rife as "each division and army was treated as independent."[68] What this meant was that troop "strength measured the wealth of the commanding general and determined not just his military status but also his political stature."[69] Funds were provided to the armies based upon their troop strength which was seldom corroborated. The potential for graft pervaded the system. Thus, commanders were unwilling to go into battle because casualties would diminish the amount that they could "squeeze" from the government's allotment since how the funds were disbursed was at their discretion; worse, defeat could result in a commander's army being disbanded. This act would, in turn, cause a drastic loss in personal income and prestige.

When war began, the Nationalist Army, though numerically superior to the Guandong Army, was at a decided disadvantage, and within no time the Japanese had conquered large swaths of Chinese territory. This does not mean to say that the Chinese did not fight bravely nor does it mean to say that individual Chinese armies did not perform well in battle.[70] What it does say is that China, despite almost a century of continuous warfare, encountered military, economic, social, and political events that were unprecedented. Militarily, the War of Resistance Against the Japanese was an example of the total war brought about by the development of the modern nation-state. In total war there are no civilians, and Japan took this belief to heart, particularly in its serious mistreatment of noncombatants in Nanjing and Jiujiang. As such, it employed the modern tools of war on what was primarily a premodern society. Economically, the "Japanese might not hold much of the region, but they did dominate its modern economy, its commerce, its cultural world, and its transport."[71] That is, the Japanese, like the warlords before them, controlled the cities and transportation lines of the most developed provinces in China. Further, Nationalist monetary policies contributed to rampant inflation as the war dragged on. This was in marked contrast to the Communist-held areas where the economic situation was relatively stable. Socially, the "Japanese invasion disrupted all of the densely populated parts of China."[72] According to figures cited by Stephen MacKinnon, over one-quarter of China's population, some ninety-five million people, became internal refugees between 1937 and 1945.[73] The gist of this is that although the Japanese did not actually control much Chinese territory, their invasion resulted in a vast movement of people. In many ways this internal migration challenged the regional nature of Chinese society and it also challenged the extant landlord-controlled rural social structure, particularly in the Communist-held areas where land reform was instituted. Politically, the nature of the government changed. The Nationalists—the leaders of "Free China"—controlled Sichuan (where Chongqing became the capital following the evacuation of Wuhan in 1938), Guizhou, Yunnan, and Xikang Provinces.[74] Although real power was vested in their Japanese overlords, the collaborationist government of Chiang Kai-shek's longtime GMD opponent, Wang Jingwei, oversaw more provinces than the Nationalists did. While it will not be seen on too many maps, the Communists controlled a fair portion of China as well. Further, in the interstices between these "spheres of influence" existed a kind of no-man's-land where guerrilla (or bandit) activity predominated.[75]

After 1938 the situation in China remained fairly stable as the Japanese "chose not to pursue the Nationalist government into Sichuan and turned their attention to expanding their grip on the north (and fighting Soviet Russia for control of Mongolia in 1939)."[76] Outer Mongolia (or the Mongolian People's Republic after 1924) was a client state of the Soviet Union. When they invaded Mongolia, the Japanese discovered that the Soviet Army they encountered was not analogous to the Tsarist Army they had so easily defeated in Manchuria in 1904–5; rather, "six months of fighting between the [Guandong] Army and the Soviet Red Army (along with their respective puppet troops) culminated in a resounding Japanese defeat in September 1939."[77] With this defeat, the Japanese bided their time in China as they sought to expand their Greater East Asia Co-prosperity Sphere. As such, occupied China was a great contributor to the Japanese war effort; however, as U.S. Army Air Corps campaigns began to affect Japan's increasingly precarious military position, the war in China drastically changed in 1944.[78]

In March, Japan launched its "do-or-die Operation ICHIGO."[79] Initially the Japanese offensive was impressive, another three provinces fell under partial Japanese control before the Chinese lines held.[80] In this case the brunt of the fighting was borne by the Nationalist Army which could not sit idly by as it had been wont to do. Strategically, Operation ICHIGO was fought for nought. In June B-29 Superfortresses, based near Chengdu in Sichuan Province, began bombing Japan. Thus while most of the Allied bases were in south-central China, the one that actually mattered to Japan's homeland security was not.[81] By mid-August the United States occupied the Mariana Islands, and the U.S. Army Air Corps no longer needed bases in China as a means for launching bombing raids on Japan.

When World War II finally ended, the situation in China was far different from what it had been prior to the war. While the "Nationalist government used the war years to win important diplomatic concessions, including the ending of the unequal treaty regime (1943) and formal recognition as a Great Power (1944),"[82] its army was demoralized, it had failed to address the issue of land tenure, and its economic failings had bankrupted the people in the areas it controlled. The Communists had "concentrated their efforts on the political organization of the areas behind Japanese lines,"[83] and in doing so, won the undying gratitude of the peasant masses. When the Civil War began, the Communists were in an enviable position: the PLA was disciplined and respectful of the Chinese people,[84] the CCP was perceived as incorruptible, and the promulgation of land reform won over the peasantry to the Communist cause. Mao declared the founding of the People's Republic of China (PRC) on October 1, 1949, and by 1950 the Civil War was over as the Nationalist forces fled to Taiwan. It only took the rest of the world until October 25, 1971, when the PRC gained China's seat in the United Nations, to officially recognize the fact that the Communists won the Civil War.

Appendix B: An American Context

IN 1893 FREDERICK JACKSON TURNER DELIVERED A PAPER TO THE AMERICAN Historical Association on "The Significance of the Frontier in American Life."[1] According to Turner the ever-present frontier created the conditions that fostered "America's unique and true democracy."[2] From their flouting of George III's Proclamation Line of 1763, Americans had pushed the frontier across the continent, "decade after decade, West after West."[3] Yet, the Census Bureau reported in 1890 that a "frontier line" no longer existed; the forty-four states that comprised the United States had been settled. Readily available land—"the life blood of American democracy"[4]—could no longer be had.[5]

Whether or not one accepts this view of American exceptionalism, the fact remains that in the decades surrounding the start of the twentieth century, the United States was undergoing significant, and frequently unwanted, social change. America was becoming a primarily urban country as industrialization and immigration occurred at unprecedented levels. The Jeffersonian ideal of a democracy of yeomen farmers was becoming more and more a country where industrial proletarians were the largest labor segment of the population. Further, these new immigrants did not come from the "usual stock" of the American "race." Rather than being northern and western Europeans of Protestant descent, they were southern and eastern Europeans of Catholic and Jewish descent. The net effect of immigration, urbanization, and industrialization on the American cultural and social milieu was monumental. Victorian gender relations were challenged; the status of farmers and small businessmen was transformed; and Protestantism was undergoing a crisis. As such, these cultural and social changes had consequences for the missionary movement.

From its inception the United States had been an agrarian country. Thus in 1790, farming accounted for 90 percent of the labor force in the United States, but by 1880 the number had dropped to 49 percent.[6] Yet, the Great American Plains were just beginning to be cultivated and the frontier remained open, but farmers were in trouble. How could this be? The Jeffersonian myth of American social equality was based on the idealization of the yeoman farmer where "independence, self-reliance, and individual moral responsibility [were] based on the economic rewards of individual productive work."[7] This myth resonated as long as farmers were engaged in subsistence agriculture that was supplemented by income gained through small-scale commercial farming, and this situation had existed for over one hundred years.

Despite an open frontier, "land prices and production costs rose sharply" in the 1880s.[8] As economic rewards increased, farmers began to transform their agricultural production from a combination of subsistence agriculture and small-scale commercial farming to larger-scale commercial farming. It made sense. Cities were growing through industrialization and immigration, and when accompanied by the burgeoning number of railroad lines, it meant that farmers had both the means and the markets to sell their products. Hence a verdict on American agriculture was handed down: self-sufficiency was out; full-scale commercial agriculture was in. The consequences were not what farmers anticipated. They now had to deal with the vicissitudes of being actively involved in a full-fledged market economy.[9]

Once farmers became thoroughly engaged in commercial agriculture, they were no longer self-sufficient, and they were also chronically in debt. Farmers live on futures. The financial rewards gained for selling a crop are used to pay off the costs incurred in sowing that crop. Thus many agrarians believed that if monetary policies were enacted that caused inflation by devaluing the currency, then the banknotes held on a farm could be paid off with cheap money. But the government maintained the gold standard, farmers suffered economically, and agrarian discontent surfaced most noticeably during the Populist Movement of the late 1880s and 1890s.

Populists were not opposed to capitalism. After all, farmers were in business to make money, but increasingly they saw that their world was being impinged upon by the economic and political evils embodied in "plutocracy." The corporate capitalism represented by "railroad companies, banks, mortgage companies, and middlemen"[10] was crushing the "proprietary, competitive capitalism"[11] represented by farmers. This form of small-scale, entrepreneurial capitalism had been the glue that bound American society together since its inception; however, farmers were now fighting a rear-guard action against the forces of modernity in a battle they could not win on the national level. But they continued to fight up through the presidential elections of 1892 and 1896 where the Populists' "People's Party" garnered twenty-two and twenty-seven electoral votes respectively.[12]

Populists, therefore, did not object to capitalism per se, but they objected to its new, corporate form that was steamrolling small, independent producers. While the Populists were ultimately unsuccessful in getting a majority of Americans to accept their political positions, they used the most powerful motivational tool they could—the language of Protestant evangelical culture—to articulate their grievances.[13] For Populists, the ever-increasing disparities in wealth threatened to rend the fabric of American society,[14] and they "called for the purification of capitalism and the revitalization of democracy"[15] in religious terms. The Populists were faced with a conundrum regarding capitalism. The Calvinist roots for so many of America's Protestant churches had long held that a relationship existed between financial success and heavenly election, and commercial agriculture had created "a new test by which the farmer had to judge himself—the test of business success."[16] Since capitalism should not or could not be eliminated, it needed to be changed. Ultimately, the Populist response was vaguely analogous to the programs espoused by European Christian Democratic parties: certain industries should be nationalized and others should be more tightly regulated for the sake of the commonweal.

Interestingly, Populism had little impact on industrial labor which was engaged in its own battles with the "monied interests." The term "Gilded Age" has been used to describe the transformation of American society following the Civil War and the institutionalization of modern corporate capitalism. This age was characterized by increasingly violent clashes between capitalists, whose tremendous wealth was generated through the triad of railroads, industry, and finance, and labor whose equally tremendous poverty was increasingly evident in their miserable working conditions and the squalor of ever-growing urban slums. Captains of industry were portrayed as enjoying unprecedented wealth made possible by corruption and exploitation, while the reality for millions of ordinary people was chronic under/unemployment and abject poverty. In response to unfettered capitalism, labor organizations bubbled up, leading to a wellspring of violent clashes where labor was at a decided economic, political, and military disadvantage.

Despite the fact that both farmers and proletarians were being adversely affected by the forces of industrialization, they had little in common socially, culturally, economically, and politically. Couching the Populist Movement in the language of Protestant evangelical culture did not resonate with the ever-growing number of non-Protestant industrial workers, and anything that would raise farm income by increasing the cost of food was anathema to cash-starved, urban residents. The lack of a common ground between the two groups can be seen in the ratification of the Eighteenth Amendment, Prohibition, in 1919. Knowing that the census of 1920 would make urban, "wet" areas more politically powerful than rural, "dry" ones, Protestant evangelicals were able to make one last, symbolic statement that American culture was a Protestant culture, even though that assertion was no longer applicable.[17]

If Populism was the rural, agrarian response to the growth of urban, industrial America, then Progressivism was the response of the "new middle class."[18] As with Populism, Progressivism "never really existed as a recognizable organization with common goals and a political machinery geared to achieve them."[19] According to Daniel T. Rodgers, Progressivism involved "three languages of discontent, the first was the rhetoric of antimonopolism, the second was an emphasis on social bonds and the social nature of human beings, and the third was the language of social efficiency."[20]

Progressive antimonopolism was, in many ways, the immediate successor to Populism's attempt to regulate big business in a more effective manner than the Sherman Antitrust Act of 1890 was able to do. While farmers could sense that some nebulous force was making their existence far more tenuous than its mythic role in the success of America should indicate, Progressives came from the group of urban individuals who sought to organize their fields of endeavor into what we now consider professions such as medicine, law, and education. Thus, Progressives, too, were capitalists at heart, but graft, corruption, and plutocracy directly or indirectly affected their bottom lines. Further, they were not political outsiders the way Populists were. So while Populists could initially call for the direct election of senators, the adoption of an eight-hour day, and the creation of a graduated income tax to virtually no effect, Progressives would get these goals accomplished as well as other "good government" programs such as the initiative, the referendum, and the recall.

The language of social bonds was the link that joined Progressivism to Protestantism. Three views concerning the "proper" role for Protestantism manifested themselves during this period—orthodox, socialist, and progressive—described by historian Henry May, as "conservative," "radical," and "progressive" social Christianity.[21] Those who adhered to the "conservative," or fundamentalist Protestant, form recognized the existence of social problems but amelioration of them was couched more in "individualistic, voluntaristic social reform movements."[22] Thus, proponents of this orthodox expression tended to promote social solutions that supported working within existing social structures to rehabilitate rather than to totally replace them. At the other extreme was "radical social Christianity" (supported by individuals who frequently referred to themselves as "Christian socialists") which argued that the laissez-faire approach of those espousing the orthodox position could do nothing to ameliorate the country's social problems. What was needed was a massive reconstruction of society creating a totally different social order. Christian socialists argued that the conservative response did little to address the institutional basis of social injustice wrought by corporate capitalism. As a consequence, a dramatic reformation was needed, but Christian socialists fell far short of advocating the radical revolution championed by Communists. Instead, their solutions recommended the creation of stronger federal intervention and the generation of new institutions that would address the nation's social ills. Somewhere in the center was "progressive social Christianity." Adherents of this position recognized the radicals' contention that the "salvation of society would require institutional as well as personal changes" but advocated "combining a call for social action with an emphasis on the importance of the individual, his rights and responsibilities."[23] It was this particular variant with which the Social Gospel was most associated.[24] Thus, the Social Gospel promoted social responsibility on an individual and on a social level through active social participation. Immigration and urbanization not only changed the face of America, but they combined to produce levels of urban poverty and squalor previously unheard of in the United States. Some form of social amelioration was needed; however, Social Gospel adherents believed that substantive social change could not take place through the individualistic nature of fundamentalist Protestantism and further, it could not take place through a total transformation of the social order. Many religious figures came to hold that Protestant beliefs needed to be socialized to include the whole of society. Underlying the Social Gospel was a belief in the "immanence of God, a conception derived from the influence of science—Darwinian evolution in particular—upon Protestant theology."[25] As such, divine judgment was "to be passed, not upon individual men only, but also upon the collective institutions which men have made."[26] Inherent in Social Gospel thought then, was the belief "that the Christian faith [viz., American Protestantism], though addressed to individuals, had social implications; that the church in its corporate capacity must deal with social issues; that socialism could not be ignored; and that positive social change must come through gradual, nonviolent means, among others."[27] These were noble goals to be sure, but this phase of the Progressive movement suffered from the sort of hubris that underlies most progressive movements. In this case "the assumption that the middle class served as a model of Christianity to be assimilated by others reinforced the middle-class sense of being the best people in the most civilized nation."[28] Thus Social Gospel ideology neither held purchase with the wealthy nor sway with the working class.[29]

In its religious guise the Social Gospel "had helped promote powerful conceptions of Christian service and example as valid modes of evangelization."[30] Until the advent of the Social Gospel, evangelism in the United States was seen solely through the lens of personal salvation. The consequences of this transformation were threefold. First, the Social Gospel became inextricably linked to Progressivism's "language of social bonds." Second, by making service an important component of evangelism, the religious message was secularized in ways that Social Gospel adherents could never have imagined.[31] Third, the Social Gospel "refused to choose between faith and reason."[32] As such the Social Gospel was irrevocably linked to Protestantism in a country that was more and more non-Protestant,[33] and as such, the equation that being an American meant being a Protestant had less and less validity.

The Social Gospel was concerned with social conditions within the United States and was decidedly postmillennial in its thought. That is: Postmillennialism is "the faith that the kingdom of God would be realized in this world; justice, peace and love would eventually reign supreme."[34] As Charles Howard Hopkins and William R. Hutchison point out, the Social Gospel was, for all its heaven-on-earth rhetoric, a militantly Protestant doctrine. Since Christians had the "right of conquest"[35] in evangelizing the world, Social Gospel adherents were "not concerned with the problems of war, imperialism, race, democracy, or the use of force."[36] In being religious and cultural chauvinists, the followers of the Social Gospel had much in common with Protestant fundamentalism's "Christian soldiers." Further Social Gospel adherents had not intentionally withdrawn from social reform nor been drawn wittingly into "beliefs about biblical inerrancy and premillennial dispensationalism"[37] the way that fundamentalists had. Nonetheless, World War I subverted the faith portion of Social Gospel Progressives' linking of faith with reason, and as such, it made Social Gospel Progressivism irrelevant throughout the 1920s.

Reason, however, was used to undergird the third language of Progressivism—social efficiency, and this is where Progressivism had its greatest impact on American society. America in the 1920s was suffering from a "religious depression."[38] The Espionage Act of 1917, the Sedition Act of 1918, and the Palmer Raids of 1919–21 effectively ended radical social Christianity in the United States. The faith component of the liberal theology of the Social Gospel, itself, was seriously wounded during World War I, but its Janus-faced twin, reason, in the guise of efficiency, survived unscathed. This situation had two noticeable consequences. "First, the strong identification of businessmen with good government and economic reforms for which the general public also had a lively concern helped preserve the good reputation of the middle-class business community . . . and helped to direct the energies of the progressive movement toward the strengthening instead of the shackling of the business community."[39] Thus a movement that began as an attempt to control the excesses of corporate capitalism became one of its major supporters. Second, as a trenchant commentator on American society stated: "America has become almost hopelessly enamoured of a religion that is little more than sanctified commercialism; it is hard in this day and this land to differentiate between religious aspiration and business prosperity. Our conception of God is that he a sort of Magnified Rotarian. . . . effiency has become the greatest of Christian virtues."[40] Further, "efficiency, rationalization, and social engineering [viz., eugenics],"[41] were, for better or worse, nonsectarian, and the tie that bound Protestantism to Progressivism was broken.

The roots of this gradual secularization of the Social Gospel can be seen as early as the Men and Religion Forward Movement of 1911 and 1912 whose motto could have been: "The women have had charge of the church work long enough."[42] The change from entrepreneurial capitalism to corporate capitalism had gender consequences for America. The Victorian gender system was based upon a clear delineation between males and females. Unlike today where we tend to view gender as a socially constructed role, Victorian gender roles were seen as immutable and God given, but American Victorians did not distinguish between a purely public space for men and a purely private space for women. Both men and women had prescribed, "separate but equal" public spheres in which to operate. Thus, men operated in the competitive sphere of business and politics; while women operated in the noncompetitive sphere of religion and morality.[43] But just as "separate but equal" did not work in terms of American race relations, it did not work for gender as well. As entrepreneurial capitalism succumbed to corporate capitalism, gender "verities" could not remain unassailable. As the male gender role of the entrepreneur became redefined into that of the corporate manager, the competitive nature of the male social realm likewise needed to be redefined. If men were losing their Victorian identity to social change and if gender was becoming less a matter of destiny and more a matter of role, then, in a patriarchal America, it was the gender role for women that had to be transformed to meet this new reality. Thus the Protestant church, which "began to seem sissified and effeminate"[44] as Victorian gender constructions ceased to be functional, would become a male bastion in the new Protestantism that was emerging out of the gender anxieties of early twentieth-century American men. Women would still be in charge of morality, but it would be confined to "the most sacred institution in the middle-class world: the family."[45] The feminized Protestantism of Victorian "producerist society" would become the manly Protestantism of the "new, consumerist world,"[46] a world which spoke a "language of virility, militarism, and Christian heroism."[47] Ironically, "many more men turned out for the social service lectures and programs than they did for the traditional evangelism or Bible study"[48] during the Men and Religion Forward Movement, but the goals of the movement were ultimately successful in the 1920s. Protestantism became more "manly," and the role of women in Protestant churches and missionary endeavors was ultimately curtailed.

What is equally interesting about the Men and Religion Forward Movement was that it was launched as an evangelical attempt at fostering the individual salvation of men, but like so many things in the world, its unintended consequences were more significant than its intended consequences. As previously mentioned, the Social Gospel components were more welcomed by the attendees of the movement's rallies. Yet, fundamentalist evangelicals, who were more interested in saving souls, tended to be openly hostile to the social reforms advocated by the followers of the Social Gospel. Thus, Protestantism was split: "In general, conservatives defined themselves as supporting evangelism but not social action, and liberals defined themselves as supporting social action but not evangelism."[49] Further, these two Protestant factions tended to split upon premillennialist and postmillennialist lines. Premillennialists, May's conservative social Christians, were "prone to see history spiraling into chaos and destruction before Jesus' return."[50] Thus, this dispensationalist-inspired fundamentalism "combined biblicist, generally Calvinist orthodoxy, an evangelistic spirit, an emphasis on the higher Christian (Holy Spirit directed) life and a millenarian eschatology."[51] Postmillennialists, May's progressive social Christians, "believed that the millennium had already come and that their job was to begin building the Kingdom then and there."[52]

Both Protestant factions were alarmed by the social and cultural changes that were occurring in the country. Whereas the conservative fundamentalists revered a Victorian ideology where women were viewed "as the pure and chaste guardians of public morality,"[53] the liberal "modernists" were no less concerned about women "getting professional educations, moving into the white-collar work force, organizing social and political reform organizations, marching for suffrage, engaging in sex before marriage, and seeking divorces."[54] Needless to say, the social changes of the 1920s were hard on American Protestantism.

Despite Warren Harding's best intentions, the 1920s were anything but normal. The decade has been called both the Age of Intolerance and the Age of Wonderful Nonsense. On the one side, the Ku Klux Klan frighteningly reappeared, immigration became highly restrictive, and Prohibition was the law of the land; on the other side, jazz transformed popular music, the flapper helped redefine women's gender role, and consumerism became as American as apple pie. In this cultural and social maelstrom, Protestantism suffered a religious depression which was not helped by the absurdity of the so-called Scopes Monkey Trial which was broadcast live on the radio, gave a forum for the discussion of evolution, and showed fundamentalism to be both intolerant and petty. Just as World War I adversely affected Social Gospel postmillennialism, the Roaring Twenties adversely affected premillennialism. The one constant of the 1920s was the cultural hegemony of Progressivism's nonreligious language of social efficiency.

The religious depression that affected American Protestantism, when combined with its new, manly manifestation, had a major impact on the missionary movement in the 1920s. The missionary enterprise had been multifaceted. Women's organizations and missionary boards had been major components within the feminized Protestant churches of the Victorian era. However, these feminized institutions were no match for the increased rationalization of the newly masculinized churches, and this change in the structure of Protestant churches would have consequences for the missionary enterprise. Missionaries were more educated than the population in general, the majority were women, and within their ranks, they were disproportionately represented by unmarried women. Since women were denied the right of ordination, how did they fit within the missionary evangelical enterprise? The exigencies faced by women missionaries in foreign countries "had necessitated broadening the meaning of evangelism to include social service."[55] Thus, women missionaries spread the word as educators, doctors, and evangelical proselytizers through social work.[56] Clearly this view of evangelism fit within liberal Protestantism's perception of evangelizing, but with the rise of fundamentalism in the early 1920s and with the delegitimizing of the Social Gospel in the aftermath of World War I, this perspective on missionary work came under siege, which led to the collapse of the women's missionary movement. That is: "In a climate where a line was being drawn in the sand between the Bible and the ministry of women, between personal salvation and the social gospel, between evangelism and education, the woman's missionary movement stood to lose."[57] Since women made up the majority of church membership and were graduating from colleges in ever-increasing numbers and since direct evangelism was no longer the major focus of missionary work, the attempt to bring evangelism back as the primary goal of missionary work was destined to have negative repercussions, and it did. The 1929 Foreign Missions Conference of North America reported that there were fewer than one-tenth as many student volunteers in 1928 as there had been in 1920.[58]

From its inception there had been two beliefs that were considered to be crucial to women's missionary work. First, only women missionaries should interact with heathen women, particularly in cultures where these women were secluded. Second, it was held that if you converted the women, then the remainder of the society would follow suit.[59] Thus, "the family was . . . the central determinant of a civilization's openness to the Gospel, and it was women therein who held the key to the heathen family's Christian potential."[60] These views made it seem that women's evangelical work was indispensable to the overall missionary enterprise, but following World War I these beliefs fell into disfavor for both modernist and fundamentalist Protestants. Since fundamentalists believed that educational and service work were not important for missionary work and since evangelism was rightly the purview of men, fundamentalists turned their interpretation of "the Bible against the ministry of women."[61] Modernists tended to maintain the values of educational and social service, but in doing so, they subverted the religiously important element of missionary evangelism.

The principal point to keep in mind is the liberating influence that missionary work provided for women. As American Christianity became more "manly," the role for women within the churches diminished, separate women's missionary societies were incorporated within the larger church organizations, and women's interest in missionary work declined. Further as more employment opportunities opened up for educated American women within the United States, the financial independence afforded by missionary work became less of an incentive. Yet for women who were truly religious and wanted to put their faith in the Social Gospel into practice, missionary work still beckoned, and it offered a place of refuge, if only for a time, from conventional societal views regarding the status of unmarried women.[62] Thus, the evolution of American Protestantism in the decades surrounding the advent of the twentieth century, particularly in relation to women and their role in the missionary movement, provides a context for understanding the transformation of American society as well.

Notes

Introduction

1. Any work on China is faced with the persistent problem of how Chinese terms and characters should be transliterated, and this book is no exception. There are two basic systems of romanization: Wade-Giles and *pinyin*. The Wade-Giles system was first developed by Thomas Wade, a nineteenth-century British army officer who spent most of his life in China and his system was further elaborated in the late nineteenth century by Cambridge University professor Herbert Giles. The *pinyin* system was developed in the People's Republic of China during the mid-1950s. This book uses a combination of both because the archival materials and most scholarly works dealing with the Republican era used the Wade-Giles system, but I prefer the *pinyin* system. As a consequence, when names or information collected from original sources used the Wade-Giles romanization, I continue to use it throughout the text; while contemporary references use the *pinyin* system. To avoid possible confusion, the practice of using the spellings of Sun Yat-sen, Chiang Kai-shek, and Whampoa Military Academy are maintained. Also, in deference to my mother's usage, I use the Wade-Giles spelling of "Yeh" for the family surname, but for the remainder of the name, I use *pinyin*.

2. All quotations and information about Yeh Yuanshuang come from a series of interviews conducted by the author and are not referenced in the text. These interviews (many of them audiotaped) were conducted from 1982 to 2009. The information about Dorothea Wakeman Howe is from interviews conducted from 1997 to 2000, letters written by Dorothea to her parents, and archival materials (reports, correspondence, magazine articles, newsletter entries, brochures, pamphlets, mission board publications, photographs, and files from the Archives of the Episcopal Church, Austin, Texas). To be as faithful to the original sources as possible, quotations from Dorothea's letters and other archival materials use the exact language, abbreviations, misspellings, and inconsistencies that exist in the originals; therefore, the frequent use of [*sic*] in these quotations, which would significantly detract from the flow of the narrative, has been purposely omitted.

3. Dorothea Kingsley Wakeman, Wuchang, to parents, San Gabriel, California, March 28, 1934, vol. 1, China Letters and Round the World, 435, private collection of Dorothea Wakeman Howe, San Diego, California.

4. Ibid., 443–48.

5. For a look at earlier efforts to educate girls in China, see: Ida Belle Lewis, *The Education of Girls in China* (New York: Teachers College, Columbia University, 1919).

6. The cities of Wuchang, Hankou, and Hanyang became collectively known as Wuhan in 1927, but the cities continued to maintain their own, separate identities even after they were merged. For my purposes, the name Wuhan will be used for the metropolitan area regardless of the time frame being discussed.

Chapter 1. Yeh Yuanshuang

1. Hugh B. O'Neill, *Companion to Chinese History* (New York: Facts on File Publications, 1987), 369–70. Liangguang refers to the "two Guangs" which meant that the viceroy of Liangguang was the governor-general in charge of Guangdong, which included Hainan Island, and Guangxi Provinces. Following the Treaty of Nanjing (1842) which concluded the First Opium War, Western powers were permitted into five treaty ports: Shanghai, Canton (Guangzhou), Fuzhou, Amoy (Xiamen), and Ningbo. Since the West had little to offer the Chinese in terms of trade, the British created a synthetic market for opium by importing it from India through their main port, Canton. While opium was still illegal in China, the government was powerless to stop the trade. The *Arrow* Incident gave the British (and the French) the pretext they needed to even more favorably renegotiate the Treaty of Nanjing following their defeat of the Qing army.

2. Frederick Wakeman Jr., *Strangers at the Gate: Social Disorder in South China, 1839–1861* (Berkeley: University of California Press, 1966), 159–63.

3. Ibid., 163. Yeh died of starvation on April 17, 1859, because he refused to eat anything but the Chinese food he had brought with him into exile. For a biography of Yeh, see: J. Y. Wong, *Yeh Ming-ch'en: Viceroy of Liang Kuang (1852–8)* (Cambridge: Cambridge University Press, 2009 [1976]).

4. Besides the constant foreign threats, the Qing dynasty was faced with numerous internal rebellions as well. The most famous is the Taiping Rebellion (1850–64) in south-central China that resulted in twenty to thirty million casualties. North-central China had the Nian Rebellion (1851–68). Also, there were Muslim rebellions in North China, the Dungan Rebellion (1862–77), and in South China, the Panthay Rebellion (1855–73). All of these rebellions further weakened Qing political and military power.

5. Although William T. Rowe, *Hankow: Commerce and Society in a Chinese City, 1796–1889* (Stanford, CA: Stanford University Press, 1984) indicates on pages 222 and 233 that the Hanyang branch of the Yeh family was from "P'iao-shui county in the Yangchow area of Kiangsu," Yeh Yuanshuang stated that the two Chinese characters are very similar, but the county was, in fact, Lishui.

6. The Ming dynasty ended in 1644 when it was defeated by the Manchus who then founded the Qing dynasty which lasted until 1911.

7. Zhu Jianguo and Guo Xiaohong, *Dongfang Jianmin Chao* [*Jianmin Ascending. Jianmin* is the current name for *Yeh Kai Tai*] (Beijing: Zhongguo Gongren Chubanshe [Worker's Press of China], 1992), 13. Neither Yeh Wenji's father nor younger brother's names are known, but the father was called Yeh Shenxian (Yeh, the Saintly One), because his ability to cure the ill was such that he was considered to be extraordinary, and his brother was called Yeh Laoer (Yeh Number Two), as noted on page 16 of *Jianmin Ascending*.

8. Rowe, *Commerce and Society,* 223.

9. In wealthy Chinese families, it was a common practice to assign a generational name to a child for genealogical purposes. Within the Yeh family, generational names were used beginning in the tenth generation. In this generation the generational name was the second part of the child's given name; thus, the brothers were named Yeh Rongzai, Yeh Zhizai, and Yeh Fanzai. Determination of whether the generational name was going to be the first part or the second part of the child's given name was made by the family patriarch. As such, Yeh Fengchi dictated that the eleventh generation would have the generational name of *Yuan* and that it would be the first part of the given name.

Some wealthy families made a distinction between male and female generational names. For instance, in my generation of the Liu family, males have the character *Jia* as in my brother, Liu Jiazhang; while, females have the character *Meng* as in my name, Liu Mengbai.

In large wealthy families, generational names permit members to know their "place" within the clan structure, and as a consequence, to also know to whom deference is, or is not, owed.

10. Fengchi decided to use two four-character phrases to determine the second half of his children's names. Thus the children of his oldest son, Yeh Rongzai, were Fù, Gui, Shuang, Quan—the first four characters of the phrase. For the others in the family, the four-character phrase, used were Fú, Lu, Shou, Xi. The children of his third son, Yeh Fanzai, were named Fú and Lu meaning luck and wealth. The son of his second son, Yeh Zhizai, was named Shou meaning longevity. Ironically, he died in infancy. For Zhizai's other two children, Fengchi did not follow any pattern. Rongzai's last child was supposed to have the character of Xi meaning happiness, but the character had already been assigned to one of Yeh Zhongxing's grandchildren. Consequently, when Rongzai's youngest son was born, he was named Li meaning prosperous to avoid two children in the same generation having the exact name of Yeh Yuanxi. Yuanli's nickname, however, was Tongxi meaning shared happiness.

11. The first daughter was stillborn and went unnamed. In traditional Chinese practice children are not named until they are one hundred days old.

12. As with most women in patriarchal China, the great-grandmother's name is unknown. Her sons were Yuanshuang's great uncles, Yeh Zhongxing and Yeh Mengji, and Yuanshuang's grandfather, Yeh Fengchi.

13. When Yuanshuang was six years old, her great-grandmother died. At that time, Fengchi purchased a large piece of land in Hankou's French concession where he intended to build a new, Western-style family compound for his family, complete with stables for his racehorses. His two brothers, Zhongxing and Mengji, and their families remained at the Yeh Kai Tai family compound throughout the period.

14. In China, the Yangzi River originally referred "to only the last three or four hundred miles" of the Chang Jiang (Long River). Due to the fact that the foreign missionaries initially only encountered that portion of the river, they thought that the Chang Jiang was named the Yangzi, and that is what the name has become in the West. Presiding Bishop and Council Department of Missions, *Handbooks on the Missions of the Episcopal Church No. I China* (Chicago: Hammond, 1922) 3.

15. As Rowe writes on page 233, *Commerce and Society:* "Nostalgia for one's acknowledged place of origin was both an instinct and an institution in late imperial society. Many associations . . . were formed with at least the partial purpose of promulgating remembrance of the home areas. This remembrance often operated in ways that can appear arbitrary to us. The nationally prominent Yeh clan of P'iao-shui county, Kiangsu [Jiangsu], for example, had members residing in widely scattered areas of the empire. All of them acknowledged P'iao-shui as their 'native district' (*pen-I*), although by the clan's own testimony it had a long history before any Yeh ever set foot in that county, and by the eighteenth century a great many members, such as those comprising the Hankow [Hankou] branch, had for many generations neither formally registered there nor even seen the district." Nonetheless, as Fengchi's placard showed, some family members still considered it as their "home."

16. For the importance of the natal family for women of the wealthy classes, see Susan Mann, *The Talented Women of the Zhang Family* (Berkeley: University of California Press, 2007).

17. Cai Hanqing was a commander—a high-ranking officer roughly analogous to a general—in warlord Wu Peifu's Zhili faction army during a portion of China's warlord era (1916–28).

18. Wuchang's "East" Lake was the colloquial name for this lake since the actual, much larger, East Lake (Dong Hu) was located northeast of Wuchang.

19. When Commander Cai learned that the children who visited were members of the Yeh family, he approached one of his top aides who was married to Rongzai's younger sis-

ter about arranging a marriage. There are two possible reasons for the additional request for the proposed adoption. First, this aunt was very fond of Yuanshuang, and second, a marriage between her "daughter" and the commander's son would bind the two families tightly together and "ensure" her husband's position in the warlord's army.

20. Since Chinese ages are based upon the Lunar New Year when everyone gains a year, there can be a discrepancy between the Chinese age and the Western calendar year. At birth infants are considered to be one year old; consequently, at three months, Yuanshuang would have become two years old with the advent of the new lunar year.

21. William T. Rowe, *Hankow: Conflict and Community in a Chinese City, 1796–1895* (Stanford, CA: Stanford University Press, 1989), 160.

22. When Fengchi split his family, Dexing became the matriarch for a portion of the Yeh family. She was responsible for the welfare of more than thirty people which included members of her family with its concubines and servants, Fanzai's family with its concubines and servants, as well as several girls from the Gao family who lived with the Yehs.

23. Both Rongzai and Chen Bingchen—the majordomo—became ill in early 1926. Ironically, given the Yeh family's association with Chinese medicine, a diviner was called, and he concluded that "dark spirits" resided on the property. After Chen Bingchen died, the family moved into the rented mansion in Wuchang.

24. Mary Latimer James, M.D., Wuchang, Report for Year 1926, file RG-64-206, Archives of the Episcopal Church, Mary Latimer James file, 1924–47, Austin, TX.

25. Ibid.

26. Elizabeth Mildred Buchanan, Wuchang, private diary, file PP:74.31, Archives of the Episcopal Church, Private Papers of Elizabeth Mildred Buchanan, undated [1926], Austin, TX.

27. At that time, a bride-price was unusual in China where a dowry was much more common, but with the benefits of marrying into the Yeh family so high, the Cais were willing to pay for their prospective daughter-in-law.

28. The Nationalists (Guomindang) were internally split among left, right, and far right factions. Wuhan was liberated by a force composed of left Guomindang and Communist-led armies aided by Soviet advisors. This faction then declared Hankou the new capital of China.

29. Mary Latimer James, M.D., Wuchang, Report of Associate Superintendent for the Year 1928, file RG-64-206, Archives of the Episcopal Church, Mary Latimer James file, 1924–47, Austin, TX.

30. The house has been in the possession of the Wuhan municipal government ever since that day.

31. The British, French, and Japanese concessions were "subject to strong pressure for change after the Chinese municipality took over the former German [in 1917] and Russian [in 1920] concessions as Special Administrative Districts (SADs) after World War I. These were run by a Chinese director and Sino-foreign councils of elective representatives." Robert Bickers, *Britain in China: Community, Culture and Colonialism, 1900–1949* (Manchester: Manchester University Press, 1999), 139. In 1927 the British concession was nationalized and as the seizing of Yeh Fengchi's mansion in the French concession indicates, only the Japanese concession offered the "security" that Dexing felt her family required. Stephen R. MacKinnon, *Wuhan, 1938: War, Refugees, and the Making of Modern China* (Berkeley: University of California Press, 2008), 13.

32. *The Living Church Annual and Churchman's Almanac: A Church Cyclopedia and Almanac, 1920* (Milwaukee, WI: Morehouse, 1919), 401.

33. Edith Hart, "Saint Lois's School for Girls," *Spirit of Missions: An Illustrated Monthly Review of Christian Missions* 88 (1923): 203–5.

34. Following consolidation of the Chinese educational system in 1928, Central China University was renamed Huazhong Daxue (Central China University).

Chapter 2. Dorothea Kingsley Wakeman

1. Dorothea Wakeman Howe, interview by author, July 30, 1999, Solana Beach, CA.
2. Dorothea Wakeman Howe, interview by author, May 27, 1997, Solana Beach, CA; hereafter cited as DWH interview, May 27, 1997.
3. Robert T. Handy, ed., *The Social Gospel in America, 1870–1920* (New York: Oxford University Press, 1966), 12.
4. Donald K. Gorrell, *The Age of Social Responsibility: The Social Gospel in the Progressive Era, 1900–1920* (Macon, GA: Mercer University Press, 1988), 28.
5. Ibid. During this period of time, Mott was the chairman of the Executive Committee of the SVM.
6. Handy, *Social Gospel,* 11.
7. Harriett Alice Stillson, Student Volunteer Movement for Foreign Missions application, June 4, 1904, Archives of the Student Volunteer Movement for Foreign Missions, Record Group Number 42, Yale University Library, Manuscripts and Archives, New Haven, CT.
8. Ibid.
9. Ibid.
10. Ibid.
11. Ibid.
12. Earl Seeley Wakeman, Student Volunteer Movement for Foreign Missions application, April 5, 1906, Archives of the Student Volunteer Movement for Foreign Missions, Record Group Number 42, Yale University Library, Manuscripts and Archives, New Haven, CT.
13. Ibid.
14. Ibid.
15. Ibid.
16. DWH interview, May 27, 1997.
17. Ibid.
18. Ibid.
19. Dorothea Kingsley Wakeman, Wuchang, to parents, San Gabriel, CA, May 13, 1935, vol. 4, China Letters and Round the World, 5, private collection of Dorothea Wakeman Howe, San Diego, CA.
20. Jordan was the first president (1891–1913) of the Leland Stanford Junior University.
21. Albert Nelson Marquis, ed., *Who's Who in America: A Biographical Dictionary of Notable Living Men and Women of the United States,* vol. 19, 1936–37 (Chicago: A. N. Marquis, 1936), 2503.
22. Dorothea Wakeman Howe, interview by author, June 2, 1997, Solana Beach, CA; hereafter cited as DWH interview, June 2, 1997.
23. Dorothea Wakeman Howe, interview by author, July 2, 1997, Solana Beach, CA; hereafter cited as DWH interview, July 2, 1997.
24. Dorothea Wakeman Howe, interview by the author, June 4, 1998, Solana Beach, CA; hereafter cited as DWH interview, June 4, 1998.
25. Ibid.
26. DWH interview, May 27, 1997.
27. Merrill Tucker, Los Angeles, CA, to Dorothea Kingsley Wakeman, San Gabriel, CA, April 26, 1933, private collection of Dorothea Wakeman Howe, San Diego, CA.
28. DWH interview, May 27, 1997.
29. Ibid.
30. DWH interview, June 4, 1998.
31. Dorothea Wakeman Howe, undated autobiographical note in vol. 3, China Letters

and Round the World, private collection of Dorothea Wakeman Howe, San Diego, CA; hereafter cited as DWH, undated autobiographical note.

32. DWH interview, June 4, 1998.

33. DWH, undated autobiographical note.

34. Marquis, *Who's Who,* 2502.

35. Dorothea Kingsley Wakeman, Wuchang, to parents, San Gabriel, CA, June 19, 1936, vol. 4, China Letters and Round the World, 2, private collection of Dorothea Wakeman Howe, San Diego, CA.

36. Dorothea Kingsley Wakeman, Berkeley, CA, to parents, San Gabriel, CA, undated 1933 letter labeled "Monday A.M.," vol. 3, China Letters and Round the World, private collection of Dorothea Wakeman Howe, San Diego, CA; hereafter cited as DKW, "Monday A.M."

37. Wendy J. Deichmann Edwards and Carolyn De Swarte Gifford, "Introduction: Restoring Women and Reclaiming Gender in Social Gospel Studies," in *Gender and the Social Gospel,* ed. Wendy J. Deichmann Edwards and Carolyn De Swarte Gifford (Urbana: University of Illinois Press, 2003), 7.

38. Application form from Deaconess File, UP [Unprocessed] File 187, file of Deaconess Julia A. Clark, Archives of the Episcopal Church, Austin, TX.

39. DWH interview, June 2, 1997.

40. Ibid.

41. A. B. Parson, New York, NY, to Dorothea K. Wakeman, San Gabriel, CA, January 17, 1933, private collection of Dorothea Wakeman Howe, San Diego, CA.

42. DWH interview, July 2, 1997.

43. A. B. Parson, New York, NY, to Dorothea K. Wakeman, San Gabriel, CA, June 20, 1933, private collection of Dorothea Wakeman Howe, San Diego, CA.

44. DWH interview, May 27, 1997.

45. Ibid.

46. DWH interview, June 2, 1997.

47. Ibid.

48. DKW, "Monday A.M."

49. Earl Seeley Wakeman, San Gabriel, CA, to Dorothea Kingsley Wakeman, Wuchang, n.d. [probably April 1937], private collection of Dorothea Wakeman Howe, San Diego, CA.

50. J. G. Vaughan, *Hints on Health for New Missionaries* (New York: National Council, Protestant Episcopal Church, Department of Missions, n.d.), private collection of Dorothea Wakeman Howe, San Diego, CA.

51. DWH interview, May 27, 1997.

52. Department of Foreign Missions of the Protestant Episcopal Church, *Business Arrangements in Connection with the China Mission* (New York: Church Missions House, September 1932), private collection of Dorothea Wakeman Howe, San Diego, CA.

53. A. B. Parson, New York, NY, to Dorothea K. Wakeman, San Gabriel, CA, May 17, 1933, private collection, Dorothea Wakeman Howe, San Diego, CA.

54. Katharine E. Scott, Yonkers, NY, to Mr. Belknap, New York, NY, July 14, 1922, file RG-64-241, Archives of the Episcopal Church, Katharine E. Scott file, 1922–23, Austin, TX.

55. DKH interview, May 27, 1997.

56. Dorothea Kingsley Wakeman, Palo Alto, CA, to parents, San Gabriel, CA, undated August 1933 letter labeled "Wednesday," vol. 3, China Letters and Round the World, private collection of Dorothea Wakeman Howe, San Diego, CA.

57. Dollar Steamship Lines, *Special Class, The S.S. President Hoover & The S.S. President Coolidge* (San Francisco: Dollar Steamship Lines, 1932), private collection of Dorothea Kingsley Wakeman, San Diego, CA.

58. Earl Wakeman, San Gabriel, CA, to Dorothea Kingsley Wakeman, Palo Alto, CA, August 28, 1933, private collection of Dorothea Wakeman Howe, San Diego, CA.

59. Grace [Stillson], San Francisco, CA, to Harriett Wakeman, San Gabriel, CA, September 9, 1933, private collection of Dorothea Wakeman Howe, San Diego, CA; Dorothea Kingsley Wakeman, California, to parents, San Gabriel, CA, Thursday [September 1933], private collection of Dorothea Wakeman Howe, San Diego, CA.

60. Dorothea Kingsley Wakeman, SS *Coolidge,* to parents, San Gabriel, CA, September 11, 1933, vol. 1, China Letters and Round the World, 33, private collection of Dorothea Wakeman Howe, San Diego, CA; hereafter cited as DKW, September 11, 1933.

61. Dorothea Kingsley Wakeman, SS *Coolidge,* to parents, San Gabriel, CA, September 9, 1933, vol. 1, China Letters and Round the World, 4, private collection of Dorothea Wakeman Howe, San Diego, CA; DKW, September 11, 1933, 32–3.

62. Dollar Steamship Lines; DKW, September 11, 1933, 30.

63. Dorothea Kingsley Wakeman, Shanghai, to parents, San Gabriel, CA, September 29, 1933, vol. 1, China Letters and Round the World, 134, 136, private collection of Dorothea Wakeman Howe, San Diego, CA. Beijing ("Northern Capital") was renamed Beiping (Peiping—"Northern Peace") in 1928 when the capital was moved to Nanjing ("Southern Capital"). The city was renamed Beijing in 1949 when it became the capital of the People's Republic of China. The train trip from Shanghai to Beiping required four legs: (1) Shanghai to Nanjing, (2) the train was ferried across the Yangzi River to Pukou, (3) Pukou to Tianjin, and (4) Tianjin to Beiping. Since no bridges crossed the Yangzi River until the 1950s, China had a somewhat disconnected railway system during this period. (See: http://teetee thought.blogspot.com/2008/09/jinghu-railway.html.) Thus, Wuhan had a "northern system" terminal at Hankou and a "southern system" terminal at Wuchang. River transports had to be used to ferry passengers and freight between the two terminals.

64. Dorothea Kingsley Wakeman, Beiping, to parents, San Gabriel, CA, November 9, 1933, vol. 3, China Letters and Round the World, 2, private collection of Dorothea Wakeman Howe, San Diego, CA.

65. Dorothea Kingsley Wakeman, Beiping, to parents, San Gabriel, CA, October 5, 1933, vol. 1, China Letters and Round the World, 157–59, private collection of Dorothea Wakeman Howe, San Diego, CA.

66. Dorothea Kingsley Wakeman, Beiping, to parents, San Gabriel, CA, October 16, 1933, vol. 1, China Letters and Round the World, 195, private collection of Dorothea Wakeman Howe, San Diego, CA.

67. Dorothea Kingsley Wakeman, Beiping, to parents, San Gabriel, CA, October 10, 1933, vol. 3, China Letters and Round the World, 1–2, private collection of Dorothea Wakeman Howe, San Diego, CA; DKW, October 5, 1933, 167.

68. Dorothy Kingsley Wakeman, Beiping, to parents, San Gabriel, CA, November 30, 1933, vol. 1, China Letters and Round the World, 268, private collection of Dorothea Wakeman Howe, San Diego, CA.

Chapter 3. St. Hilda's School for Girls

1. Arthur R. Gray and Arthur M. Sherman, *The Story of the Church in China* (New York: The Domestic and Foreign Missionary Society, 1913), 40, 353.

2. Ibid., 77–78, 355. Yichang, which was further west than Hankou, became a treaty port in 1876.

3. Ibid., 79, 355. Presiding Bishop, *Handbooks on the Missions,* 13.

4. "Girls' School House in Wuchang," *Spirit of Missions: An Illustrated Monthly Review of Christian Missions* 39 (August 1874): 309.

5. Henrietta F. Boone, "The Jane Bohlen Memorial School," *Spirit of Missions: An Illustrated Monthly Review of Christian Missions* 44 (1879): 174–75. "St. Hilda's School,

Wuchang, China: Looking Backward," *Spirit of Missions: An Illustrated Monthly Review of Christian Missions* 65 (1900): 374–76.

6. Although China did not have a national currency until 1933 and different localities used varying scales of measurement, a tael was normally a unit of weight equivalent to 1.2 troy ounces of silver; whereas, the U.S. silver dollar was slightly more than .77 troy ounces. Thus, $4,500 in silver dollars is roughly equivalent to 3,000 taels.

7. "The Bohlen Memorial Girls' School," *Spirit of Missions: An Illustrated Monthly Review of Christian Missions* 39 (August 1874): 501–2.

8. William J. Boone, Wuchang, to Rev. R. B. Duane, New York, NY, September 11, 1874, file RG-64-5, Archives of the Episcopal Church, William J. Boone file, 1870–74, Austin, TX.

9. Rev. William J. Boone was the son of Bishop William J. Boone, the first Episcopal bishop of China, who died in 1864. Rev. William J. Boone became the Episcopal bishop of China on October 28, 1884. Gray and Sherman, *Story of the Church,* 71, 125.

10. William J. Boone, Wuchang, to Rev. R. B. Duane, New York, NY, May 22, 1875, file RG-64-5, Archives of the Episcopal Church, William J. Boone file, 1875–76, Austin, TX.

11. Ibid.

12. Gray and Sherman, *Story of the Church,* 94–95.

13. William J. Boone, Wuchang, to Rev. S. D. Denison, New York, NY, June 22, 1876, file RG-64-5, Archives of the Episcopal Church, William J. Boone file, 1875–76, Austin, TX; William J. Boone, Shanghai, to Rev. Joshua Kimber, New York, NY, August 18, 1882, file RG-64-6, Archives of the Episcopal Church, William J. Boone file, 1882, Austin, TX.

14. William J. Boone, Wuchang, to Rev. Joshua Kimber, New York, NY, July 7, 1877, file RG-64-5, Archives of the Episcopal Church, William J. Boone file, 1877–79, Austin, TX.

15. Boone, "Jane Bohlen Memorial School," 174.

16. Gray and Sherman, *Story of the Church,* 103.

17. William J. Boone, Shanghai, to Rev. Joshua Kimber, New York, NY, August 24, 1880, file RG-64-5, Archives of the Episcopal Church, William J. Boone file, 1880, Austin, TX.

18. Ibid.

19. William J. Boone, Shanghai, to Rev. Joshua Kimber, New York, NY, March 22, 1881, file RG-64-6, Archives of the Episcopal Church, William J. Boone file, 1881, Austin, TX.

20. William J. Boone, Shanghai, to Rev. Secretary of the Foreign Committee, New York, NY, May 2, 1882, letter, file RG-64-6, Archives of the Episcopal Church, William J. Boone file, 1882, Austin, TX.

21. William J. Boone, Shanghai, to Rev. Secretary of the Foreign Committee, New York, NY, May 2, 1882, Private enclosure A, file RG-64-6, Archives of the Episcopal Church, William J. Boone file, 1882, Austin, TX.

22. William J. Boone, Shanghai, to Rev. Secretary of the Foreign Committee, New York, NY, June 30, 1882, Appendix to Foreign Committee's Report—II, file RG-64-6, Archives of the Episcopal Church, William J. Boone file, 1882, Austin, TX.

23. "St. Hilda's School, Wuchang, China: Looking Backward," 374–75.

24. American Church Mission in the Valley of the Yang-tsz, *The Church in China: A Bi-monthly Magazine* 1, no. 6 (November 1894): 118.

25. "St. Hilda's School, Wuchang, China: Looking Backward," 375.

26. William J. Boone, Shanghai, to Rev. Joshua Kimber, New York, NY, August 18, 1882, file RG-64-6, Archives of the Episcopal Church, William J. Boone file, 1882, Austin, TX.

27. "St. Hilda's School, Wuchang, China: Looking Backward," 375.

28. Ibid., 374–76; Pauline Austin Osgood, Shanghai, to Bishop Graves, Wuchang, July 17, 1899, file RG-64-23, Archives of the Episcopal Church, Pauline A. Osgood file, 1898–

1901, Austin, TX; Gray and Sherman, *Story of the Church,* 222. The school was named in honor of Saint Hilda, who was the founding abbess of the monastery at Whitby, England, in 657 AD and who is considered to be the patron saint of learning and culture. Anne Warin, *Hilda: The Chronicle of a Saint. A Story of Saints and Kings, and the Beginnings of the English Church* (London: Marshall Morgan and Scott, Lamp Press, 1989), x.

29. Osgood, July 17, 1899.

30. Pauline Austin Osgood, "St. Hilda's School, Wuchang," *Spirit of Missions: An Illustrated Monthly Review of Christian Missions* 67 (1902): 494.

31. Pauline Austin Osgood, "Report of St. Hilda's School, Wuchang, China 1901–1902," file RG-64-72, Archives of the Episcopal Church, Pauline A. Osgood file, 1902–6, Austin, TX.

32. Pauline Austin Osgood, "Report of St. Hilda's School, Wuchang, China, For the year ending January 31, 1903," file RG-64-72, Archives of the Episcopal Church, Pauline A. Osgood file, 1902–6, Austin, TX.

33. Ibid.

34. Ibid.

35. Pauline Austin Osgood, "Annual Report of St. Hilda's School, Wuchang, China, 1904," file RG-64-72, Archives of the Episcopal Church, Pauline A. Osgood file, 1902–6, Austin, TX.

36. Pauline Austin Osgood, Wuchang, to Mr. J. W. Wood, New York, NY, May 26, 1905, file RG-64-72, Archives of the Episcopal Church, Pauline A. Osgood file, 1902–6, Austin, TX.

37. Gray and Sherman, *Story of the Church,* 280.

38. Ibid.

39. Ibid., 280–81.

40. Ibid., 308. The Bishop Boone Memorial School was founded in 1871. It became a high school in 1890, and in 1903, the high school became Boone College. According to Robert D. Stueart, "Flowers From Horseback: A Retrospective View of China—United States Library and Information Science Education Cooperation in the 20th Century"; available from http://digarc.usc.edu/search/controller/view/impa-m10743.html. Boone College became Boone University in 1909. In 1922, Boone merged with Wesley College and Griffith John College to form Central China College. Central China College became Central China University in 1926. At this point the historical record becomes murky. It appears that Boone became a college preparatory school during this period, and it was not a part of Central China University. Following Nationalist-mandated registration of all foreign schools in 1928, Central China University became Huazhong Daxue. This could explain why the missionary community always referred to the school as "Boone." Today, the Hebei University of Chinese Medicine occupies the land where the Boone campus and Church General Hospital were located. Huazhong Daxue continues to exist as a normal school in Wuchang.

41. Gray and Sherman, *Story of the Church,* 309; E. Mildred Buchanan, "Saint Hilda's School," *Spirit of Missions: An Illustrated Monthly Review of Christian Missions* 83 (1918): 510.

42. "What the Ten Thousand Dollar Gift to St. Hilda's Will Do For the Church in China," *Spirit of Missions: An Illustrated Monthly Review of Christian Missions* 76 (1911): 75.

43. Buchanan, "Saint Hilda's School," 510.

44. Gray and Sherman, *Story of the Church,* 332–34.

45. Katharine E. Scott, "Report of St. Hilda's School, 1916–1917" (Wuchang, China), file RG-64-241, Archives of the Episcopal Church, Katharine E. Scott file, 1913–21, Austin, TX.

46. Ibid.

47. Ibid.; Katharine E. Scott, Wuchang, to Dr. John W. Wood, New York, NY, February 3, 1921, file RG-64-241, Archives of the Episcopal Church, Katharine E. Scott file, 1913–21, Austin, TX.

48. Buchanan, "Saint Hilda's School," 510.

49. E. Mildred Buchanan, Wuchang, to Miss Tillotson, New York, NY, February 9, 1924, file RG-64-191, Archives of the Episcopal Church, Elizabeth Mildred Buchanan file, 1916–27, Austin, TX; E. Mildred Buchanan, "Report 1925, Saint Hilda's School" (Wuchang, China), file RG-64-191, Archives of the Episcopal Church, Elizabeth Mildred Buchanan file, 1916–27, Austin, TX.

50. E. Mildred Buchanan, "Annual Report for 1924, Saint Hilda's School," (Wuchang, China)," file RG-64-191, Archives of the Episcopal Church, Elizabeth Mildred Buchanan file, 1916–27, Austin, TX; Buchanan, "Report 1925, St. Hilda's School."

51. *Zhonghua jidujiaohui nianjian* [The China Christian year book], vol. 8 (1925; repr., Shanghai: Gan lan wen hua ji jin hui, 1983), 347.

52. Buchanan, "Report 1925, Saint Hilda's School."

53. E. Mildred Buchanan, August 26, 1926 "Siege diary," file PP:74.31, Archives of the Episcopal Church, Private Papers of Elizabeth Mildred Buchanan, Austin, TX.

54. Mary Latimer James, "Report of Associate Superintendent, The Church General Hospital, 1928" (Wuchang, China), file RG-64-206, Archives of the Episcopal Church, Mary Latimer James, MD, 1924–47, Austin, TX.

55. Arthur M. Sherman, "Story of a Beleaguered City: Thrilling Account of the Siege of Wuchang by an Eye-Witness," *Spirit of Missions: An Illustrated Monthly Review of Christian Missions* 91 (1926): 671.

56. Ibid.

57. E. Mildred Buchanan, September 7, 1926, "Siege diary," file PP:74.31, Archives of the Episcopal Church, Private Papers of Elizabeth Mildred Buchanan, Austin, TX.

58. Ibid.; Sherman, "Beleaguered City," 672.

59. Buchanan, September 7, 1926; Sherman, "Beleaguered City," 672.

60. E. Mildred Buchanan, October 11, 1926 "Siege diary," file PP:74.31, Archives of the Episcopal Church, Private Papers of Elizabeth Mildred Buchanan, Austin, TX.

61. James, "Report of Associate Superintendent, The Church General Hospital, 1928."

62. Gertrude Carter Gilman, "Wuhan Revisited After Two Years: The Vast Changes Which have Emerged from the Chinese Turmoil of Recent Years Augur Well for the New China that is Building," *Spirit of Missions: An Illustrated Monthly Review of Christian Missions* 94 (1929): 359.

63. The 1927 split in the Guomindang pitted the militaristic or right faction against the political or left faction. The left, which was based in Hankou, was "defeated" by the right which made Nanjing the new capital of China.

64. Milton W. Meyer, *China: A Concise History*. 2nd ed., rev. (Lanham, MD: Littlefield Adams Quality Paperback, 1994), 275–76.

65. *Zhonghua jidujiaohui nianjian* [The China Christian year book], vol. 9 (1927; repr., Shanghai: Gan lan wen hua ji jin hui, 1983), 337. The fourteen educational institutions included three in Hankou: one elementary (St. Lois's), one middle (St. Margaret's), and one vocational training center; ten in Wuchang: one college (Central China University), eight middle schools (including St. Hilda's), and one college preparatory school (Boone); and in Hanyang: one middle school; John W. Wood, New York, NY, to Olive B. Tomlin, Columbus, OH, April 28, 1927, file RG-64-246, Archives of the Episcopal Church, Olive B. Tomlin file, 1917–29, Austin, TX.

66. E. Mildred Buchanan, Wuchang, to John W. Wood, New York, NY, memorandum of cable, April 11, 1927, file RG-64-191, Archives of the Episcopal Church, Elizabeth Mildred Buchanan file, 1916–27, Austin, TX; Logan H. Roots, Hankow, to John W. Wood, New York, NY, letter, April 1, 1927, file RG-64-236, Archives of the Episcopal Church, Bishop Logan H. Roots files, January–June 1927, Austin, TX.

67. Logan H. Roots, April 1, 1927.

68. See John W. Wood, "The Pro and Con of Registration of Christian Schools in China: A Symposium of the Views Held by Missionaries in all Three Districts in China on a Grave Question Which May Influence Future Policy," *Spirit of Missions: An Illustrated Monthly Review of Christian Missions* 93 (1928): 653—55.

69. The Restore Educational Rights Movement from 1924 advocated the nationalization of foreign missionary schools along with several other policies that were adopted by the Nationalist government following the success of the Northern Expedition. See Jessie G. Lutz, "Chinese Nationalism and the Anti-Christian Campaigns of the 1920s," *Modern Asian Studies* 10, no. 3 (1976): 395–416.

70. Logan H. Roots, Hankow, to John W. Wood, D.C.L., New York, NY, December 24, 1926, file RG-64-235, Archives of the Episcopal Church, Bishop Logan H. Roots file, 1926, Austin, TX. That both Bishop Roots and Bishop Gilman had considered the impact of Chinese government registration of mission schools is not surprising. The Educational Rights Movement, which began in 1924, sought the nationalization of foreign missionary schools and became an integral element of Guomindang ideology.

71. Edward M. Merrins, "The Progress of China," *Spirit of Missions: An Illustrated Monthly Review of Christian Missions* 78 (1913): 590.

72. "An Attempt to Analyze the Situation in China: The Bearings of the Present Disturbances Upon Mission Work, Especially That of Christian Education," *Spirit of Missions: An Illustrated Monthly Review of Christian Missions* 92 (1927): 199.

73. Ibid.

74. Ibid., 200.

75. Ibid.

76. Frederick R. Graves, "Kuomintang Bans Christian Schools: Bishop of Shanghai Reviews the Implications of Registering Our Schools in China and Reports Recent Proposals of Shanghai Kuomintang," *Spirit of Missions: An Illustrated Monthly Review of Christian Missions* 95 (1930): 576.

77. John W. Wood, New York, NY, to Bishop Alfred A. Gilman, Wuchang, "Subject: Plans for Cooperative Board of Christian Education in Wuhan," December 5, 1929, Archives of the Episcopal Church, Alfred A. Gilman file, file RG-64-199, 1924–35, Austin, TX; Alfred A. Gilman, "The Christian Schools of Central China," *Chinese Recorder* (October 1932): 2, Archives of the Episcopal Church, Alfred A. Gilman file, file RG-64-199, 1924–35, Austin, TX.

78. Wood, "Plans for Cooperative Board."

79. Regulations Re Private Schools, "Chap. 1: General Regulations," file RG-64-238, Archives of the Episcopal Church, Bishop Logan H. Roots file, 1928–29, Austin, TX.

80. Ibid., "Chap. IV: Ptivate [*sic*] Middle and Primary Schools."

81. Julia A. Clark, "Voluntary Religious Education in China: Survey of Religious Teaching at St. Hilda's, Wuchang, Reveals Opportunity to Enrich the Kingdom Through Intelligent Christian Women," *Spirit of Missions: An Illustrated Monthly Review of Christian Missions* 95 (1930): 380.

82. Julia A. Clark, Wuchang, to John W. Wood, New York, NY, October 6, 1929, file RG-64-193, Archives of the Episcopal Church, Julia A. Clark file, 1923–30, Austin, TX.

83. Julia A. Clark, Wuchang, to Rt. Rev. L. H. Roots, Hankow, January 1, 1929, file RG-64-193, Archives of the Episcopal Church, Julia A. Clark file, 1923–30, Austin, TX.

84. Julia A. Clark, Wuchang, to Rt. Rev. L. H. Roots, Hankow, January 29, 1932, "Annual Report for St. Hilda's School, 1931," file RG-64-193, Archives of the Episcopal Church, Julia A. Clark file, 1930–39, Austin, TX.

85. H. Owen Chapman, *The Chinese Revolution: A Record of the Period Under Communist Control as Seen from the Nationalist Capitol Hankow* (Westport, CT: Hyperion Reprint Edition, 1977), 64. It is interesting to observe that a wide gulf separated the world

views of the West and the Chinese. To the West, the Nationalists' attempt to create a strong Chinese nation-state (as it existed in the West) was seen as nationalistic "propaganda"; while to the Chinese, the West's attempt to spread Christianity into China (as it existed in the West) was seen as religious "propaganda." That is, with both nationalism and Christianity coming out of the West, the Chinese accepted the ideology of nationalism, but tended to reject the ideology of Christianity.

86. From the newspaper report of the Government Educators Conference, held in Nanking, May 1928, Archives of the Episcopal Church, Bishop Alfred A. Gilman file, file RG-64-199, 1924–35, Austin, TX.

87. John W. Wood, New York, NY, to Julia A. Clark, Wuchang, November 30, 1929, file RG-64-193, Archives of the Episcopal Church, Julia A. Clark file, 1923–30, Austin, TX.

88. Julia A. Clark, Wuchang, to Rt. Rev. L. H. Roots, Hankow, January 1, 1929, file RG-64-193, Archives of the Episcopal Church, Julia A. Clark file, 1923–30, Austin, TX.

89. Ibid.

90. Julia A. Clark, "St. Hilda's Reopened," *Hankow Newsletter* 7, no. 8 (October 1928): 8.

91. Ibid.

92. Ibid.

93. Ibid.

94. Alfred A. Gilman, Hankow, to Dr. John W. Wood, New York, NY, July 3, 1929, file RG-64-199, Archives of the Episcopal Church, Bishop Alfred A. Gilman file, 1924–35, Austin, TX.

95. Julia A. Clark, January 1, 1929.

96. Julia A. Clark, SS *Shasi,* to Bishop Logan H. Roots, Hankow, January 27, 1930, Report of St. Hilda's School, 1929, file RG-64-193, Archives of the Episcopal Church, Julia A. Clark file, 1923–30, Austin, TX.

97. Julia A. Clark, Wuchang, to John W. Wood, New York, NY, September 15, 1930, file RG-64-193, Archives of the Episcopal Church, Julia A. Clark file, 1930–39, Austin, TX.

98. Julia A. Clark, Wuchang, to Rt. Rev. Logan H. Roots, Hankow, January 17, 1931, "Annual Report for St. Hilda's School, 1930," file RG-64-239, Archives of the Episcopal Church, Bishop Logan H. Roots file, 1930–32, Austin, TX.

99. Julia A. Clark, Wuchang, to Dr. John W. Wood, New York, NY, May 17, 1931, file RG-64-193, Archives of the Episcopal Church, Julia A. Clark file, 1930–39, Austin, TX.

100. Logan H. Roots, Hankow, to Louise Boynton, New York, NY, May 30, 1930, file RG-64-239, Archives of the Episcopal Church, Bishop Logan H. Roots file, 1930–32, Austin, TX.

101. Ibid.

102. Julia A. Clark, September 15, 1930.

103. Julia A. Clark, January 17, 1931.

104. Julia A. Clark, "St. Hilda's Reopened," 9.

105. Julia A. Clark, January 17, 1931.

106. Logan H. Roots, Hankow, to John W. Wood, New York, NY, "1931 Annual Report" (Hankou, China), file RG-74-239, Archives of the Episcopal Church, Bishop Logan H. Roots file, 1930–32, Austin, TX; Stephen C. Clark, Jr., "Flood Days in Central China," *Los Angeles Churchman,*" n.d., file RG-64-193, Archives of the Episcopal Church, Julia A. Clark file, 1930–39, Austin, TX.

107. Stephen C. Clark, Jr., "Flood Days," 8.

108. Julia A. Clark, Wuchang, to John W. Wood, New York, NY, August 20, 1931, file RG-64-193, Archives of the Episcopal Church, Julia A. Clark file, 1930–39, Austin, TX.

109. Logan H. Roots, "1931 Annual Report," 4.

110. Julia A. Clark, August 20, 1931.

111. Julia A. Clark, Wuchang, to John W. Wood, New York, NY, November 29, 1931, file RG-64-193, Archives of the Episcopal Church, Julia A. Clark file, 1930–39, Austin, TX.

112. Ibid.

113. Grace Miller Clark, Pasadena, CA, to John W. Wood, New York, NY, November 5, 1931, file RG-64-193, Archives of the Episcopal Church, Julia A. Clark file, 1930–39, Austin, TX; Grace Miller Clark, Pasadena, CA, to John W. Wood, New York, NY, November 6, 1931, file RG-64-193, Archives of the Episcopal Church, Julia A. Clark file, 1930–39, Austin, TX.

114. Julia A. Clark, January 17, 1931; Gilman, "Christian Schools of Central China," 3.

115. Julia A. Clark, Pasadena, CA, to Rt. Rev. L. H. Roots, Hankow, "Personal Report of Julia A. Clark" (1932), file RG-64-193, Archives of the Episcopal Church, Julia A. Clark file, 1930–39, Austin, TX.

116. Alfred A. Gilman, Hankow, to Dr. John W. Wood and Rt. Rev. Logan H. Roots, New York, NY, October 13, 1933, file RG-64-199, Archives of the Episcopal Church, Alfred A. Gilman file, 1924–35, Austin, TX.

117. Wang Yingan, interview by author, San Diego, CA, 1989; hereafter cited as Wang Yingan interview, San Diego, 1989.

118. Having to do manual labor and having to deal with the poor meant that many of the wealthy girls at St. Hilda's were encountering life experiences that were completely foreign to their upbringing. The egalitarianism of the Social Gospel was antithetical to the hierarchical structure of Chinese society, and as such, its inculcation into the girls of St. Hilda's was revelatory.

119. Wang Yingan interview, San Diego, 1989.

120. The notion of Communist control of state schools was a holdover from the 1927 split in the Guomindang. Despite the victory by the right Guomindang, many of the more conservative, wealthy Wuhan families believed that a leftist philosophy continued to pervade the state schools.

121. Dorothy Tso, Wuchang, to Rt. Rev. L. H. Roots, Hankow, February 8, 1933, file RG-64-248, Archives of the Episcopal Church, Dorothy Tso file, 1933, Austin, TX.

122. Olive Bird Tomlin, "Report for 1928," Wuchang, China, file RG-64-246, Archives of the Episcopal Church, Olive Bird Tomlin file, 1917–29, Austin, TX.

123. Tso, February 8, 1933. Fortunately, the principal was not the math teacher as the figures she provided do not add up. This gives credence to the perception held by missiologists that missionary figures are notoriously inaccurate.

124. Olive Bird Tomlin, Wuchang, to Dr. John Wood, New York, NY, October 23, 1932, file RG-64-246, Archives of the Episcopal Church, Olive Bird Tomlin file, 1917–50, Austin, TX.

125. Logan H. Roots, Hankow, to John W. Wood, New York, NY, August 2, 1933, file RG-64-240, Archives of the Episcopal Church, Bishop Logan H. Roots file, 1933–38, Austin, TX.

126. Ibid.

127. A. B. Parson, New York, NY, to Dorothea K. Wakeman, San Gabriel, CA, June 20, 1933, private collection of Dorothea Wakeman Howe, San Diego, CA.

Chapter 4. Yeh Yuanshuang at St. Hilda's

1. Julia A. Clark, SS *Shasi,* to Bishop Logan H. Roots, Hankow, January 27, 1930, Report of St. Hilda's School, 1929, file RG-64-193, Archives of the Episcopal Church, Julia A. Clark file, 1923–30, Austin, TX.

2. Ibid.

3. Dorothy Mills, "St. Hilda's Wuchang," *Spirit of Missions: An Illustrated Monthly Review of Christian Missions* 81 (1916), 228.

4. Fu Huaqing, interview by author, 1982, Shanghai; hereafter cited as Fu interview, 1982.

5. Yu Shuming, interview by author, 1982, Beijing; hereafter cited as Yu interview, 1982. Wang Yingan interview, San Diego, 1989.

6. The Paris Peace Conference sparked major demonstrations in China when the German concessions in Shandong Province were "officially" reassigned to the Japanese. The May Fourth Movement, so named to commemorate the first demonstration held by the students, launched an effort that criticized Confucianism and patriarchy. Hair was a target because the braided queue was the mark of citizenship during the Qing dynasty. It also led to a move away from classical Chinese to a more vernacular form as the new genre for literary expression.

7. Julia A. Clark, Wuchang, to Bishop Logan Roots, Hankow, January 17, 1931, Annual Report for St. Hilda's School, 1930, RG-64-193, Archives of the Episcopal Church, Julia A. Clark file, 1930–39, Austin, TX.

8. Margaret Roberts, Wuchang, to Bishop Logan H. Roots, Hankow, Annual Report of 1928, file RG-64-217, Archives of the Episcopal Church, Margaret Roberts file, 1925–28, Austin, TX.

9. Julia A. Clark, Hankow, to Dr. John W. Wood, New York, NY, letter, March 3, 1929, file RG-193, Archives of the Episcopal Church, Julia A. Clark file, 1923–30, Austin, TX.

10. Fu interview, 1982.

11. Margaret Roberts, Annual Report of 1928. (Clearly Miss Roberts's "watchful eye" was somewhat shortsighted.)

12. Julia A. Clark, January 1, 1929.

13. Logan H. Roots, Hankow, to John W. Wood, New York, NY, letter, December 24, 1926, file RG-64-235, Archives of the Episcopal Church, Bishop Logan H. Roots file, 1926, Austin, TX.

14. Fu interview, 1982.

15. Dorothy Tso, Wuchang, to Bishop Logan H. Roots, Hankow, February 8, 1933, Annual Report of 1932, p. 4, file RG-64-248, Archives of the Episcopal Church, Dorothy Tso file, Austin, TX.

16. Yu interview, 1982.

17. Ibid.

18. Zhong Limin, interview by author, 1982, Shanghai.

19. Yu interview, 1982.

20. Chen Siyu, interview by author, 1982, Shanghai; hereafter cited as Chen interview, 1982.

21. Wang Yingan interview, San Diego, 1989.

22. Julia A. Clark, Wuchang, to Rev. Logan H. Roots, Hankow, letter, January 1, 1929, file RG-64-193, Archives of the Episcopal Church, Julia A. Clark file, 1923–30, Austin, TX.

23. Margaret Roberts, Annual Report of 1928; Olive Bird Tomlin, Wuchang, to Bishop Logan H. Roots, Hankow, Report for 1928, file RG-64-246, Archives of the Episcopal Church, Olive Bird Tomlin file, 1917–19, Austin, TX.

24. Olive Bird Tomlin, Report for 1928.

25. Julia A. Clark, Wuchang, to Rt. Rev. L. H. Roots, Hankow, January 17, 1931, Annual Report for 1930, file RG-64-193, Archives of the Episcopal Church, Julia A. Clark file, 1930–39, Austin, TX.

26. Wang Yingan, interview by author, 1989, Los Angeles, CA; hereafter cited as Wang Yingan interview, Los Angeles, 1989.

27. Fu interview, 1982.
28. Julia A. Clark, Annual Report for 1930.
29. Wang Yingan interview, Los Angeles, 1989.
30. Zhou Zezhen, interview by author, 1982, Shanghai.
31. Yu interview, 1982.
32. Dorothy Tso, Annual Report of 1932, 2.
33. While Yuanquan remained at St. Hilda's and graduated in 1936, Yuanlu left St. Hilda's after her Junior III year in 1933.
34. For a comparison with English boarding schools, see Mallory Wober, *English Girls' Boarding Schools* (London: Allen Lane The Penguin Press, 1971).
35. Wang Guifen, interview by author, 1982, Shanghai.
36. Dorothy Tso, Annual Report of 1932, 3.
37. Ibid.
38. Fu interview, 1982.
39. Ibid.
40. Although Yuanlu was a first cousin, in Chinese families, cousins who are raised together in the same household are often referred to as siblings rather than cousins.
41. Logan H. Roots, December 24, 1926.
42. Dorothy Tso, Annual Report of 1932, 3.
43. Margaret E. Spurr, Wuchang, to Bishop Logan H. Roots, Hankow, Annual Report for the Year 1931, file RG-64-239, Archives of the Episcopal Church, Bishop Logan H. Roots files, 1930–32, Austin, TX.
44. Julia A. Clark, Annual Report for 1930.
45. Yu interview, 1982.
46. Julia A. Clark, Wuchang, to Bishop Logan H. Roots, Hankow, January 30, 1932, Annual Report for 1931, file RG-64-239, Archives of the Episcopal Church, Bishop Logan H. Roots file, 1930–32, Austin, TX.
47. Margaret E. Spurr, Wuchang, to Bishop Logan H. Roots, Hankow, March 17, 1931, Annual Report for the Year 1930, file RG-64-239, Archives of the Episcopal Church, Bishop Logan H. Roots files, 1930–32, Austin, TX.
48. Margaret E. Spurr, Annual Report for 1931.
49. Julia A. Clark, Annual Report for 1930.
50. Julia A. Clark, Annual Report for 1931.
51. Ibid.
52. Yu interview, 1982.
53. Dorothy Tso, Annual Report of 1932, 1.
54. Yu interview, 1982.
55. Ibid.
56. Wang Yingan, interview by author, 1982, Shanghai; hereafter cited as Wang Yingan interview, Shanghai, 1982.
57. Chen interview, 1982.
58. Yu interview, 1982.
59. Wang Yingan, interview, Shanghai, 1982.
60. Dorothy Tso, Annual Report of 1932, 2.
61. Although Deaconess Clark was no longer at the school, Principal Tso supported her recommendation that Yuanshuang not be allowed to participate in her junior middle graduation because of her previous misbehavior.
62. Dorothy Tso, Annual Report of 1932, 4.
63. Ibid.; Julia A. Clark, Wuchang, to Bishop Logan H. Roots, Hankow, Annual Report of Julia A. Clark, Deaconess, 1931, file RG-64-239, Bishop Logan H. Roots, 1930–32, Archives of the Episcopal Church, Bishop Logan H. Roots files, 1930–32, Austin, TX.

64. Julia A. Clark, "Voluntary Religious Education in China," 380.
65. Ibid.
66. Lloyd E. Eastman, *The Abortive Revolution: China under Nationalist Rule, 1927–1937* (Cambridge: Harvard University Press, 1990 [1974]), 246–47.
67. District of Hankow, "In Remembrance, Eliza McCook Roots, October 22, 1869–August 4, 1934," *Newsletter,* 7, 14.
68. Liu Defu interview by author, 1982, Shanghai.
69. For a description of Jimmy Yen's life and work, see Charles W. Hayford, *To the People: James Yen and Village China* (New York: Columbia University Press, 1990); Charles W. Hayford, "Y. C. James Yen and Rural Reconstruction in China" (Phd diss., Harvard University, 1973); and John Hershey, "Jimmy Yen: Crusader for Mankind," *Reader's Digest* (October 1987): 138–45, 233–64.
70. Julia A. Clark, Annual Report for 1930.
71. Ibid.

Chapter 5. Dorothea and the "Saints"

1. Dorothea Kingsley Wakeman, Wuchang, to parents, San Gabriel, CA, April 2, 1934, vol. 1, China Letters and Round the World, 450, 452, private collection of Dorothea Wakeman Howe, San Diego, CA; hereafter cited as DKW, April 2, 1934.
2. Ibid., 448.
3. Ibid.
4. Ibid., 451, 452; Dorothea Wakeman Howe interview by author, May 27, 1997, Solana Beach, CA; hereafter referred to as DWH, May 27, 1997.
5. Dorothea Kingsley Wakeman, Wuchang, to parents, San Gabriel, CA, March 28, 1934, vol. 1, China Letters and Round the World, 448, private collection of Dorothea Wakeman Howe, San Diego, CA.
6. DWH, May 27, 1997.
7. Dorothea Kingsley Wakeman, Wuchang, to parents, San Gabriel, CA, December 29, 1935, vol. 2, China Letters and Round the World, 1022, private collection of Dorothea Wakeman Howe, San Diego, CA.
8. The portion of the city wall along Serpent Hill was removed sometime between 1915 and 1918 for the building of the Wuchang-Changsha railroad line. MacKinnon, *Wuhan, 1938,* 12.
9. Dorothea Kingsley Wakeman, Wuchang, to parents, San Gabriel, CA, May 1, 1934, vol. 1, China Letters and Round the World, 478, private collection of Dorothea Wakeman Howe, San Diego, CA.
10. DKW, April 2, 1934, 449.
11. Dorothea Kingsley Wakeman, Wuchang, to parents, San Gabriel, CA, March 28, 1934, vol. 1, China Letters and Round the World, 447, private collection of Dorothea Wakeman Howe, San Diego, CA.
12. Dorothea Kingsley Wakeman, Wuchang, to parents, San Gabriel, CA, April 13, 1934, vol. 1, China Letters and Round the World, floor plans, private collection of Dorothea Wakeman Howe, San Diego, CA.
13. The term "Amah," from the Portugese "Ama," was used by foreigners to refer to Chinese women who cared for their children. Eventually, the term was used as an honorific to any Chinese woman who took care of the foreign women.
14. Dorothea Kingsley Wakeman, Wuchang, to parents, San Gabriel, CA, June 27, 1934, vol. 1, China Letters and Round the World, 525, private collection of Dorothea Wakeman Howe, San Diego, CA.

15. Rowe, *Commerce and Society,* 23.
16. Dorothea Kingsley Wakeman, Wuchang, to parents, San Gabriel, CA, March 21, 1937, vol. 4, China Letters and Round the World, 1, private collection of Dorothea Wakeman Howe, San Diego, CA.
17. Dorothea Kingsley Wakeman, Wuchang, to parents, San Gabriel, CA, March 3, 1937, vol. 4, China Letters and Round the World, 2, private collection of Dorothea Wakeman Howe, San Diego, CA.
18. Dorothea Kingsley Wakeman, Wuchang, to parents, San Gabriel, CA, April 8, 1934, vol. 1, China Letters and Round the World, 459, private collection of Dorothea Wakeman Howe, San Diego, CA.
19. Ibid., 460.
20. Dorothea Kingsley Wakeman, Wuchang, to parents, San Gabriel, CA, May 14, 1934, vol. 1, China Letters and Round the World, 486, 1–4, private collection of Dorothea Wakeman Howe, San Diego, CA; hereafter cited as DKW, May 14, 1934.
21. Dorothea Kingsley Wakeman, Wuchang, to parents, San Gabriel, CA, January 30, 1936, vol. 4, China Letters and Round the World, 1, private collection of Dorothea Wakeman Howe, San Diego, CA; hereafter cited as DKW, January 30, 1936.
22. The Oxford Group was a movement founded by an American Lutheran minister, Frank Buchman, that had a significant impact on Christianity during the 1920s and '30s. It was based upon four points: (1) Absolute Honesty, (2) Absolute Purity, (3) Absolute Unselfishness, and (4) Absolute Love (7). To be spiritually reborn, and to live in the state in which these four points are the guides to our life in God, the Oxford Group advocate four practical spiritual activities: (1) The Sharing of our sins and temptations with another Christian life given to God, and to use Sharing as Witness to help others, still unchanged, to recognize and acknowledge their sins; (2) Surrender of our life, past, present, and future, into God's keeping and direction; (3) Restitution to all whom we have wronged directly or indirectly; and (4) Listening to, accepting, relying on God's Guidance, and carrying it out in everything we do or say, great or small (8–9). The Layman with a Notebook, *What is the Oxford Group?* (New York: Oxford University Press, 1937), 7–9.

According to Maisie Ward, who attended several Oxford Group meetings in England, the following rhyme was an integral feature of every meeting:

> It's not an institution,
> It's not a point of view,
> It starts a revolution
> By starting it in you.
>
> (Maisie Ward, *The Oxford Groups,* 12)

Two years later Dorothea made the observation that: "If you know anything of the Ox[ford] G[roup] you know that their appeal is made mainly to the 'smart set', the people with money or position" (DKW, January 30, 1936). (The Oxford Group's "four points," "practical spiritual activities," and house meetings provided an impetus for the founding of Alcoholics Anonymous and its twelve-step program.)

23. Dorothea Kingsley Wakeman, Wuchang, to parents, San Gabriel, CA, May 16, 1934, vol. 1, China Letters and Round the World, 502–3, private collection of Dorothea Wakeman Howe, San Diego, CA.
24. Dorothea Kingsley Wakeman, Wuchang, to parents, San Gabriel, CA, June 3, 1934, vol. 1, China Letters and Round the World, 510, private collection of Dorothea Wakeman Howe, San Diego, CA.
25. DKW, May 14, 1934, 488.
26. See Robert T. Handy, "The American Religious Depression, 1926–1935," *Church History* 29, no. 1 (March 1960): 3–16.

27. Dorothea Kingsley Wakeman, Kuling [Guling], Kwangsi [Jiangxi], to parents, San Gabriel, CA, June 25, 1934, vol. 1, China Letters and Round the World, 520, private collection of Dorothea Wakeman Howe, San Diego, CA.

28. Dorothea Kingsley Wakeman, Kuling, Kwangsi, to parents, San Gabriel, CA, June 27, 1934, vol. 1, China Letters and Round the World, 521, private collection of Dorothea Wakeman Howe, San Diego, CA.

29. Dorothea Wakeman Howe, interview by author, October 7, 1997, Solana Beach, CA.

30. Dorothea Kingsley Wakeman, Kuling, Kwangsi, to parents, San Gabriel, CA, July 27, 1934, vol. 3, China Letters and Round the World, 1, private collection of Dorothea Wakeman Howe, San Diego, CA.

31. Ibid.; Dorothea Kingsley Wakeman, Kuling, Kwangsi, to parents, San Gabriel, CA, July 21, 1934, vol. 1, China Letters and Round the World, 555, private collection of Dorothea Wakeman Howe, San Diego, CA.

32. Dorothea Kingsley Wakeman, Wuchang, to parents, San Gabriel, CA, April 24, 1936, vol. 4, China Letters and Round the World, private collection of Dorothea Wakeman Howe, San Diego, CA.

33. Dorothea Kingsley Wakeman, Kuling, Kiukiang, to parents, San Gabriel, CA, August 12, 1934, vol. 2, China Letters and Round the World, 573–74, private collection of Dorothea Wakeman Howe, San Diego, CA.

34. Dorothea Kingsley Wakeman Howe, interview by author, September 25, 1997, Solana Beach, CA; hereafter cited as DWH interview, September 25, 1997.

35. Dorothea Kingsley Wakeman, Wuchang, to parents, San Gabriel, CA, September 14, 1934, vol. 2, China Letters and Round the World, 608, private collection of Dorothea Wakeman Howe, San Diego, CA.

36. Dorothea Kingsley Wakeman, Wuchang, to parents, San Gabriel, CA, June 3, 1934, vol. 1, China Letters and Round the World, 510, private collection of Dorothea Wakeman Howe, San Diego, CA.

37. Tiffin was the term used to designate lunch; its derivation is English and Indian.

38. St. Andrew's Day, November 30, honors the patron saint of Scotland. Guy Fawkes Day celebrates the man executed for his unsuccessful attempt to blow up the English Parliament on November 5, 1605.

39. One of the major reasons for Dorothea's active social life was that it provided a way to diffuse her father's criticism of her decision to become a missionary by showing him that her behavior was totally unlike that of Julia Clark.

40. Dorothea Kingsley Wakeman, Wuchang, to parents, San Gabriel, CA, October 9, 1935, vol. 2, China Letters and Round the World, 978, private collection of Dorothea Wakeman Howe, San Diego, CA.

41. Dorothea Kingsley Wakeman, Wuchang, to parents, San Gabriel, CA, May 3, 1934, vol. 1, China Letters and Round the World, 483, private collection of Dorothea Wakeman Howe, San Diego, CA; hereafter cited as DKW, May 3, 1934.

42. The "recent trouble" was actually the Japanese invasion of northeast China from their puppet state of Manzhouguo in 1933. Manchuria was occupied by the Japanese in 1931 when they invaded with virtually no resistance from Zhang Xueliang's warlord army. The Japanese installed the last Qing emperor, Puyi, as the so-called head of state in 1932. Puyi was further declared emperor in 1934. Only Axis or Axis-occupied countries ever recognized Manzhouguo as a legitimate state; DKW, May 3, 1934, 483.

43. Dorothea Wakeman Howe, interview by author, November 11, 1997, Solana Beach, CA.

44. Dorothea Kingsley Wakeman, Wuchang, to parents, San Gabriel, CA, April 27, 1935, vol. 2, China Letters and Round the World, 862–83, private collection of Dorothea Wakeman Howe, San Diego, CA; hereafter cited as DKW, April 27, 1935.

45. Ibid., 863.

46. The New Life Movement was Chiang Kai-shek's attempt to develop a unifying ideology for China that drew upon the doctrines of Sun Yat-sen, reformist social strategies of Christian missionaries, and his own views on Confucian tenets with regard to the formation of a loyal and moral human character. He declared " 'a new national consciousness and mass psychology' that, through the revived force of the virtues of 'etiquette, justice, integrity, and conscientiousness' would lead to 'the social regeneration of China.' " Jonathan D. Spence, *The Search for Modern China* (New York: W.W. Norton, 1990), 414.

47. DKW, April 27, 1935, 863–64.

48. Dorothea Kingsley Wakeman, Wuchang, to parents, San Gabriel, CA, June 13, [1935], vol. 2, China Letters and Round the World, 892, private collection of Dorothea Wakeman Howe, San Diego, CA.

49. Dorothea Kingsley Wakeman, Kuling, Kwangsi, letter to parents, San Gabriel, CA, July 27, 1935, vol. 2, China Letters and Round the World, 3, private collection of Dorothea Wakeman Howe, San Diego, CA.

50. Venetia Cox, Wuchang, to Bishop [Logan H. Roots], Hankow, January 14, 1933, file RG-64-196, Archives of the Episcopal Church, Venetia Cox file, 1930–39, Austin, TX.

51. Dorothea Kingsley Wakeman, Wuchang, to parents, San Gabriel, CA, September 14, 1935, vol. 2, China Letters and Round the World, 956, private collection of Dorothea Wakeman Howe, San Diego, CA.

52. Ibid., 956–57.

53. Ibid., 959.

54. Dorothea Wakeman Howe, interview by author, July 2, 1997, Solana Beach, CA.

55. Dorothea Wakeman Howe, interview by author, May 27, 1997, Solana Beach, CA. If one was going to use a "squeeze," then salt was a good choice whether it was purchased or not. If you purchased it, salt could be used as an important source of exchange. In dynastic China, from the mid-1700s until 1850, salt was such an important commodity that it ranked "either first or second (to grain) in the total value of commodities" traded at Hankou. Although its value declined in importance during the latter part of the nineteenth century, it continued to be used as a medium of exchange in Republican China. Rowe, *Commerce and Society,* 90–91.

56. Dorothea Kingsley Wakeman, Wuchang, to parents, San Gabriel, CA, March 31, 1937, vol. 4, China Letters and Round the World, 1, private collection of Dorothea Wakeman Howe, San Diego, CA; Dorothea Kingsley Wakeman, Wuchang, to parents, San Gabriel, CA, July 7, 1936, vol. 4, China Letters and Round the World, 1, private collection of Dorothea Wakeman Howe, San Diego, CA.

57. Dorothea Kingsley Wakeman, Wuchang, to parents, San Gabriel, CA, February 25, 1935, vol. 2, China Letters and Round the World, 820–21, private collection of Dorothea Wakeman Howe, San Diego, CA.

58. Dorothea Kingsley Wakeman, Wuchang, to parents, San Gabriel, CA, November 10, 1935, vol. 2, China Letters and Round the World, 1, private collection of Dorothea Wakeman Howe, San Diego, CA.

59. Dorothea Kingsley Wakeman, Wuchang, to parents, San Gabriel, CA, November 8, 1935, vol. 3, China Letters and Round the World, 1–2, private collection of Dorothea Wakeman Howe, San Diego, CA; Dorothea Kingsley Wakeman, Wuchang, to parents, San Gabriel, CA, January 19, 1936, vol. 3, China Letters and Round the World, 2, private collection of Dorothea Wakeman Howe, San Diego, CA.

60. The Tanggu Truce ended the fighting between the Chinese and the Japanese that had been occurring since the Japanese invaded Manchuria. Under the truce the Chinese agreed to the creation of Manzhouguo and to the Japanese occupation of Rehe and the land north

of the Great Wall. Once the Japanese crossed into southern Hebei following the Marco Polo Bridge incident, the War of Resistance Against the Japanese began.

61. Dorothea Kingsley Wakeman, Wuchang, to parents, San Gabriel, CA, December 20, 1935, vol. 2, China Letters and Round the World, 1000, private collection of Dorothea Wakeman Howe, San Diego, CA; hereafter cited as DKW, December 20, 1935. Located to the east of St Hilda's, Wuhan University was completed in 1932. It was the sole public university in Wuhan. MacKinnon, *Wuhan, 1938,* 15.

62. DKW, December 20, 1935.

63. Dorothea Kingsley Wakeman, to parents, San Gabriel, CA, December 29, 1935, vol. 2, China Letters and Round the World, 1006, private collection of Dorothea Wakeman Howe, San Diego, CA; hereafter cited as DKW, December 29, 1935.

64. D.K.W., "St. Hilda's Notes," *Hankow Newsletter* 15 (March 1935): 7; D.K.W., "St. Hilda's Notes," *Hankow Newsletter* 15 (May 1935): 7–8; D.K.W., "St. Hilda's Notes," *Hankow Newsletter* 15 (June 1935): 8–9; D.K.W., "St. Hilda's Notes," *Hankow Newsletter* 15 (September 1935): 15.

65. DKW, December 29, 1935, 1022.

66. The relatively quiescent reaction of the girls in 1935 contrasts significantly from the reaction of the girls, under Yuanshuang's leadership, in 1931 and 1933 to Japanese military advances into Chinese territory. Clearly Principal Tso's curtailment of free speech on the campus was successful in controlling political movements at St. Hilda's; ibid., 1023–24.

67. Ibid., 1024.

68. Dorothea Kingsley Wakeman, Wuchang, to parents, San Gabriel, CA, January 9, 1936, vol. 3, China Letters and Round the World, 1, private collection of Dorothea Wakeman Howe, San Diego, CA.

69. Dorothea Kingsley Wakeman, Wuchang, to parents, San Gabriel, CA, January 15, 1936, vol. 3, China Letters and Round the World, private collection of Dorothea Wakeman Howe, San Diego, CA. Zhili Province became Hebei Province in 1928.

70. Dorothea Kingsley Wakeman, Wuchang, to parents, San Gabriel, CA, April 23, 1936, vol. 4, China Letters and Round the World, 1, private collection of Dorothea Wakeman Howe, San Diego, CA; hereafter cited as DKW, April 23, 1936.

71. Hazel F. Gosline, Wuchang, to Miss Grace Lindley, New York, NY, April 7, 1936, file RG-64-202, Archives of the Episcopal Church, Hazel F. Gosline file, 1925–39, Austin, TX.

72. Dorothea Kingsley Wakeman, Wuchang, to parents, San Gabriel, CA, March 22, [1936], vol. 4, China Letters and Round the World, 1, private collection of Dorothea Wakeman Howe, San Diego, CA; DKW, April 23, 1936.

73. "St. Hilda's Concert and Operetta," *Hankow Newsletter* 16 (May 1936): 6.

74. Dorothea Kingsley Wakeman, Wuchang, to parents, San Gabriel, CA, May 19, 1936, vol. 3, China Letters and Round the World, 1–2, private collection of Dorothea Wakeman Howe, San Diego, CA.

75. Ibid., 1. Gilmore Brown was the founder of the Pasadena Playhouse in California.

76. Ibid., 2.

77. "St. Hilda's Concert," *Hankow Newsletter,* 6–7.

78. Dorothea Kingsley Wakeman, Wuchang, to parents, San Gabriel, CA, July 15, 1936, vol. 4, China Letters and Round the World, 2, private collection of Dorothea Wakeman Howe, San Diego, CA.

79. Dorothea Kingsley Wakeman, Wuchang, to parents, San Gabriel, CA, June 19, 1936, vol. 4, China Letters and Round the World, 2, private collection of Dorothea Wakeman Howe, San Diego, CA.

80. Dorothea Kingsley Wakeman, Peiping, to parents, San Gabriel, CA, August 6, 1936, vol. 4, China Letters and Round the World, 2, private collection of Dorothea Wakeman Howe, San Diego, CA.
81. Ibid.
82. Ibid., 4.
83. Ibid., 3.
84. Dorothea Kingsley Wakeman, Wuchang, to parents, San Gabriel, CA, September 24, 1936, vol. 4, China Letters and Round the World, private collection of Dorothea Wakeman Howe, San Diego, CA; Dorothea Kingsley Wakeman, Wuchang, to parents, San Gabriel, CA, October 1, 1936, vol. 4, China Letters and Round the World, private collection of Dorothea Wakeman Howe, San Diego, CA; hereafter cited as DKW, October 1, 1936.
85. DKW, October 1, 1936.
86. Zhang Xueliang helped kidnap Chiang on the morning of December 12, 1936. Chiang's obsession with eradicating the Communist bases served as an impetus for his abduction. Zhang was anxious to get Chiang to form a second "United Front" with the Communists so that together they could prepare for the coming war with the Japanese instead of fighting with each other. After Chiang agreed, he was released. At that point Zhang accompanied Chiang to Nanjing where he was placed under house arrest for the next 55 years. After his sentence was commuted, Zhang moved to Hawaii where he died in 2001 at the age of 100. For an account of the events of the so-called "Xi'an Incident," see Spence, *Modern China,* 418–24.
87. Dorothea Kingsley Wakeman, Wuchang, to parents, San Gabriel, CA, December 16, 1936, vol. 4, China Letters and Round the World, 1, private collection of Dorothea Wakeman Howe, San Diego, CA.
88. Dorothea Kingsley Wakeman, Wuchang, to parents, San Gabriel, CA, January 17, 1936, vol. 4, China Letters and Round the World, 3, private collection of Dorothea Wakeman Howe, San Diego, CA.
89. DKW, January 30, 1937.
90. Ibid., 2.
91. Dorothea Kingsley Wakeman, Wuchang, to parents, San Gabriel, CA, March 13, 1937, vol. 4, China Letters and Round the World, 4, private collection of Dorothea Wakeman Howe, San Diego, CA.
92. Earl Seeley Wakeman, San Gabriel, CA, to Dorothea Kingsley Wakeman, Wuchang, n.d. [probably April 1937], private collection of Dorothea Wakeman Howe, San Diego, CA.
93. Ibid.
94. Dorothea Kingsley Wakeman, Wuchang, to parents, San Gabriel, CA, June 5, 1937, vol. 4, China Letters and Round the World, 1, private collection of Dorothea Wakeman Howe, San Diego, CA; hereafter cited as DKW, June 5, 1937.
95. Ibid., 2.
96. Dorothea Kingsley Wakeman, Wuchang, letter to parents, San Gabriel, CA, May 15, 1937, vol. 4, China Letters and Round the World, 1, private collection of Dorothea Wakeman Howe, San Diego, CA.
97. Ibid., 2.
98. DKW, June 5, 1937.
99. Dorothea Kingsley Wakeman, Wuchang, to parents, San Gabriel, CA, May 20, 1937, vol. 4, China Letters and Round the World, private collection of Dorothea Wakeman Howe, San Diego, CA.
100. Dorothea Kingsley Wakeman, Wuchang, to parents, San Gabriel, CA, June 5, 1937, vol. 4, China Letters and Round the World, 2, private collection of Dorothea Wakeman Howe, San Diego, CA.

Chapter 6. Into the West

1. Hazel F. Gosline, Sagada, Philippines, to Friends at Saint John's [Church], Georgetown, Washington, DC, November 14, 1962, private collection of Hazel F. Gosline, Eleanor Wheeler, Bainbridge Island, WA; hereafter cited as Gosline, November 14, 1962.

2. Olive B. Tomlin, "Saint Hilda's," *Hankow Newsletter* 17, no. 7–8 (September–October 1937): 20.

3. Ibid.

4. Hazel F. Gosline, Annual Report for the Year 1937, Wuchang, January 10, 1938, file RG-64-70-15, Archives of the Episcopal Church, Hazel Gosline file, 1930–39, Austin, TX; hereafter cited as Gosline, Annual Report 1937; L[ogan] H. R[oots], "Bishop's Column," *Hankow Newsletter* 18, no. 1 (January–February 1938): 1; O[live] B. T[omlin], "Saint Hilda's," *Hankow Newsletter* 18, no. 1 (January–February 1938): 5.

5. Tomlin, "Saint Hilda's," January–February 1938.

6. Ibid.

7. Ibid.

8. Ibid.

9. A[lfred] A. G[ilman], "An Appeal to the Government and People of Japan," *Hankow Newsletter* 18, nos. 5–8 (May–August 1938): 2.

10. Ibid.

11. Wuhan served as the provisional capital of Nationalist China from the fall of Nanjing in December 1937 until its occupation by the Japanese in October 1938.

12. Alfred A. Gilman, Hankou, to Dear Folks, United States, July 19, 1938, file RG-64-69-13, Archives of the Episcopal Church, Alfred A. Gilman file, 1938, Austin, TX; MacKinnon, 121.

13. Arthur and Netta Allen, "The *An Chia Pao*" [Allen Family Newspaper], La Jolla, CA, to Dear Friends, United States, June 28, 1940, file RG-64-63-2, Archives of the Episcopal Church, Arthur J. Allen file, 1940–41, Austin, TX; Arthur and Netta Allen, "The *An Chia Pao* [Allen Family Newspaper], Chennan, Yunnan to Dear Friends, United States, August 1941, file RG-64-63-2, Archives of the Episcopal Church, Arthur J. Allen file, 1940–41, Austin, TX; hereafter cited as Allen and Allen, August 1941. Li Xueying, interview by author, 1990, Wuchang; hereafter cited as Li interview, 1990. Venetia Cox, Chuan Hsien, Kwangsi, to Friends, United States, November 9, 1938, file RG-64-67-10, Archives of the Episcopal Church, Venetia Cox file, 1930–39, Austin, TX.

14. Gosline, November 14, 1962. Hazel F. Gosline, "Notes for a speech," n.d., private collection of Hazel F. Gosline, Eleanor Wheeler, Bainbridge Island, WA; hereafter cited as Gosline, "Speech."

15. Gosline, November 14, 1962.

16. Hazel F. Gosline, Hong Kong, to Dr. [John W.] Wood, New York, NY, June 21, 1939, file RG-64-70-15, Archives of the Episcopal Church, Hazel Gosline file, 1930–39, Austin, TX.

17. Yang Kongxian, interview by author, 1990, Wuchang; hereafter cited as Yang interview, 1990.

18. Ibid.; Gosline, June 21, 1939.

19. Gosline, June 21, 1939.

20. Yang interview, 1990.

21. Ibid.; Allen and Allen, August 1941; Arthur J. Allen, Chennan, Yunnan, to Mr. James E. Whitney, New York, NY, July 20, 1941, file RG-64-63-2, Archives of the Episcopal Church, Arthur J. Allen file, 1940–41, Austin, TX; Gosline, June 21, 1939.

22. Allen and Allen, August 1941.

23. Ibid.

24. Ibid.
25. Arthur J. Allen, Chennan, Yunnan, to Rev. A. B. Parson, New York, NY, July 19, 1941, file RG-64-63-2, Archives of the Episcopal Church, Arthur J. Allen file, 1940–41, Austin, TX.
26. Ibid.; Yang interview, 1990.
27. Yang interview, 1990.
28. Venetia Cox, Chennan, Yunnan, to Mr. [John W.] Wood, New York, NY, April 25, 1940, file RG-64-67-11, Archives of the Episcopal Church, Venetia Cox file, 1940–50, Austin, TX
29. Venetia Cox, Chennan, Yunnan, to Dr. [John W.]Wood, New York, NY, September 2, 1940, file RG-64-67-11, Archives of the Episcopal Church, Venetia Cox file, 1940–50, Austin, TX.
30. Yang interview, 1990.
31. Ibid.; Li interview, 1990. For a hilarious description of dealing with body lice, see William Hinton, *Fanshen: A Documentary of Revolution in a Chinese Village* (New York: Vintage Books, 1966).
32. Yang interview, 1990.
33. Cox, September 2, 1940.
34. Yang interview, 1990; Gosline, November 14, 1962; Alfred A. Gilman, Tsingchen, Kweichow, to My Dear Folks, September 11, 1944, file RG-64-70-2, Archives of the Episcopal Church, Alfred A. Gilman file, 1944, Austin, TX.
35. Yang interview, 1990; Li interview, 1990.
36. Wuhan was used as the staging area for the launching of the ICHIGO offensive in the south; consequently, the city was heavily bombarded by the U.S. Air Force in December 1944. See MacKinnon, *Wuhan, 1938,* 112–13.
37. Venetia Cox, Wuchang, to Father [A. Ervine] Swift, Wuchang, June 9, 1946, file RG-64-67-11, Archives of the Episcopal Church, Venetia Cox file, 1940–50, Austin, TX.
38. Ibid.
39. Alfred A. Gilman, Kunming, to Dr. [James Thayer] Addison, New York, NY, October 4, 1943, file RG-64-70-1, Archives of the Episcopal Church, Alfred A. Gilman file, 1942–43, Austin, TX; Gosline, "Speech."
40. Gosline, November 14, 1962.
41. Zhen Yifang, interview by author, August 4, 1990, Wuchang.
42. Hazel F. Gosline, Wuchang, to Earl [Fowler], New York, NY, May 28, 1950, file RG-64-70-16, Archives of the Episcopal Church, Hazel Gosline file, 1942–50, Austin, TX.
43. Olive Bird Tomlin, Hong Kong, to Bishop [John B.] Bentley, New York, NY, September 10, 1950, file RG-64-94-16, Archives of the Episcopal Church, Olive Bird Tomlin file, 1947–50, Austin, TX; Olive Bird Tomlin, Hong Kong, to J. Earl Fowler, New York, NY, September 13, 1950, file RG-64-94-16, Archives of the Episcopal Church, Olive Bird Tomlin file, 1947–50, Austin, TX; Hazel F. Gosline, Hong Kong, to Margaret, September 27, 1950, file RG-64-70-16, Archives of the Episcopal Church, Hazel F. Gosline file, 1942–50, Austin, TX.
44. Gosline, September 27, 1950.
45. With careful looking, the chapel building can be seen on the Web site: http://www.panoramio.com/photo/1335429.
46. For an interesting study of the YMCA (and by inference, the YWCA), the Social Gospel, and their impact on China, see Jun Xing, *Baptized in the Fire of Revolution: The American Social Gospel and the YMCA in China: 1919–1937* (Bethlehem, PA: Lehigh University Press, 1996).
47. While the foreigners virtually excluded the Chinese, except for their servants, from their area in Guling, the wealthy Chinese virtually excluded foreigners from theirs. While both groups may have been *in* the same place, they were not *of* the same place, and this dichotomy explains much of the missionary experience in China.

48. Patty [Margaret] Sherman, Chuan Hsien, Kwangsi, to Dorothea Kingsley Wakeman, New Canaan, CT, October 1, 1938, private collection of Dorothea Wakeman Howe, San Diego, CA.

49. Huang Shan is a mountain that sits above the city of Chongqing. During the sweltering summers, high-ranking officials, professionals, and the wealthy retreated to their summer homes to escape the heat.

50. Liu's great-great-grandfather and great-grandfather had been high-ranking officials in the Qing dynasty, and he had been the "Tupan" (duban—military governor) of Shaanxi Province. See James E. Sheridan, *Chinese Warlord: The Career of Feng Yüshiang* (Stanford, CA: Stanford University Press, 1966), 207. With the revolution he became a powerful warlord, and following the Northern Expedition he "assumed the office of the pacification governor of Henan, Shaanxi, and Shanxi provincial border area." Available from: http://english.gongyi.gov.cn/content.asp?id=1389&id_type=46. In 1934 he became the " 'Bandits Exterminating' commander in chief about the border area of Henan, Hubei and Anhui" Provinces. Available from: http://english.gongyi.gov.cn/content.asp?id=1389&id_type=44. By 1937 he became "morally disabled" due to tertiary syphilis and quit politics. Available from: http://rulers.org/index13.htm.

51. According to Shu Hsin-ch'eng, Chin-tai Chung-kuo liu-sheh shin (Shanghai, 1933) cited in Tse-tsung Chow: "Statistics show that during this period [1903–19] 41.51 per cent of the Chinese students abroad were in Japan, 33.85 per cent in the United States, and 24.64 in European countries, mostly Germany, France, and Great Britain." Tse-tsung Chow, *The May Fourth Movement: Intellectual Revolution in Modern China* (Stanford, CA: Stanford University Press, 1960), 31n.

52. After the capture of Wuhan, the front between Chinese and Japanese lines remained relatively stable until the Japanese launched Operation ICHIGO in 1944.

53. Available from: http://generals.dk/general/Liu_Xianjie/_/China.html. Following this defeat, Liu Maoen's Fourteenth Army Group was disbanded, and he became the chairman of Henan Province and the commander of the Henan Province Garrison. Available from: http://pwencycl.kgbudge.com/L/i/Liu_Mao-en.htm; and http://english.gongyi.gov.cn/content.asp?id=1389&id_type=46.

54.The Allens were able to eventually return to China by taking the Burma Road from India to Zhenan, Yunnan Province, where they remained with the Hankou Diocesan Union School.

55. Dorothea Kingsley Wakeman, letter to parents, San Gabriel, CA, undated 1937 letter, vol. 4, private collection of Dorothea Wakeman Howe, San Diego, CA.

56. Dorothea Kingsley Wakeman, Oberhofen, Switzerland, letter to parents, San Gabriel, CA, August 10, 1937, vol. 4, private collection of Dorothea Wakeman Howe, San Diego, CA; hereafter cited as DKW, August 10, 1937.

57. Dorothea Kingsley Wakeman, Magdeburg, Germany, letter to parents, San Gabriel, CA, August 14, 1937, vol. 4, private collection of Dorothea Wakeman Howe, San Diego, CA.

58. Ibid.

59. Dorothea Kingsley Wakeman, Stockholm, letter to parents, San Gabriel, CA, August 24, 1937, vol. 4, private collection of Dorothea Wakeman Howe, San Diego, CA.

60. DKW, August 10, 1937.

61. Dorothea Kingsley Wakeman, London, letter to parents, San Gabriel, CA, September 7, 1937, vol. 4, private collection of Dorothea Wakeman Howe, San Diego, CA.

62. Ibid.

63. DKW, August 10, 1937.

64. Dorothea Wakeman Howe, interview by author, March 10, 1998, Solana Beach, CA; hereafter cited as DWH interview, March 10, 1998.

65. Dorothea Kingsley Wakeman, personal note, December 24, 1937, private collection of Dorothea Wakeman Howe, San Diego, CA.

66. *The Industrial Arts Cooperative Service* (New York: Industrial Arts Cooperative Service, 1939).

67. DWH interview, March 10, 1998.

68. DWH interview, July 2, 1997.

69. Ibid.

70. Ibid.

71. DWH interview, March 10, 1998. Dorothea Kingsley Wakeman, personal note, n.d. [probably 1938], private collection of Dorothea Wakeman Howe, San Diego, CA; hereafter cited as DKW personal note 1938.

72. DWH interview, March 10, 1998.

73. DKW personal note 1938.

74. DWH interview, March 10, 1998.

75. Ibid.

76. Ibid.

77. Ibid.

78. Ibid.

79. Family e-mail correspondence to Judith Liu, July 2006, San Diego, CA. Margaret Bowlus Stehle to Judith Liu, San Diego, CA, e-mail correspondence, June 13, 2009; hereafter cited as Stehle, June 13, 2009.

80. Stehle, June 13, 2009.

81. DWH interview, June 4, 1998.

82. "Peking Premiere, October 3, 1972. Piano Duo-logues with the Haddens" flyer, private collection of Dorothea Wakeman Howe; Donal Henahan, "U.S. Pianists Give China Taste of Rock (and Bach)," *New York Times,* November 8, 1972.

83. Dorothea Wakeman Howe, interview by author, June 16, 1997, Solana Beach, CA.

84. Episcopal News Service: Press Release # 79122, April 19, 1979. Available from: http://www.episcopalarchives.org/cgi-bin/ENS/ENSpress_release.pl?pr_number=79122.

85. Eleanor Wheeler, e-mail correspondence to Judith Liu, June 28, 2009.

86. DWH interview, June 2, 1997.

87. St. Hilda's School for Girls no longer physically exists as a missionary school—it became Wuchang's Number 25 Middle School in 1953. In honor of its Christian roots, however, the name of a small shop selling student-made products contains the Chinese characters of Xilida—used in the transliteration of the word "Hilda." St. Hilda's does, however, continue to exist in the vividly recalled memories and recollections of its ever-diminishing number of graduates. More importantly, its legacy lives on through the impact it made on the lives of those of us who are the friends and families of the graduates and teachers of St. Hilda's.

Appendix A: A Chinese Context

1. Edward A. McCord, *The Power of the Gun: The Emergence of Modern Chinese Warlordism* (Berkeley: University of California Press, 1993), 23.

2. See Hsi-Sheng Ch'i, *Warlord Politics in China, 1916–1928* (Stanford, CA: Stanford University Press, 1976), 11–12.

3. McCord, *Power of the Gun,* 23.

4. "Beiyang, meaning literally 'Northern Ocean', refers to the customs revenues collected in North China, which were used to fund first the Beiyang Fleet and later the Beiyang Army." Edward L. Dreyer, *China at War, 1901–1949* (New York: Longman, 1995), 14.

5. The Treaty of Shimonoseki which ended the war, in essence, made Korea a tributary state of Japan and ceded Taiwan to Japan.

6. James E. Sheridan, *China in Disintegration: The Republican Era in Chinese History, 1912–1949* (New York: Free Press, 1977), 15.

7. Ibid., 39.

8. See Lucien Pye, "How China's Nationalism was Shanghaied," *Australian Journal of Chinese Affairs* 29 (January 1993): 107–33.

9. Marie-Claire Bergère, *The Golden Age of the Chinese Bourgeoisie, 1911–1937,* trans. Janet Lloyd (Cambridge: Cambridge University Press, 1989, 28.

10. Ibid., 279.

11. Pye, "China's Nationalism," 115. (This is not a novel situation, however. Even in the United States the "real America" is somehow associated with the nonurban areas of the country despite the fact that they do not represent the social reality faced by the majority of Americans.)

12. Jessie Gregory Lutz, "Chinese Nationalism and the Anti-Christian Campaigns of the 1920s," *Modern Asian Studies* 10, no. 3 (1976): 396.

13. Chün-tu Hsüeh, *Huang Hsing and the Chinese Revolution* (Stanford, CA: Stanford University Press, 1961), 135.

14. Sheridan, *China,* 49.

15. McCord, *Power of the Gun,* 162.

16. The Twenty-one Demands were promulgated in January 1915. If Yuan had accepted all of Japan's Twenty-one Demands, then China would have become a tributary state of Japan. In the end thirteen of the twenty-one demands were accepted, but the most nettlesome was the agreement that the existing German concessions in Shandong Province would be turned over to the Japanese. This was seen, not unjustifiably, as another imperialist affront to Chinese sovereignty. The Twenty-one Demands seriously undermined Yuan's authority by making China's strongest political and military figure acquiesce to the leaders of a former tributary state. Is it possible that Yuan and his supporters felt his position in China would be strengthened if he became the new emperor? If that is possible, then they seriously miscalculated the situation.

17. Sheridan, *Chinese Warlord,* 10.

18. See Gavan McCormack, *Chang Tso-lin in Northeast China, 1911–1928: China, Japan, and the Manchurian Idea* (Stanford, CA: Stanford University Press, 1977), 45–47.

19. As McCormack points out, the term, "Manchuria," is primarily an imperialist shortcut used to describe the non-Han-majority provinces of Heilongjiang, Jilin, and Liaoning that comprised what the Chinese called Dongbei—the Northeast—following the 1911 Revolution. Ibid., 4. While these provinces were sparsely populated, they provided a disproportionate share of China's export income. For example, Liaoning with 3.2 percent of China's population accounted for 33.0 percent of its coal output; 32.7 percent of its iron output; and 21.5 percent of its foreign trade in 1929. Ibid., 7.

20. The movement received its name from a protest held in Beijing on May 4, 1919. The term, May Fourth Movement, is a historical shortcut. The actual movement roughly covers the period from the upsurge in patriotic fervor resulting from the promulgation of the Twenty-one Demands by Japan in 1915 through the Paris Peace Conference of 1919 and into the anti-Christian crusade of 1920–22. All of these were instances where the Chinese intelligentsia recognized the need for substantive social change if China was to regain its place on the world stage. In essence, "the May Fourth Movement was the source from which sprang the principal ideological currents that gave direction to the history of contemporary China—liberalism, nationalism, and communism." Bergère, *Golden Age,* 209.

21. Tse-tsung Chow, *May Fourth Movement,* 1.

22. Because of its relative geographical isolation, Yan was able to rule Shanxi Province from 1911 until 1949 (with a brief hiatus in the early 1930s).

23. Other than the size of their armies, what differentiated a bandit from a warlord? "The bandit had no official position; he killed and stole and fled. The warlord had military rank; he killed and stole and stayed." Sheridan, *China,* 92.

24. For an excellent look at Chinese banditry, see Phil Billingsley, *Bandits in Republican China* (Stanford, CA: Stanford University Press, 1988).

25. Ibid., 43. Exploitation of the peasantry by landlords was nothing new, and "a landlord's seizure of 50 percent or even 75 percent of a tenant's crop as rent was accepted as normal" (ibid., 273). The crops that were accepted as rent, however, were changing. By forcing the peasants to grow nonedible, cash crops, the warlords and landlords diminished the peasantry's ability to feed itself.

26. The name, Zhongguo Tongmenghui, is normally shortened to Tongmenghui. Hsüeh, *Huang Hsing,* 42.

27. McCord, *Power of the Gun,* 268.

28. Ibid., 277.

29. The people involved with the academy reads like a "Who's Who" of Chinese figures. The academy's first commandant was Chiang Kai-shek. The political affairs part of the academy had the Communist, Zhou Enlai, the GMD rightist, Hu Hanmin, and the GMD leftist, Wang Jingwei, who would become the putative leader of occupied China during the War of Resistance Against the Japanese.

30. McCormack, *Chang Tso-lin,* 209.

31. Ch'i, *Warlord Politics,* 229–30.

32. Ibid., 230.

33. Lloyd Eastman considers that part of the GMD controlled by Chiang as "Centrists," but they had much more in common with the right GMD than they did with the left GMD. Lloyd E. Eastman, "Nationalist China during the Nanking decade, 1927–1937" in *The Nationalist Era in China, 1927–1949,* Lloyd E. Eastman et al. (Cambridge: Cambridge University Press, 1991): 2.

34. Michael G. Murdock, "Exploiting Anti-Imperialism: Popular Forces and Nation-State-Building During China's Northern Expedition, 1926 1927," *Modern China* 35, no. 1 (January 2009): 77. Up until this point, foreign governments recognized whatever government was in power in Beijing as the legitimate government of China. As Ch'i notes: "The trouble is, however, that in the thirteen years after the founding of the Republic, China had at least four different constitutions, and all of them became dead letters as soon as they were promulgated. . . . Most political institutions were also in a state of flux; the form of government alternated among monarchy, republic, regency, etc., a number of times during this brief period. In addition to the major institutional changes, the head of state changed nine times in less than twelve years between 1916 and 1928 in the north alone; the average tenure was less than sixteen months. In the south the same 'musical chairs' phenomenon was occurring in the rival [GMD] government with equal abandon" (Ch'i, *Warlord Politics,* 2).

35. While the CCP had been successful in organizing industrial workers and the peasantry, they did not have a military wing. Thus on August 1, 1927 (Dreyer, *China at War,* 5), the People's Liberation Army (PLA) was born, and within two weeks the main party apparatus in Shanghai was attacked. Neither the warlord factions nor the GMD had any desire for a strong CCP because it was considered to be a threat to both of them. If the CCP organized the proletariat as part of the United Front with the GMD, it alienated the Chinese business elite—traditionally the main group to support liberal democracy—and if it organized the peasantry to overthrow the existing rural social structure, it endangered a major source of income available for financing warlord armies—the cash crops peasants were increasingly being forced to cultivate.

36. Sheridan, *China,* 172–73.

37. Eastman, "Nationlist China," 2.

38. Sheridan, *China,* 176.

39. Ibid.

40. Harold R. Isaacs, *The Tragedy of the Chinese Revolution,* 2nd rev. ed. (Stanford, CA: Stanford University Press, 1961), 255.

41. Dreyer, *China at War,* 147. The Song family was one of China's most prominent families. Song Qingling, Meiling's older sister, was Sun Yat-sen's widow and the Nationalist government's finance minister was their brother, Song Ziwen (T. V. Soong). Chiang Kai-shek and Song Meiling were married on December 1, 1927.

42. Eastman, "Nationalist China," 2.

43. Ibid., 3.

44. Ibid., 9.

45. Interestingly, the two provinces whose names represented the two major factions that challenged the Guomindang/Guominjun alliance—Fengtian and Zhili—had their names changed following the reunification of the country. Fengtian became Liaoning; Zhili became Hebei.

46. See C. Martin Wilbur, *The Nationalist Revolution in China, 1923–1928* (Cambridge: Cambridge University Press, 1983), 193–94, and Sheridan, *China,* 184. The remaining provinces, Qahar and Ningxia in the north, Yunnan and Guizhou in the southwest, Sichuan and Xikang in the near west, and Qinghai and Xinjiang in the far west were reasonably independent because of their physical isolation from provinces directly controlled by the GMD. Tibet considered itself to be independent from 1913 until the People's Liberation Army reoccupied it in 1950–51.

47. Lloyd E. Eastman, *Seeds of Destruction: Nationalist China in War and Revolution 1937–1949* (Stanford, CA: Stanford University Press, 1984), 2.

48. Ch'i, *Warlord Politics,* 56.

49. Chinese nationalism was anti-imperialist in essence; thus, the GMD based some of its legitimacy on its goal of ending the treaty port system. On this score it was only partially successful, and most of China's "successes" in ending the concessions to imperialist powers were not of its doing. First, the German concessions fell during World War I and the most important one—the Shandong concession—was ceded to the Japanese. Second, the Russian concessions were returned to the Chinese by the Soviets who, at least in their initial ideology, were decidedly anti-imperialist. Third, the anti-British May Thirtieth Movement of 1925 occurred as a consequence of Shanghai's International Settlement police firing on anti-imperialist demonstrators. It changed British policy toward China and remained a cause célèbre for Chinese nationalists. See Bickers, *Britain in China,* 4. Fourth, the most noticeable success the Northern Expedition produced—the seizing of the British concessions in Hankou and Jiujiang—was done by agents of the left GMD/CCP United Front as a result of the fervor caused by the May Thirtieth Movement.

50. For a firsthand account of the peasant movement in Hunan during the initial phase of the Northern Expedition, see Mao Zedong, "Report on an Investigation of the Peasant Movement in Hunan," in *Selected Readings from the Works of Mao Tse-tung* (Peking: Foreign Languages Press, 1967), 20–32.

51. Paul Linebarger, *The China of Chiang K'ai-shek: A Political Study* (Boston: World Peace Foundation, 1941), 7.

52. Dreyer, *China at War,* 356.

53. In 1932 Manchuria became the "independent" state of Manzhouguo ("land of the Manchus") with the last Qing emperor, Puyi, installed as its leader.

54. Eastman, "Nationalist China," 14.

55. Chiang Kai-shek quoted in Sheridan, *China,* 217.

56. Chiang ended the Blue Shirts in 1938 following the start of the Second United Front with the CCP. Eastman, *Abortive Revolution,* 79.

57. Eastman, "Nationalist China," 9.

58. Mary Wright, "From Revolution to Restoration: The Transformation of Kuomintang Ideology," *Far Eastern Quarterly* 14, no. 4 (August 1955): 524.
59. Eastman, *Abortive Revolution,* 67.
60. Ibid., 279.
61. Bergère, *Golden Age,* 286.
62. Eastman, *Seeds,* 89.
63. In actuality both groups maintained a top-down form of organization, but the CCP's increasingly Maoist version of communism held that it was the role of the party to formalize the "pure" but unfocused thoughts of the peasantry into a coherent plan and then explain to the peasants what their thoughts meant. While this argument may seem to verge on being balderdash, it provided the CCP with an enormous propaganda tool to use against the GMD. That is, the CCP showed that it cared about the peasants while the GMD showed that all it cared about was preserving the power of the landlords over the peasants. Thus while one party was perceived to be creating substantive social change, the other party was perceived to be inhibiting substantive social change. In the end this difference in perception on the value of social change for China meant that the CCP occupied the countryside while the GMD continued the warlord/occupying-army model of controlling the cities and transportation lines.
64. Guandong refers to an area in Liaoning (Fengtian) Province where the Japanese garrisoned soldiers assigned to protect its South Manchurian Railway. The most militaristic segment of the Japanese army came from the officer corps of the Guandong Army which, over time, became the name for the entire Japanese force in northern China. Much of the Japanese aggression directed at China prior to the War of Resistance was instigated by the Guandong Army.
65. See David Curtis Wright, *The History of China* (Westport, CT: Greenwood, 2001), 135–38.
66. Chiang never forgave their treachery. Both were placed under arrest. Yang was executed in 1949, and Zhang remained under house arrest until 1990 when he was pardoned by Li Denghui (Lee Teng-hui), Jiang Jingguo's (Chiang Ching-kuo—Chiang Kai-shek's son) successor as president of the Republic of China (Taiwan).
67. John Hunter Boyle, *China and Japan at War, 1937–1945: The Politics of Collaboration* (Stanford, CA: Stanford University Press, 1972), 109.
68. Theodore H. White and Annalee Jacoby, *Thunder Out of China* (New York: William Sloane, 1946), 139.
69. Boyle, *China and Japan,* 318.
70. For example, see MacKinnon, *Wuhan, 1938,* for riveting examples of Chinese victories and defeats during the period when Wuhan served as the capital of Nationalist China.
71. Diana Lary, "Introduction: The Context of War," in *China at War: Regions of China, 1937–1945,* ed. Stephen R. MacKinnon, Diana Lary, and Ezra F. Vogel (Stanford, CA: Stanford University Press): 9.
72. Stephen R. MacKinnon, "Conclusion: Wartime China" in *China at War: Regions of China, 1937–1945,* ed. Stephen R. MacKinnon, Diana Lary, and Ezra F. Vogel (Stanford, CA: Stanford University Press, 2007), 336.
73. MacKinnon, *Wuhan, 1938,* 48.
74. Lary, "Context of War," 11.
75. According to figures cited by Boyle, 70 million people lived in occupied Chinese territory; 43 million in guerrilla areas; 54 million in Communist-controlled areas; and 16 million in Free China. See note on page 315, Boyle, *China and Japan.* As with many statistics the numbers must not be taken as gospel. The total of 183 million people is roughly twice the number of people that MacKinnon cites as refugees, and this number, 95 million, is given as one-quarter of China's population. Given that some provinces may be included

in one survey and not in the other, the discrepancy between them is, nonetheless, large. What can be inferred, however, is that large numbers of Chinese became refugees during the war and that what passes as the actual political control of an area is a somewhat fluid concept.

76. MacKinnon, *Wuhan, 1938,* 2.

77. Boyle, *China and Japan,* 257.

78. Dreyer, *China at War,* 307.

79. Boyle, *China and Japan,* 319.

80. Ibid.

81. See http://www.history.army.mil/brochures/72-38/map3.JPG.

82. Dreyer, *China at War,* 266.

83. Ibid.

84. According to Maoist philosophy, not all Chinese were a part of "the people." See Mao Zedong, "On the Correct Handling of Contradictions among the People," in *Selected Readings,* 350–87.

Appendix B: An American Context

1. Frederick Jackson Turner, "The Significance of the Frontier in American History," in *The Frontier in American History* (New York: Henry Holt, 1920), 1–38.

2. William Appleman Williams, "The Frontier Thesis and American Foreign Policy," *The Pacific Historical Review* 24, no. 4 (November 1955): 380.

3. Frederick Jackson Turner, "The Problem of the West," in *The Frontier in American History* (New York: Henry Holt, 1920), 205.

4. Williams, "Frontier Thesis," 382.

5. The frontier was such an integral part of American mythology that John F. Kennedy used the term "New Frontier" as the motto for his presidential campaign in 1960 and it came to represent the catchphrase for his administration's programs.

6. Percentages available from: www.agclassroom.org/gan/timeline/index.htm. By 1930, the number had decreased to 21 percent of the labor force.

7. Rhys H. Williams and Susan M. Alexander, "Religious Rhetoric in American Populism: Civil Religion as Movement Ideology," *Journal for the Scientific Study of Religion* 33, no. 1 (March 1994): 11.

8. William F. Holmes, "Populism: In Search of Context," *Agricultural History* 64, no. 4 (Autumn 1990): 43.

9. But the underlying rationale of their market economy did not resemble ours. Currency had to be backed by hard metal reserves, and from 1873, that meant gold and only gold. For decades, gold and silver had been used for backing currency based on a ratio of sixteen ounces of silver being equal to one ounce of gold. Ironically at nearly the same time that silver was demonetized, the Comstock Lode was discovered, and the United States had the potential of being awash in silver. If the United States had returned to bimetallism based on the traditional sixteen to one ratio, inflation would have resulted, and even though the U.S. government exchanged silver for gold in various ratios from 1875 to 1900, the United States remained nominally on the gold standard, and the question of bimetallism remained a political "hot button" issue through the presidential election of 1900 when, after the Republican victory, gold became the sole currency standard.

10. Anne Mayhew, "A Reappraisal of the Causes of Farm Protest in the United States, 1870–1900," *Journal of Economic History* 32, no. 2 (June 1972): 468.

11. Ibid., 58.

12. In 1896 both the Democratic Party and the People's Party nominated William Jennings Bryan as their standard bearer though they each nominated different vice-presidential candidates. Bryan received 46.7 percent of the popular vote and 176 total electoral votes (149 as a Democrat; 27 as a Populist) to Republican William McKinley's 51 percent and 271 electoral votes.

13. See Williams and Alexander, "Religious," 3–9, and Holmes, "Populism," 33.

14. See Henry Demarest Lloyd, *Wealth Against Commonwealth* (New York: Harper & Brothers, 1894).

15. Holmes, "Populism," 44.

16. Mayhew, "Reappraisal," 473.

17. See Joseph R. Gusfield, *Symbolic Crusade: Status Politics and the American Temperance Movement,* 2nd ed. (Urbana: University of Illinois, 1986).

18. See Robert H. Wiebe, *The Search for Order, 1877–1920* (New York: Hill and Wang, 1967).

19. Arthur S. Link, "What Happened to the Progressive Movement in the 1920's," *American Historical Review* 64, no. 4 (July 1959): 836.

20. Daniel T. Rodgers, "In Search of Progressivism," in "The Promise of American History: Progress and Prospects," *Reviews in American History* 10, no. 4 (December 1982): 123.

21. See Henry F. May, *Protestant Churches and Industrial America* (New York: Harper & Brothers, 1949).

22. Paul A. Carter, *The Decline and Revival of the Social Gospel: Social and Political Liberalism in American Protestant Churches, 1920–1940* (Ithaca: Cornell University Press, 1954), 12.

23. Ibid., 13; Handy, *Social Gospel,* 5.

24. Handy, *Social Gospel,* 6.

25. Charles Howard Hopkins, *The Rise of the Social Gospel in American Protestantism, 1865–1915* (New Haven: Yale University Press, 1940), 320.

26. Carter, *Decline,* 4.

27. Jacob H. Dorn, "The Social Gospel and Socialism: A Comparison of the Thought of Francis Greenwood Peabody, Washington Gladden, and Walter Rauschenbusch," *Church History* 62, no. 1 (March 1993): 83.

28. Janet Forsythe Fishburn, *The Fatherhood of God and the Victorian Family: The Social Gospel in America* (Philadelphia: Fortress, 1981), 168.

29. See Carter, *Decline,* 13–14.

30. William R. Hutchison, *Errand to the World: American Protestant Thought and Foreign Missions* (Chicago: University of Chicago Press, 1987), 111.

31. See Jean B. Quandt, "Religion and Social Thought: The Secularization of Postmillennialism," *American Quarterly* 25, no. 4 (October 1973): 391.

32. Richard Wightman Fox, "The Culture of Liberal Protestant Progressivism, 1875–1925," in "Religion and History," *Journal of Interdisciplinary History* 23, no. 3 (Winter 1993): 640.

33. See Bradley W. Bateman, "Make a Righteous Number: Social Surveys, the Men and Religion Forward Movement and Quantification in American Economics, " in *The Age of Economic Measurement,* ed. Judy L. Klein and Mary S. Morgan, *History of Political Economy* Annual Supplement, vol. 33 (Durham, NC: Duke University Press, 2001), 72–73.

34. Quandt, "Religion," 391.

35. See Hutchison, *Errand,* 111.

36. Hopkins, *Rise,* 319.

37. David G. Hackett, "Gender and Religion in American Culture, 1870–1930," *Religion and American Culture* 5, no. 2 (Summer 1995): 130.

38. See Robert T. Handy, "The American Religious Depression, 1925–1935," *Church History* 29, no. 1 (March 1960): 3–16.
39. Link, "What Happened," 836.
40. Charles Fiske quoted in Handy, "Religious Depression," 8.
41. Rodgers, "In Search," 126.
42. See Gail Bederman, " 'The Women Have Had Charge of the Church Work Long Enough': The Men and Religion Forward Movement of 1911–1912 and the Masculinization of Middle-Class Protestantism," *American Quarterly* 41, no. 3 (September 1989): 432–65.
43. Ibid., 435.
44. Ibid., 436.
45. Fishburn, *Fatherhood,* 95.
46. Bederman, "Women," 444.
47. Betty A. DeBerg, *Ungodly Women: Gender and the First Wave of American Fundamentalism* (Minneapolis, MN: Fortress, 1990), 76.
48. Bateman, "Make," 60.
49. Fishburn, *Fatherhood,* 175.
50. Randall Stephens, "More Recovered: A Review of Recent Historical Literature on Evangelicalism in the Late Victorian Era," *Quodlibet Journal* 3, no. 1 (Winter 2001), http://www.quodlibet.net/articles/stephens-victorian.shtml.
51. Joel A. Carpenter, "Fundamentalist Institutions and the Rise of Evangelical Protestantism, 1929–1942," *Church History* 49, no. 1 (March 1980): 64.
52. Bateman, "Make," 67.
53. DeBerg, *Ungodly,* 109.
54. Ibid., vii.
55. Patricia R. Hill, *The World Their Household: The American Woman's Foreign Mission Movement and Cultural Transformation, 1870–1920* (Ann Arbor: University of Michigan Press, 1985), 4.
56. "In 1919, 13 percent of all missionary centers in China were entirely staffed by single women." Jane Hunter, *The Gospel of Gentility: American Women Missionaries in Turn-of-the-Century China* (New Haven: Yale University Press, 1984), 52. St. Hilda's was one of these centers.
57. Dana L. Robert, "American Women in Mission: A Social History of Their Thought and Practice," in *The Modern Mission Era, 1792–1992: An Appraisal,* ed. Wilbert F. Shenk (Macon, GA: Mercer University Press, 1996), 312.
58. See Handy, "Religious Depression," 4.
59. See Hill, *World,* 58.
60. Susan Thorne, "Missionary-Imperial Feminism," in *Gendered Mission: Women and Men in Missionary Discourse and Practice,* ed. Mary Taylor Huber and Nancy C. Lutkehaus (Ann Arbor: University of Michigan Press, 1999), 43.
61. See Robert, "American Women," 307–8.
62. See Hunter, *Gospel,* 255.

Bibliography

Archival Holdings

The correspondence and papers of the following individuals are taken from the China Missions Record—Record Group 64—at the Archives of the Episcopal Church, Austin, TX:

Allen, Arthur J.
Boone, William J.
Buchanan, Elizabeth Mildred
Clark, Julia A.
Cox, Venetia
Gilman, Alfred A.
Gosline, Hazel F.
James, Mary Latimer
Osgood, Pauline Austin
Roberts, Margaret
Roots, Logan H.
Scott, Katharine E.
Spurr, Margaret E.
Tomlin, Olive Bird
Tso, Dorothy
Wakeman, Dorothea Kingsley

The missionary applications of the following people are taken from the Archives of the Student Volunteer Movement for Foreign Missions—Record Group Number 42—at the Yale University Divinity School Library, Manuscripts and Archives, New Haven, CT:

Stillson, Harriett Alice
Wakeman, Earl Seeley

Private Collections

The correspondence and papers of the following individuals are taken from private collections:

Gosline, Hazel. Papers. Private collection of Eleanor Wheeler. Bainbridge Island, WA.

Sherman, Patty [Margaret]. Letter to Dorothea Kingsley Wakeman, New Canaan, CT. Private collection of Dorothea Wakeman Howe. San Diego, CA.

[Stillson], Grace. Letter to Harriett Wakeman, San Gabriel, CA. Private collection of Dorothea Wakeman Howe. San Diego, CA.

Wakeman, Dorothea Kingsley. "Letters from China and Around the World." Vols. 1–4, June 1933–September 1937. Private collection of Dorothea Wakeman Howe. San Diego, CA.

———. Papers. Private collection of Dorothea Wakeman Howe. San Diego, CA.

Wakeman, Earl Seeley. Letter to Dorothea Kingsley Wakeman, Palo Alto. Private collection of Dorothea Wakeman Howe. San Diego, CA.

Interviews

Chen, Siyu. Interview by author. Shanghai, People's Republic of China, 1982.

Fu, Huaqing. Interview by author. Shanghai, People's Republic of China, 1982.

Howe, Dorothea Kingsley Wakeman. Interviews by author. Solana Beach, CA., 1997–2000.

Li, Xueying. Interview by author. Wuchang, People's Republic of China, 1990.

Liu, Defu. Interview by author. Shanghai, People's Republic of China, 1982.

Wang, Guifen. Interview by author. Shanghai, People's Republic of China, 1982.

Wang, Yingan. Interviews by author. Shanghai, People's Republic of China, 1982; Los Angeles, CA, 1989; San Diego, CA, 1989.

Yang, Kongxian. Interview by author. Wuchang, People's Republic of China, 1990.

Yeh, Yuanshuang. Interviews by author. Los Angeles and San Diego, CA., 1982–2009.

Yu, Shuming. Interview by author. Beijing, People's Republic of China, 1982.

Zhen, Yifang. Interview by author. Wuchang, People's Republic of China, 1990.

Zhong, Limin. Interview by author. Shanghai, People's Republic of China, 1982.

Zhou, Zezhen. Interview by author. Shanghai, People's Republic of China, 1982.

Published Books and Articles

Bateman, Bradley W. "Make a Righteous Number: Social Surveys, the Men and Religion Forward Movement and Quantification in American Economics." In *The Age of Economic Measurement,* edited by Judy L. Klein and Mary S. Morgan, 57–85. Vol. 33, *History of Political Economy* Annual Supplement. Durham, NC: Duke University Press, 2001.

Bederman, Gail. " 'The Women Have Had Charge of the Church Work Long Enough': The Men and Religion Forward Movement of 1911–1912 and the Masculinization of Middle-Class Protestantism." *American Quarterly* 41, no. 3 (September 1989): 432–65.

Bergère, Marie-Claire. *The Golden Age of the Chinese of the Chinese Bourgeoisie, 1911–1937.* Translated by Janet Lloyd. Cambridge: Cambridge University Press, 1989.

Bickers, Robert. *Britain in China: Community, Culture and Colonialism, 1900–1949.* Manchester: Manchester University Press, 1999.

Billingsley, Phil. *Bandits in Republican China.* Stanford, CA: Stanford University Press, 1988.

Boyle, John Hunter. *China and Japan at War, 1937–1945: The Politics of Collaboration.* Stanford, CA: Stanford University Press, 1972.

Carpenter, Joel A. "Fundamentalist Institutions and the Rise of Evangelical Protestantism, 1929–1942." *Church History* 49, no. 1 (March 1980): 62–75.

Carter, Paul A. *The Decline and Revival of the Social Gospel: Social and Political Liberalism in American Protestant Churches, 1920–1940.* Ithaca: Cornell University Press, 1954.

Chapman, H. Owen. *The Chinese Revolution: A Record of the Period Under Communist Control as Seen from the Nationalist Capitol Hankow.* Westport, CT: Hyperion Reprint Edition, 1977.

Ch'i, Hsi-Sheng. *Warlord Politics in China, 1916–1928.* Stanford, CA: Stanford University Press, 1976.

Chow, Tse-tsung. *The May Fourth Movement: Intellectual Revolution in Modern China.* Stanford, CA: Stanford University Press, 1960.

DeBerg, Betty A. *Ungodly Women: Gender and the First Wave of American Fundamentalis.* Minneapolis, MN: Fortress, 1990.

Dorn, Jacob H. "The Social Gospel and Socialism: A Comparison of the Thought of Francis Greenwood Peabody, Washington Gladden, and Walter Rauschenbusch." *Church History* 62, no. 1 (March 1993): 82–100.

Dreyer, Edward L. *China at War, 1901–1949.* New York: Longman, 1995.

Eastman, Lloyd E. *The Abortive Revolution: China under Nationalist Rule, 1927–1937.* Cambridge: Harvard University Press, 1990.

———. "Nationalist China during the Nanking decade, 1927–1937." In *The Nationalist Era in China, 1927–1949,* edited by Lloyd E. Eastman, Jerome Ch'en, Suzanne Pepper, and Lyman P. Van Slyke, 1–52. Cambridge: Cambridge University Press, 1991.

———. *Seeds of Destruction: Nationalist China in War and Revolution, 1937–1949.* Stanford, CA: Stanford University Press, 1984.

Edwards, Wendy J. Deichmann, and Carolyn De Swarte Gifford. "Introduction: Restoring Women and Reclaiming Gender in Social Gospel Studies." In *Gender and the Social Gospel,* edited by Wendy J. Deichmann Edwards and Carolyn De Swarte Gifford, 1–17. Urbana: University of Illinois Press, 2003.

Fishburn, Janet Forsythe. *The Fatherhood of God and the Victorian Family: The Social Gospel in America.* Philadelphia: Fortress, 1981.

Fox, Richard Wightman. "The Culture of Liberal Protestant Progressivism, 1875–1925." *Journal of Interdisciplinary History* 23, no. 3, Religion and History (Winter 1993): 639–60.

Gorrell, Donald K. *The Age of Social Responsibility: The Social Gospel in the Progressive Era, 1900–1920.* Macon, GA: Mercer University Press, 1988.

Gray, Arthur R. and Arthur M. Sherman. *The Story of the Church in China.* New York: Domestic and Foreign Missionary Society, 1913.

Gusfield, Joseph R. *Symbolic Crusade: Status Politics and the American Temperance Movement.* 2nd ed. Urbana: University of Illinois, 1986.

Hackett, David G. "Gender and Religion in American Culture, 1870–1930." *Religion and American Culture* 5, no. 2 (Summer 1995): 127–57.

Handy, Robert T. "The American Religious Depression, 1925–1935." *Church History* 29, no. 1 (March 1960): 3–16.

———. "Introduction." In *The Social Gospel in America, 1870–1920,* edited by Robert T. Handy, 3–16. New York: Oxford University Press, 1966.

Hayford, Charles W. *To the People: James Yen and Village China.* New York: Columbia University Press, 1990.

Hill, Patricia R. *The World Their Household: The American Woman's Foreign Mission Movement and Cultural Transformation, 1870–1920.* Ann Arbor: University of Michigan Press, 1985.

Hinton, William. *Fanshen: A Documentary of Revolution in a Chinese Village.* New York: Vintage Books, 1966.

Holmes, William F. "Populism: In Search of Context." *Agricultural History* 64, no. 4 (Autumn 1990): 26–58.

Hopkins, Charles Howard. *The Rise of the Social Gospel in American Protestantism, 1865–1915.* New Haven: Yale University Press, 1940.

Hsüeh, Chün-tu. *Huang Hsing and the Chinese Revolution.* Stanford, CA: Stanford University Press, 1961.

Hunter, Jane. *The Gospel of Gentility: American Women Missionaries in Turn-of-the-Century China.* New Haven: Yale University Press, 1984.

Hutchison, William R. *Errand to the World: American Protestant Thought and Foreign Missions.* Chicago: University of Chicago Press, 1987.

Issacs, Harold R. *The Tragedy of the Chinese Revolution,* 2nd rev. ed. Stanford, CA: Stanford University Press, 1961.

Lary, Diana. "Introduction: The Context of War." In *China At War: Regions of China, 1937–1945,* edited by Stephen R. MacKinnon, Diana Lary, and Ezra F. Vogel, 1–16. Stanford, CA: Stanford University Press, 2007.

Layman with a Notebook. *What is the Oxford Group?* New York: Oxford University Press, 1937.

Lewis, Ida Belle. *The Education of Girls in China.* New York: Teachers College, Columbia University, 1919.

Linebarger, Paul M. A. *The China of Chiang K'ai-shek: A Political Study.* Boston: World Peace Foundation, 1941.

Link, Arthur S. "What Happened to the Progressive Movement in the 1920's." *American Historical Review* 64, no. 4 (July 1959): 833–51.

The Living Church Annual and Churchman's Almanac: A Church Cyclopedia and Almanac, 1920. Milwaukee, WI: Morehouse, 1919.

Lloyd, Henry Demarest. *Wealth Against Commonwealth.* New York: Harper & Brothers, 1894.

Lutz, Jessie G. "Chinese Nationalism and the Anti-Christian Campaigns of the 1920s." *Modern Asian Studies* 10, no. 3 (1976): 395–416.

MacKinnon, Stephen R. "Conclusion: Wartime China." In *China At War: Regions of China, 1937–1945,* edited by Stephen R. MacKinnon, Diana Lary, and Ezra F. Vogel, 335–54. Stanford, CA: Stanford University Press, 2007.

———. *Wuhan, 1938: War, Refugees, and the Making of Modern China.* Berkeley: University of California Press, 2008.

Mann, Susan. *The Talented Women of the Zhang Family.* Berkeley: University of California Press, 2007.

Mao, Zedong. *Selected Readings from the Works of Mao Tse-tung.* Peking: Foreign Languages Press, 1967.

Marquis, Albert Nelson, ed. *Who's Who in America: A Biographical Dictionary of Notable Living Men and Women of the United States.* Vol. 19, 1936–37. Chicago: A. N. Marquis, 1936.

May, Henry F. *Protestant Churches and Industrial America.* New York: Harper & Brothers, 1949.

Mayhew, Anne. "A Reappraisal of the Causes of Farm Protest in the United States, 1870–1900." *Journal of Economic History* 32, no. 2 (June 1972): 464–75.

McCord, Edward A. *The Power of the Gun: The Emergence of Modern Chinese Warlordism.* Berkeley: University of California Press, 1993.

McCormack, Gavan. *Chang Tso-lin in Northeast China, 1911–1928: China, Japan, and the Manchurian Idea.* Stanford, CA: Stanford University Press, 1977.

Meyer, Milton W. *China: A Concise History.* 2nd rev. ed. Lanham, MD: Littlefield Adams Quality Paperback, 1994.

Murdock, Michael G. "Exploiting Anti-Imperialism: Popular Forces and Nation-State-Building During China's Northern Expedition, 1926–1927." *Modern China* 35, no. 1 (January 2009): 65–95.

O'Neill, Hugh B. *Companion to Chinese History.* New York: Facts on File Publications, 1987.

Presiding Bishop and Council Department of Missions. *Handbooks on the Missions of the Episcopal Church No. I China.* Chicago: Hammond, 1922.

Pye, Lucian W. "How China's Nationalism was Shanghaied." *Australian Journal of Chinese Affairs,* no. 29 (January 1993): 107–33.

Quandt, Jean B. "Religion and Social Thought: The Secularization of Postmillennialism." *American Quarterly* 25, no. 4 (October 1973): 390–409.

Robert, Dana L. "American Women in Mission: A Social History of Their Thought and Practice." In *The Modern Mission Era, 1792–1992: An Appraisal,* edited by Wilbert F. Shenk. Macon, GA: Mercer University Press, 1996.

Rodgers, Daniel T. "In Search of Progressivism." In "The Promise of American History: Progress and Prospects." *Reviews in American History* 10, no. 4 (December 1982): 113–32.

Rowe, William T. *Hankow: Commerce and Society in a Chinese City, 1796–1889.* Stanford, CA: Stanford University Press, 1984.

———. *Hankow: Conflict and Community in a Chinese City, 1796–1895.* Stanford: Stanford University Press, 1989.

Sheridan, James E. *China in Disintegration: The Republican Era in Chinese History, 1912–1949.* New York: Free Press, 1977.

———. *Chinese Warlord: The Career of Feng Yüshiang.* Stanford, CA: Stanford University Press, 1966.

Spence, Jonathan D. *The Search for Modern China.* New York: W. W. Norton, 1990.

Stephens, Randall. "More Recovered: A Review of Recent Historical Literature on Evangelicalism in the Late Victorian Era." *Quodlibet Journal* 3, no. 1 (Winter 2001). http://www.quodlibet.net/articles/stephens-victorian.shtml.

Thorne, Susan. "Missionary-Imperial Feminism." In *Gendered Mission: Women and Men in Missionary Discourse and Practice,* edited by Mary Taylor Huber and Nancy C. Lutkehaus. Ann Arbor: University of Michigan Press, 1999.

Turner, Frederick Jackson. "The Problem of the West." In *The Frontier in American History.* New York: Henry Holt, 1920.

———. "The Significance of the Frontier in American History." In *The Frontier in American History.* New York: Henry Holt, 1920.

Wakeman, Frederick, Jr. *Strangers at the Gate: Social Disorder in South China, 1839–1861.* Berkeley: University of California Press, 1966.

Ward, Maisie. *The Oxford Groups.* London: Sheed & Ward, 1937.

Warin, Anne. *Hilda: The Chronicle of a Saint. A Story of Saints and Kings, and the Beginnings of the English Church.* London: Lamp Press, 1989.

White, Theodore H., and Annalee Jacoby. *Thunder Out of China.* New York: William Sloane, 1946.

Wiebe, Robert H. *The Search for Order, 1877–1920.* New York: Hill and Wang, 1967.

Wilbur, C. Martin. *The Nationalist Revolution in China, 1923–1928.* Cambridge: Cambridge University Press, 1983.

Williams, Rhys H., and Susan M. Alexander. "Religious Rhetoric in American Populism: Civil Religion as Movement Ideology." *Journal for the Scientific Study of Religion* 33, no. 1 (March 1994): 1–15.

Williams, William Appleman. "The Frontier Thesis and American Foreign Policy." *Pacific Historical Review* 24, no. 4 (November 1955): 379–95.

Wober, Mallory. *English Girls' Boarding Schools.* London: Allen Lane The Penguin Press, 1971.

Wong, J. Y. *Yeh Ming-ch'en: Viceroy of Liang Kuang (1852–8).* Cambridge: Cambridge University Press, 2009.

Wright, David Curtis. *The History of China.* Westport, CT: Greenwood, 2001.

Wright, Mary. "From Revolution to Restoration: The Transformation of Kuomintang Ideology." Special Number on Chinese History and Society, *Far Eastern Quarterly* 14, no. 4 (August 1955): 515–32.

Xing, Jun. *Baptized in the Fire of Revolution: The American Social Gospel and the YMCA in China: 1919–1937.* Bethlehem, PA: Lehigh University Press, 1996.

Zhonghua jidujiaohui nianjian [The China Christian year book]. Vol. 8, 1925. Shanghai: Zhonguo jiao hui yan jiu zhong xin, 1925; repr., Shanghai: Gan lan wen hua ji jin hui, 1983.

Zhonghua jidujiaohui nianjian [The China Christian year book]. Vol. 9, 1927. Shanghai: Zhonguo jiao hui yan jiu zhong xin, 1927; repr., Shanghai: Gan lan wen hua ji jin hui, 1983.

Zhu, Jianguo, and Guo Xiaohong. *Dongfang Jianming Chao* [Jianmin Ascending]. Beijing: Zhongguo Gongren Chubanshe [Worker's Press of China], 1992.

Periodicals, Pamphlets, and Dissertations

American Church Mission in the Valley of the Yang-tsz. *Church in China: A Bi-monthly Magazine* 1, no. 6 (November 1894): 118.

"An Attempt to Analyze the Situation in China: The Bearings of the Present Disturbances Upon Mission Work, Especially That of Christian Education." *Spirit of Missions: An Illustrated Monthly Review of Christian Missions* 92 (1927): 197–200.

"The Bohlen Memorial Girls' School." *Spirit of Missions: An Illustrated Monthly Review of Christian Missions* 39 (1874): 501–2.

Boone, Henrietta F. "The Jane Bohlen Memorial School." *Spirit of Missions: An Illustrated Monthly Review of Christian Missions* 44 (1879): 174–75.

Buchanan, Elizabeth Mildred. "Saint Hilda's School." *Spirit of Missions: An Illustrated Monthly Review of Christian Missions* 83 (1918): 509–11.

Clark, Julia A. "Voluntary Religious Education in China: Survey of Religious Teaching at St. Hilda's, Wuchang, Reveals Opportunity to Enrich the Kingdom Through Intelligent Christian Women." *Spirit of Missions: An Illustrated Monthly Review of Christian Missions* 95 (1930): 380–81, 402.

Department of Foreign Missions of the Protestant Episcopal Church. "Business Arrangements in Connection with the China Mission." Brochure dated September 1932. Private collection of Dorothea Wakeman Howe. San Diego, CA.

District of Hankow. *Hankow Newsletter.* Hankow: Diocese of Hankow, Domestic and Foreign Missionary Society of the Protestant Episcopal Church in the United States, December 1919–February 1941. Archives of the Episcopal Church. Austin, TX.

Dollar Steamship Lines. *Special Class, S.S. The President Hoover & S.S. The President Coolidge.* San Francisco: Dollar Steamship Lines, 1932. Private collection of Dorothea Wakeman Howe. San Diego, CA.

Gilman, Gertrude Carter. "Wuhan Revisited After Two Years: The Vast Changes Which have Emerged from the Chinese Turmoil of Recent Years Augur Well for the New China that is Building." *Spirit of Missions: An Illustrated Monthly Review of Christian Missions* 94 (1929): 357–64.

"Girls' School House in Wuchang." *Spirit of Missions: An Illustrated Monthly Review of Christian Missions* 39 (1874): 309.

Graves, Frederick R. "Kuomintang Bans Christian Schools: Bishop of Shanghai Reviews the Implications of Registering Our Schools in China and Reports Recent Proposals of Shanghai Kuomintang." *Spirit of Missions: An Illustrated Monthly Review of Christian Missions* 95 (1930): 576.

Hart, Deaconess [Edith]. "Saint Lois's School for Girls." *Spirit of Missions: An Illustrated Monthly Review of Christian Missions* 88 (1923): 203–5.

Hayford, Charles W. "Y. C. James Yen and Rural Reconstruction in China." PhD diss., Harvard University, 1973.

Hershey, John. "Jimmy Yen: Crusader for Mankind." *Reader's Digest* (October 1987): 138–45, 233–64.

The Industrial Arts Cooperative Service. New York: Industrial Arts Cooperative Service, 1939. Private collection of Dorothea Wakeman Howe. San Diego, CA.

Merrins, Edward M. "The Progress of China." *Spirit of Missions: An Illustrated Monthly Review of Christian Missions* 78 (1913): 589–53.

Mills, Dorothy. "St. Hilda's Wuchang." *Spirit of Missions: An Illustrated Monthly Review of Christian Missions* 81 (1916): 227–31.

Osgood, Pauline Austin. "St. Hilda's School. Wuchang." *Spirit of Missions: An Illustrated Monthly Review of Christian Missions* 67 (1902): 493–94.

"Peking Premiere, October 3, 1972. Piano Duo-logues with the Haddens." Flyer. Private collection of Dorothea Wakeman Howe. San Diego, CA.

"St. Hilda's School, Wuchang China: Looking Backward." *Spirit of Missions: An Illustrated Monthly Review of Christian Missions* 65 (1900): 374–76.

Sherman, Arthur M. "Story of a Beleaguered City: Thrilling Account of the Siege of Wuchang by an Eye-Witness." *Spirit of Missions: An Illustrated Monthly Review of Christian Missions* 91 (1926): 671–73.

Stueart, Robert D. "Flowers From Horseback: A Retrospective View of China—United States Library and Information Science Education Cooperation in the 20th Century." http://digarc.usc.edu/search/controller/view/impa-m10743.html.

Vaughan, J. G. *Hints on Health for New Missionaries.* New York: National Council, Protestant Episcopal Church, Department of Missions. Brochure, n.d. Private collection of Dorothea Wakeman Howe. San Diego, CA.

"What the Ten Thousand Dollar Gift to St. Hilda's Will Do For the Church in China." *Spirit of Missions: An Illustrated Monthly Review of Christian Missions* 76 (1911): 75–77.

Wood, John W. "The Pro and Con of Registration of Christian Schools in China: A Symposium of the Views Held by Missionaries in all Three Districts in China on a Grave Question Which May Influence Future Policy." *Spirit of Missions: An Illustrated Monthly Review of Christian Missions* 93 (1928): 653–55.

Electronic Sources

Information: Liu Maoen. http://pwencycl.kgbudge.com/L/i/Liu_Mao-en.htm; http://english.gongyi.gov.cn/content.asp?id=1389&id_type=46.

Information: Liu Xianjie. http://generals.dk/general/Liu_Xianjie/_/China.html.

Information: Liu Zhenhua. http://english.gongyi.gov.cn/content.asp?id=1389&id_type=44; 46. http://rulers.org/index13.htm.

Map: Hankow with Hanyang and Wuchang 1915. http://www.lib.utexas.edu/maps/historical/hankow_1915.jpg.

Map: Hankow 1945. http://www.lib.utexas.edu/maps/ams/china_city_plans/txu-oclc-6566099.jpg.

Map: Japanese Occupation 1940. http://www.dean.usma.edu/history/web03/atlases/china%20civil %20war/chinese%20civil%20war%20pages/chinese%20civil%20war%2 0map%2004.htm.

Map: Japanese Occupation 1945. http://www.dean.usma.edu/history/web03/atlases/china%20civil %20war/chinese%20civil%20war%20pages/chinese%20civil%20war%2 0map%2005.htm.

Photograph: Wuchang Number 25 Middle School (St. Hilda's Chapel). http://www.panoramio.com/photo/1335429.

Railroad information: http://teeteethought.blogspot.com/2008/09/jinghu-railway.html.

Index

Note: Numbers in italic reference a photograph